A SHORT H

BALI

DATE DUE SLIP
renew by phone or online
Overdue Fines Apply

Short History of Asia Series

Series Editor: Milton Osborne
Milton Osborne has had an association with the Asian region for over 40 years as an academic, public servant and independent writer. He is the author of nine books on Asian topics, including *Southeast Asia: An Introductory History*, first published in 1979 and now in its eighth edition, and, most recently, *The Mekong: Turbulent Past, Uncertain Future*, published in 2000.

A SHORT HISTORY OF

BALI

INDONESIA'S HINDU REALM

Robert Pringle

ALLEN&UNWIN

Cover: Water Temple on Lake Bratan

First published in 2004 by Allen & Unwin

Allen & Unwin
83 Alexander Street
Crows Nest NSW 2065
Australia
Phone: (61 2) 8425 0100
Fax: (61 2) 9906 2218
Email: info@allenandunwin.com
Web: www.allenandunwin.com

National Library of Australia
Cataloguing-in-Publication entry:

Pringle, Robert, 1936– .
    A short history of Bali, Indonesia's Hindu realm.

    Bibliography.
    Includes index.
    ISBN 1 86508 863 3.

    1. Bali (Indonesia) – History. 2. Bali (Indonesia) –
    Politics and government. 3. Bali (Indonesia) – Social life
    and customs. I. Title.

959.86

Set in 11/14 pt Goudy by Midland Typesetters, Maryborough, Victoria
Printed by South Wind Production, Singapore

10 9 8 7 6 5 4 3 2 1

For my granddaughters,
Ni Wayan Zoe and Ni Made Penelope,
to read before they visit Bali.

Contents

Acknowledgments and a word on names, spelling and sources

Writing this book would have been impossible without the expertise of others. Many Bali specialists were generous in sharing their insights with me, and two of them deserve special mention. Chapter 4 is in the main a condensation of Henk Schulte Nordholt's *The Spell of Power*. He both read this chapter in draft and offered much assistance on other chapters as well. Chapter 8 relies almost as heavily on Geoffrey Robinson's *The Dark Side of Paradise*, and again the author was extremely generous with his commentary. Any factual mistakes or divergences in interpretation in these two chapters or elsewhere are, of course, solely my responsibility. I owe another special debt of gratitude to Hildred Geertz, who offered invaluable advice on the entire draft. In Bali, historian I Nyoman Wijaya provided me with extensive research and production assistance over several months.

Others who gave generously of their time and expertise include archaeologist I Wayan Ardika, whose views on prehistory substantially influenced my treatment of this subject. Anthropologist J. Stephen Lansing and Alit Artawiguna of the Bali agricultural extension service helped me understand the impact of the Green Revolution. Gloria Davis did the same for transmigration. Dewa N. Wirawan was a major source of insight into Bali's family planning success, as was one of its pioneers, A.A.M. Djelantik. Andrew Toth, an ethnomusicologist who doubles as US Honorary Consul on Bali, assisted with music and many other subjects. Economist I Nyoman Erawan helped with the tourism sector, as did Jack Daniels of Bali Discovery Tours (who also produces the very informative *Bali Update* online newsletter) and I Nyoman

Suamba of the provincial tourism office. Peter Stowell and Walter Sullivan shared their expertise on Walter Spies and Margaret Mead respectively and more generally helped me to understand Bali in the 1930s.

Suteja Neka and I Made Parnatha of the Neka Art Museum, and Gusti Ayu Indrayana Karya of the Museum Puri Lukisan, as well as Tjokorda Putra Sukawati, all in Ubud, allowed me generous access to their respective collections and permission to reproduce certain items. Jos Pet and Tim Jessup of the Nature Conservancy and Ketut Sarjana Putra of the World Wide Fund for Nature explained the turtle project and other environmental issues. Barbara Harvey, Sean Foley, Merle Ricklefs and Debe Campbell read and commented on the draft in whole or in part. Others who helped along the way include A.A. Gde Putra Agung, Clifford Geertz, *Latitudes* editor Degung Santikarma, Leslie Dwyer, John MacDougall, Bill Liddle, Adrian Vickers, Helen Jessup, Greta Morris, Christopher Purdy, Yanti Spooner, Dan and Margaret Sullivan, Ketut Sudhana Astika, Surya Dharma, the editors of Joyo Indonesia News Service, the unfailingly helpful management of the Puri Kelapa Hotel in Sanur, and the miracle-working inter-library loan staff of the Alexandria, Virginia, Public Library, and I thank them all.

I owe special thanks to the United States – Indonesia Society for a travel grant which enabled me to explore Bali's recent history and made possible the interviews on which the final two chapters are largely based. Milton Osborne encouraged me to undertake the project and waited patiently for years until retirement from the US Foreign Service gave me time to work on it. Both he and the staff at Allen & Unwin, especially Claire Murdoch and Rebecca Kaiser, have been unfailingly helpful and supportive. My wife Barbara provided editorial supervision and proofreading capacity and, as she always does, sustained the project from beginning to end.

I have adhered to modern Indonesian and Balinese spelling ('c' is pronounced 'ch', and so on.) rather than the older Dutch-derived usage. Proper names have been treated the same way except in a few cases where an individual is known to favour the old spelling. Thus I have used 'Sukarno', but 'Soeharto'; 'Jelantik' in most cases, but 'Djelantik' for one prominent member of the family who himself uses that spelling. In Indonesia, names are still a matter of personal choice. The complex Balinese naming system is briefly explained in Chapter 1. For Balinese place names I have followed prevailing current practice, which often runs together names which were previously split (for example, 'Bayunggede' instead of 'Bayung Gede').

There is a brief guide to further reading at the end of this book, which includes those general works upon which I have relied most heavily. Notes have been kept to a minimum and used mainly to document direct quotations, to indicate unpublished or obscure sources and, in a few cases, to document statements which might be debatable. Anyone seeking additional information on sources is welcome to contact me directly.

Robert Pringle
Alexandria, Virginia

Abbreviations

BTI	*Barisan Tani Indonesia* (Indonesian Farmers' Front), the farmers' organisation of the PKI
DPR	*Dewan Perwakilan Rakyat* (People's Representative Council), established at the national level by the 1945 constitution. Together with appointed members it makes up the MPR.
DPRD	*Dewan Perwakilan Rakyat Daerah* (Regional People's Representative Council) which exists at two levels, province and district
Gestapu	*Gerakan September Tigapuluh* (30th September Movement), which launched the coup attempt of 1965
Lekra	*Lembaga Kebudayaan Rakyat* (Institute for People's Culture), the PKI artists' and writers' institute
LOGIS	*Lanjutan Organizasi Gerilya Indonesia Seluruhnya* (Continuation of the All-Indonesia Guerrilla Organisation), a private army on Bali at the time of the Indonesian Revolution
MPR	*Majelis Permusyarawatan Rakyat* (People's Consultative Assembly), supreme national council created by the 1945 constitution
NASAKOM	'*Nasionalisme, Agama, Komunism*', Sukarno's acronym for an idealogy which embraced nationalism, religion and communism
NIT	*Negara Indonesia Timur* (State of Eastern Indonesia, including Bali), created by the Dutch in 1946
NU	*Nahdlatul Ulama* (Muslim Scholars' Party)
PDI	*Partai Demokrasi Indonesia* (Indonesian Democracy Party)

Peta	*Pembela Tanah Air* (Protectors of the Fatherland), a Japanese-sponsored Indonesian militia
Petani	*Petani Nasionalis Indonesia* (PNI farmers' organisation)
PKI	*Partai Komunis Indonesia* (Indonesian Communist Party)
PNI	*Partai Nasionalis Indonesia* (Indonesian Nationalist Party)
PSI	*Partai Sosialis Indonesia* (Indonesian Socialist Party)
STSI	*Sekolah Tinggi Seni Indonesia* (College of Indonesian Arts)

Introduction

In the early 1980s I was sitting in the coffee shop of the Bali Beach Hotel in Sanur, reflecting on the strange fact that Dutch troops had come ashore nearby, less than 80 years previously, on their way to perpetrate one of the more extraordinary massacres in the history of colonialism. I did not know that the Japanese had also landed in this same area in 1942, or that the Dutch had returned here to Bali in 1946, or that an important relic of Bali's ancient history, the tenth-century Sanur inscription, was only a few kilometres away. I did realise that it was difficult for the average visitor to know about such details or indeed to read anything about Bali's obviously intriguing history. It occurred to me that someone should do something about that. Today more books on Bali are available, and many of them contain varying amounts of history, often of high quality. But there has been nothing designed for the general reader which covers the whole sweep of Bali's past, including aspects about which we still have a great deal to learn.

In undertaking to write a short history of Bali I had a number of subsidiary concerns. First there is the problem of context. All too often Bali is perceived as an almost mythological realm, devoid of any national character. I have tried to place Balinese history in its Indonesian context because it cannot be understood any other way. Second, I have avoided the clichés spawned by tourism, and such terms as 'paradise' or 'Island of the Gods' do not occur in the pages that follow. But I have also avoided implying that because Bali was never the idyll of the tourist brochures, the entire tourist industry was built on false premises, the product of manipulation by non-Balinese. Bali's attractive force is genuine, not created by outsiders, and the island loses none of its appeal if one understands the truth about its often turbulent past, or the challenges and debates that abound today. One of the central, defining characteristics of modern Bali is that it has limited physical resources but an exceptional wealth of cultural and aesthetic capital. The great questions of Bali's recent past and present revolve around the dilemma of using this wealth in a sustainable way.

As I write this, many people, Balinese and non-Balinese alike, are worried about the island's future in the wake of the Kuta bombing of October, 2002, and its severe impact on tourism, which now dominates the local economy. While there is certainly reason for concern, Bali's history is nothing if not testimony to the creativity and resilience of the Balinese people. This historical record makes clear that these qualities extend well beyond art and drama, and I think should give everyone cause for optimism.

This book was written primarily for non-Balinese, including other Indonesians. While I have tried to understand Balinese viewpoints— not always easy, especially for the pre-colonial periods—I make no claim to have written from a Balinese perspective, and I have hardly addressed a number of issues which feature prominently in Balinese historiography. For example, I have said little about the detailed histories of most of the pre-colonial kingdoms, much less about their complex relationships with each other. On these subjects and others, many volumes remain to be written by Balinese historians interpreting traditional Balinese sources, which exist in abundance. It is nonetheless my hope that this book will prove useful to visitors and others who seek a starting point for the historical study of this superb island and its people.

Robert Pringle
Alexandria, Virginia

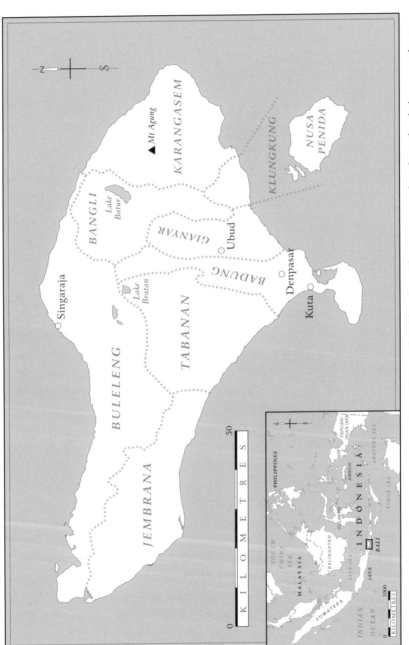

The boundaries indicated on this map are those of the eight pre-colonial kingdoms. They are more or less identical with the current districts (kabupaten) but not as exact.

1
A SNUG LITTLE AMPHITHEATRE: THE BALINESE SETTING

Visitors often come to Bali without going to other provinces of Indonesia. Some are mildly surprised when they are greeted at the airport by 'Indonesian' and not 'Balinese' immigration officials. So it is worth emphasising that Bali is indeed and profoundly part of Indonesia. Culturally, it is one bright flash in an archipelagic kaleidoscope. Geologically, it is one link in a chain of volcanoes which created soils of exceptional fertility. Historically, it has always been part of a broader island world. No aspect of the history of Bali can be fully understood divorced from its Indonesian context.

Born of fire and water

Bali is small—only 5633 square kilometres, less than one-third of one per cent of Indonesia's land area. Despite the narrow congested roads, one can drive around the island in a day. It is shaped like a flattened diamond, with the long dimension running east-west and a significant bulge to the south.

Bali is the first link in a chain of islands which stretches eastward from Java. Although Java doesn't look big on a map of Indonesia, it is huge compared to Bali, 60 times larger in area, with more than 30 times Bali's population of 3.2 million. Seen from a Balinese perspective, Java looms even larger politically than it does geographically, and this has been true for over a thousand years.

To the north, Bali is bordered by the Java Sea, a passageway between major islands of the Indonesian archipelago. Southwards, the vast expanses of the Indian Ocean drop away unbroken toward Australia, except for the eastern extremity of Java, which protrudes directly south of western Bali. Like the island of Lombok, this eastern salient of Java was ruled by Balinese in the past.

The two straits which border the island are radically different. On the west, the Bali Strait is only 2.5 kilometres wide and very shallow. It was dry more than once during the ice ages, most recently about 18 000 years ago. Even when flooded, it has never been a major barrier to the passage of ideas or people.

To the east, the Lombok Strait is a different matter, more than 30 kilometres wide and 1300 metres deep. It is of interest to modern navies because it is one of only two major passages between the South China Sea and Australia, the other being the Sunda Strait between Java and Sumatra, which modern submarines can navigate submerged. The Lombok Strait did not go dry during the ice ages. For that reason it marks a very approximate border, usually known as the Wallace Line, between the fauna of southeast Asia to the west, and that of Australasia (including, for example, marsupials) to the east. It was named after Alfred Russel Wallace, co-originator with Charles Darwin of evolution theory, and a nineteenth-century visitor to Bali.

Bali is surrounded by coral reefs which were once famous as a hazard to navigation and the cause of numerous shipwrecks. In the nineteenth century, the Balinese rulers' insistence that they were entitled to any cargo they could salvage from such wrecks became a pretext for Dutch intervention. Today the reefs are touted as a tourist attraction, but the sad truth is that they have been badly damaged in most areas by fishing with explosives, coral mining to make lime for cement and other problems, including those associated with global warming. It will take an intensive conservation effort to save or restore some of them.

The climate is tropical, with the northeast monsoon bringing wetter weather from November to April, and the southwest monsoon relatively dry and somewhat cooler weather from May to October. There are a surprising number of microclimates on Bali, some of them of historical significance. The dryness of the east and west inhibited agriculture, hence human settlement. Even in the lush south, where Balinese civilisation developed, variations in rainfall may have influenced the density of the forest, so that some regions were cleared and settled more easily, hence earlier, than others.

Most of the island was covered with tropical forest until at least the mid-nineteenth century. Today there is virtually no undisturbed old-growth forest left except for a few patches on the steepest slopes and in the relatively arid west. Most of the wood consumed by Bali's booming handicraft and furniture industries is imported from other provinces. There are very few large wild animals. Tigers were allegedly seen on the island as recently as the 1930s, but there are none today.

Like Java, most of Bali is young geologically. There are exceptions, including the uplifted coral of the Bukit Peninsula, south of the airport, and the nearby island of Nusa Penida. But the Bali of song and story is the product of ongoing volcanic activity along a grinding intersection of tectonic plates, part of the longer volcanic chain which is the backbone of the Indonesian archipelago.

One volcano is rarely out of sight of the next. From the western end of the island, the nearest volcano on Java dominates the horizon, and if one didn't know better one would assume it was on Bali. The most famous and historically significant Balinese peaks are Batur (1717 metres above the lake of the same name) and Gunung Agung or 'Great Mountain' (3142 metres), which dominates the eastern half of the island. Both of them are dangerously active. Bali was also affected by the tremendous 1815 eruption of Mount Tambora on Sumbawa, the second island to the east, the most violent anywhere on earth in historic times.

These mountains have always figured prominently in the mythology and economics of the island. The Balinese regard Gunung Agung as a replica of the sacred Mount Meru of Hindu mythology, the central axis of the universe. According to one legend it originated as a fragment of Mount Meru which the first Hindus brought to Bali. The mother temple, Besakih, is located on its slopes.

Bali's volcanic uplands anchor one end of a sacred axis between mountains and sea which is a central feature of Balinese belief and ritual. The Balinese believe the crater lakes in two of the volcanoes are the source of irrigation water for much of the island. (In fact, the water is generated by heavier rainfall around the peaks.) Major religious observances which oversee the complex management of south Bali's irrigation systems take place at regional water temples on the shores of these lakes.

As is the case on Java, the ash and lava ejected by the Balinese volcanoes weather into soil of great fertility. This is not true everywhere in Indonesia. For example, the ejecta from Sumatran volcanoes are more acidic, and therefore less fertile, which is the main reason Java and Bali are so much more densely populated than Sumatra.

Bali remains one of the most crowded provinces in Indonesia, although not quite as crowded as Central or East Java. The current population of over 3 million is more than ten times what it was at the time of first contact with Europeans in the late sixteenth century, and three times what it was in 1930. But if the volcanoes are economically essential over time, they are also dangerous in the short run. They are one reason, along with warfare and epidemic disease, why life on Bali has been fraught with uncertainty and mortal peril until recently.

Drive north from the provincial capital of Denpasar or the luxury hotel complex at Nusa Dua on either of two roads across the centre of the island. It will take you only about three hours to reach the north coast, notwithstanding overloaded trucks, lumbering tour buses and hordes of motorcycles, all competing for space on roads little changed since Dutch times.

You will drive up a long sloping plain covered on its lower and middle portions with villages, 'art shops' and irrigated rice fields, until the increasingly steep road crests a divide at around 1300 metres above sea level. Either route will take you close to one of the two major volcanic lakes, Bratan and Batur, with their important water temples. Once you are on the north side, the roads drop much more suddenly, there are no expanses of rice fields, and in less than an hour you will arrive at the Java Sea coast. On a good day you can see it from the top of the pass.

Such a journey dramatically illustrates the geopolitical implications of Balinese topography. The fertile, gently sloping rice fields of the well-watered south provided the economic basis for the full flowering of Balinese culture. But areas of cultivation are divided by streams which have cut precipitous north-south valleys through the rich volcanic debris. You will understand why, even today, most of the roads in south Bali run north-south, not east-west, except along the coast.

Anthropologist Clifford Geertz wrote of this densely settled area: 'If ever there was a forcing house for the growth of a singular civilization, this snug little amphitheater was it; and if what was produced turned out to be a rather special orchid, perhaps we should not be altogether surprised.'[1] Yet, as Geertz also emphasised, the south Bali amphitheatre had some real limitations. The difficulty of east-west travel was conducive to political fragmentation. Equally significant was the fact that, from a trade perspective, the amphitheatre was on the wrong side of the island. South Bali was isolated from the major trade routes between Java and the rest of the Indonesian archipelago, not to mention India and China. These sea lanes were and still are on Bali's northern side. There are no harbours truly suitable for modern shipping on either side.

It is interesting to speculate how Bali might have fared historically had the rich rice amphitheatre been on the same side of the island as the favoured trading coast.[2] Surely Bali would have been a more important political force in pre-colonial Indonesia, and surely the Dutch would not have refrained from direct intervention for as long as they did.

What is 'Bali'?

'Bali' can be understood in at least three ways. One way, perhaps the most common, is to equate it with the south-central, rice-growing amphitheatre described above, where the orchid of Balinese culture has bloomed most profusely. Here, as we shall see, the states of pre-colonial Bali flourished in all their intricacy, and here the tourists are now concentrated.

A second Bali is geographic, coincident with the entire island. But to understand the history of Bali it is critical to recognise important regional variations, rooted in geography, among south, north, east and west.

The north, as we have already seen, is crowded against the Java Sea by the central mountain mass, a narrow coastal plain bordered by a sudden escarpment, with the even higher volcanoes behind. With agricultural land in short supply and important sea lanes close at hand, commerce has been a far more important influence here than elsewhere. The port city of Singaraja is a polyglot mix of Chinese, Arabs, Javanese, Buginese, Balinese and others, resembling in spirit the old and equally diverse trading ports of north Java, with which it has been directly related for centuries. Although the north is predominantly Hindu-Balinese, there has been more cultural cross-fertilisation among Hindu, Chinese and Islamic traditions, there is a strong element of Bali Aga (see below), and even the Hindu temples are quite different from those in the south.

The history of north Bali contrasts in important ways with that of the south. In late bronze–iron age and early Hindu times, Bali's centre of political gravity may have been initially in the north, based on trade.

Puri Beji at Sangsit, not far from Singaraja, is typical of the 'baroque' style of the little-visited north Bali temples, which are also famous for their humorous reliefs. Pura Beji is an irrigation society (subak) temple. (Source: Robert Pringle)

If so, the circumstances under which it shifted to the agricultural south remain unknown. Much later, resistance to the Dutch was bitter and protracted in the north. There was more fighting, but only one example of the ritual suicide episodes which helped make the south famous. The colonial experience, beginning in 1849, was more than twice as long, and the Dutch administrative presence in Singaraja brought greater exposure to modernising influences than in the south.

In eastern Bali, the kingdom of Karangasem was of major importance by the seventeenth century, thanks to its key role in the Balinese expansion onto the island of Lombok and its intense political interaction with both north and south Bali. But economic development of the east was limited by lack of rainfall and mountainous terrain, much of its land area being occupied by the great mass of Gunung Agung. As early as 1905 a perceptive Dutch visitor noted that Karangasem appeared to be overpopulated.

The western province of Jembrana was mostly empty until the twentieth century. Relatively dry forest and scrub, it is today the site of the only national park on the island. Things began to change when the Dutch encouraged migration to Jembrana from elsewhere in Bali. Most of the few foreign-owned plantations which the Dutch allowed were also located there. But until the road connecting Bali to Java via the ferry at Gilimanuk was completed in the 1930s, Jembrana was a backwater, and to some extent it still is.

A third Bali is cultural. Here the main standards are language and Balinese religion. Cultural Bali includes the 3.2 million inhabitants of geographic Bali, roughly 100 000 Balinese on the island of Lombok, and those Balinese who live and work elsewhere in Indonesia. Beginning early in the twentieth century, over 200 000 Balinese 'transmigrants' moved, with government encouragement, to other less populated islands. The objectives of this programme were to ease population pressure on Bali itself and to spread advanced irrigation technology to new areas. The majority of these people have retained their Balinese culture (see Chapter 9).

In general, there is no argument about who is Balinese in a cultural sense, for although the Balinese love nothing better than debating major aspects of their own civilisation, they are in agreement about who is a member, broadly speaking, of the family.

The native language of Bali is Balinese. Most Balinese learn the national language, Indonesian, a modernised version of nineteenth-century Malay, only in school. Most of Indonesia's languages, including Balinese, belong to the great Austronesian family, formerly known as Malayo-Polynesian, which stretches from Taiwan and the highlands of Indochina to Madagascar.

Somewhat surprisingly, Balinese is closer in syntax to Sasak, a language spoken on Lombok, its neighbour to the east, than it is to Javanese, despite the historic ties between Java and Bali. However, over time Balinese has picked up an extensive vocabulary from Javanese, much as English, syntax-wise a Germanic language, has over time picked up vocabulary from Greek and Latin (often via French). Like Javanese, Balinese has alternative vocabularies, the use of which depends on whether the person addressed is equal, inferior or superior in social status to the speaker.

Who is Balinese and who might not be?

Using the cultural definition of Bali, more than 87 per cent of the island's present population is Balinese, categorised as Hindu in the 2000 census figures. There are minorities of Muslims (9.7 per cent), Protestants (1 per cent), Catholics (0.8 per cent), and Buddhists (0.5 per cent) concentrated in the urban centres of Denpasar and Singaraja, and in the west. The majority of Buddhists and some of the Christians are probably ethnic Chinese who, under Indonesian law, have been pressured to choose a recognised state religion.

Today a newly prosperous Bali is attracting migrants from other parts of Indonesia and beyond, drawn primarily by employment opportunities. Javanese migrant labour is harvesting rice in south Bali, Roman Catholics from Flores are driving taxis in Denpasar, and Indonesians of all kinds have found work in the tourist industry. In addition, despite the questionable legality of such practice, upscale expatriates are 'buying' land and houses in Ubud and elsewhere.

Muslims first came to Bali centuries ago as traders and as military mercenaries in the service of Balinese rulers. They were of diverse origins. There were Arabs from the Hadramaut in modern Yemen, often claiming descent from the Prophet with the title 'Sheik' or 'Sayid', who circulated throughout the archipelago trading and getting into politics. There were Buginese from Makasar who were both merchants and soldiers for hire. A few were Javanese who, like the father of Indonesia's first president, Sukarno, were employed as clerks and teachers by the colonial administration. Muslims often formed their own communities, especially in trading centres and around the rulers' courts. One of the oldest such communities is at Gelgel, the site of an important sixteenth-century Balinese kingdom, a few minutes' drive south of Klungkung.

Chinese were trading with Bali from an early period, although Ma-Li gets only passing mention in early Chinese sources. Recent archaeological discoveries suggest that India rather than China was the first and most important trading partner with pre-Hindu Bali. But well before the Dutch conquest the Chinese had established themselves as resident merchants, typically in the service of Balinese rulers or under their protection. They flourished under the Dutch and dominated local trade, but many were driven out of business or forced to operate with Balinese partners during the early independence period.

Strings of Chinese copper coins known as *kepeng* were the standard of Balinese currency until Dutch times. Today Chinese coins dating to the Tang dynasty and even earlier are readily obtained on Bali, and they remain important for certain kinds of offerings. Chinese influence on Balinese art is obvious, especially in some of the design features of temples and religious regalia, not least the lion-like Barong which manifests the forces of 'good' in opposition to the 'evil' sorceress, Rangda.

Well before the Kuta bombing in October 2002, the Balinese were nervous about the growing influx of 'foreigners' from other parts of Indonesia. But they remained proud of their traditional tolerance of the Chinese and Muslim minorities which have been with them for hundreds of years. Especially in the north, the degree of cultural mingling at the local level between Muslims and Hindus has been substantial and there has been considerable intermarriage. The Balinese relationship with the resident Chinese has been helped by the entrepreneurial aptitude of the Balinese themselves. By and large, and despite the sometimes harsh role of Chinese money lenders during the colonial period, the Balinese have never felt economically marginalised by the Chinese minority.

Christians, both Catholics and Protestants, are a third important and growing minority on Bali. Some are non-Balinese who have moved to the island, while others are Balinese converts whose numbers have increased modestly since the relaxation of Dutch restrictions on missionary activity. Christianity undoubtedly appeals to some Balinese who are offended by caste distinctions, but the cost of conversion, in terms of isolation from family and community ties, can be high.

The fact that many Christians are converts from Hinduism, not historically discrete 'foreigners', has no doubt been the main cause of some Hindu-Christian tension evident recently. But it is less significant than the ongoing debate over caste and priestly authority within the Hindu community itself, which is discussed in a later chapter.

There is a fourth important and often misunderstood social category, the Bali Aga or Mountain Balinese. *Aga* derives from a word meaning 'mountain' in the Old Javanese language. The Bali Aga are distinguished by their mountain environment and, in some cases, distinctive village style. They live mainly around the volcanic uplands, but also in the village of Tenganan, a popular tourist destination located near the seaside resort town of Candidasa in eastern Bali and famous for its unique double–*ikat* textiles.

Too often tourist guides and others depict the Bali Aga as an earlier, older substratum of the population who were conquered by a later wave of orthodox Hindus from the Javanese kingdom of Majapahit and their Balinese followers. In fact, there is no evidence that the ancestors of the Bali Aga arrived on the island earlier than other Balinese. However, there are important religious and kinship distinctions between them and other Balinese, above all the absence of caste.

In the 1930s, anthropologist Margaret Mead chose a Bali Aga village for her field work (Bayunggede, near Lake Batur) because she felt it represented a more essential version of Balinese culture than the wealthier, ceremonial-encrusted communities of south Bali. But in modern times some Bali Aga have come to feel that they are treated as less then wholly Balinese.

How did the distinction between Bali Aga and other Balinese originate? We do not know, but it probably occurred because the ancestors of the Bali Aga were closely associated with the kingdoms which existed before the Majapahit conquest and were never fully subjugated by the new Majapahit rulers and their Balinese heirs. Today the Bali Aga comprise between 2 and 3 per cent of the total population.

Intricate and formal delights: The appeal of Balinese culture

This is a book about Balinese history, not Balinese culture, using 'culture' in its anthropological sense to cover the totality of social structure and behaviour. Hundreds of books, many of them excellent, describe the art, art history, architecture, cosmology, ethnography, literature, dance, drama, music, religion and social structure of Bali. Here I will do no more than outline a few characteristics which have greatly influenced the history and politics of the island. Among the most important of these is Bali's aesthetic appeal, initially to Westerners but more recently to others, including other Indonesians. This attractive force became obvious soon after the Dutch conquered south Bali, when reports from dazzled visitors made the island famous in less than three decades.

Then as now, Bali's appeal had many facets. As the sole survivor of a great Indonesian Hindu civilisation, long isolated from the outside world, Bali seemed ineffably romantic. Bali's music, art and dance were prolific, ranging in form from refined to earthy, the product of participation by all social classes, often humorous and always changing. It was, unlike much of the high art of Asia, easy for outsiders to enjoy. The Balinese welcomed foreign observers and were quick to recognise them as a source of income. They seemed contented and harmonious. Few foreign visitors were sensitive to evidence of poverty and social stress, or stayed long enough to encounter it. In any case, Balinese poverty was less extreme than in most other parts of Asia.

Bali's people were beautiful, although the lure of bare breasts, long since covered except for a few expatriates on Kuta Beach, has been exaggerated. Bali appealed above all because it was something very rare, a high civilisation in a rural setting of unsurpassed beauty. It combined the fascinations of a South Sea idyll with those of the Timeless East.

Margaret Mead caught it when she said of Balinese villagers, 'Their lives were packed with intricate and formal delights'.[3]

Bali's cultural appeal was of critical importance because it led in time to the development of tourism, which has today overshadowed agriculture as the island's most important economic activity. Tourism made Bali one of the wealthiest Indonesian provinces, and in time generated a new set of problems, from water shortages to terrorism, which could hardly have been imagined 50 years ago.

Recent writing often suggests that the growth of Bali's tourist industry was primarily the result of clever marketing, first by the Dutch, later by the Indonesian national government, and that many if not most Balinese were exploited in the process. There is some truth in this approach, but it tends to discount unduly the more important reality that no such effort could have succeeded had Balinese culture not generated admiration on its own merits.

In my final chapter I discuss the results of tourism development as they appear today. For the moment it is sufficient to be aware that all the fuss has not been about nothing. That Balinese culture has also generated half a century of pop clichés and commercial fluff, from Bali H'ai to Bali bras, does not make its legitimate appeal any less genuine.

But there are other, more specific features of Balinese culture which need to be comprehended in order to understand Balinese history and politics. These features can be divided into two broad categories, one illustrating the often playful intricacy of Balinese social and artistic culture, the other helping to explain the competitiveness between elements in Balinese society. This competitive streak has been an important although far from exclusive cause of the faction-riddled, often violent character of the island's history.

Intricacy is inherent to Bali's appeal, as Margaret Mead noted. Balinese social order is rarely chaotic. At any level there is a design which befuddled foreigners can sometimes appreciate, whether or not they ever master its details—and if they do, they will discover that, in another village down the road, things are done differently.

The intricate patterns of Bali's culture have been a gold mine for students of human behaviour. A good example is the classic essay by anthropologist Clifford Geertz on the Balinese way of keeping time. The Balinese system has two calendar years, one more or less like our own 365-day solar calendar and one of 210 days arranged in 30 seven-day weeks, plus a variety of additional week cycles of differing lengths, all of which run simultaneously. The intersection of the cycles tells the expert interpreter whether any given day is auspicious or inauspicious, or somewhere in between, for performing various activities, ritual and otherwise. Thus it is that the unfortunate tourist who arrives in Bali at the most inauspicious of times may find the island devoid of activity, and consider demanding a refund.

Geertz concludes:

> The cycles and supercycles are endless, unanchored, and uncountable and, as their internal order has no significance, without climax. They do not accumulate, they do not build, and they are not consumed. *They don't tell you what time it is, they tell you what kind of time it is.*[4] (emphasis added)

Geertz goes on to explain that the Balinese find this kind of complexity, which is reflected in almost all aspects of their art and social behaviour, pleasing and beautiful both to themselves and to the gods. Manipulating the intricate forms is amusing to humans and at the same time a form of worship.

To cite another example, it should come as no surprise that the Balinese system of personal naming, while not quite as complex as the calendar system, is rather more elaborate and informative than most. Thus, to cover just the main points, Balinese names typically consist of three elements. The first tells you the bearer's birth order from first through fourth, after which the cycle begins again. In numerical order these names are Wayan (or Putu), Made, Nyoman and Ketut; they are the same for both sexes, but are not always used by the nobility. The second element is a title, which indicates caste. Ida Bagus (male) or Ida Ayu (female) identifies a member of the highest, *brahmana* or priestly, caste. Dewa (male) or Desak (female) denotes the warrior or kingly (*satria*) caste. Cokorde is a royal *satria* title. Gede (or Gde) is another *satria* title indicating that the person is important within his clan, while Anak Agung is a title that was bestowed by the Dutch on those who held official positions under them. I Gusti denotes *wesia* status, the lowest order of nobility, while I (male) and Ni (female) are indicators of commoner or *sudra* status.

The third element in Balinese naming is a personal or given name or names; there may be two. But there are no family names, so you won't learn who the bearer's father or mother is. And the full-blown system becomes much more complicated when the widespread use of tekonyms—terms derived from family status used in place of a name, for example, 'mother of so-and-so'—is taken into account. In the broader Indonesian context, Balinese are instantly identifiable as such by their names. Warning: there are regional variations in Balinese naming, as in almost everything else.

Temple organisation is another example of the Balinese propensity for intricate social structure. Each village has at minimum a trilogy of important temples—a village-origin temple concerned primarily with ancestor worship, a death temple concerned with the correct handling of malevolent forces and death, and a third temple concerned primarily with the spiritual oversight of irrigated rice land.

Most village-origin temples have a written charter which spells out the rules and obligations which their membership is supposed to follow. This document, written on *lontar* (palm leaf material), is itself an object of worship and can be read only under proper ritual circumstances. It defines numerous aspects of social life, some of which go well beyond the purely religious, such as the rules for membership in various local councils. It also specifies fines for breaking any of the rules. The regulations themselves have sacred character, and to transgress them puts the entire community at risk of supernatural punishment. These temple charters vary considerably in content from one village to another, generating well-honed awareness of the difference between 'us' and 'them'.

Every Balinese temple, regardless of its size or function, has a specified membership responsible for its ritual observances. The term for such a congregation, *pemaksan*, is drawn from the word *paksa*, meaning 'obligatory work', which is revealing. Even if you are Balinese, you can't just wander into a temple and worship; you must be a member, although you may be a non-resident member.

But this is only the beginning of the temple story. There are state temples for each of the major traditional kingdoms, usually at the three points of the sacred axis between sea, royal centre and mountain. There are national temples, of which the most important is the mother temple, Besakih, high on the slopes of Gunung Agung. At this complex of more than 20 shrines, some dating to pre-Hindu times, all Balinese can worship regardless of their social status.

The major water temples mentioned earlier, Pura Ulun Danu Batur and Pura Ulun Danu Bratan, each serve the entire region covered by their respective outflow systems. Downstream from them, each irrigation association (*subak*) has its own temple in addition to the village agricultural temple mentioned above.

Since Balinese gods are constantly on the move there are, quite considerately, temples where they can come down to rest in mid-passage. There are temples at bridges, at dangerous intersections, at sharp turns in roads, under huge dark banyan trees, and anywhere else where malevolent forces are probably lurking. There are temples in offices and of course in homes. The preparation and presentation of offerings, largely the business of women, is constantly and visibly under way everywhere, from hotels and office buildings to the most remote villages, a constant reminder of the pervasive importance of Balinese religion.

There were 53 temples in the village of Sukawati, not counting household temples, when anthropologist Stephen Lansing studied there

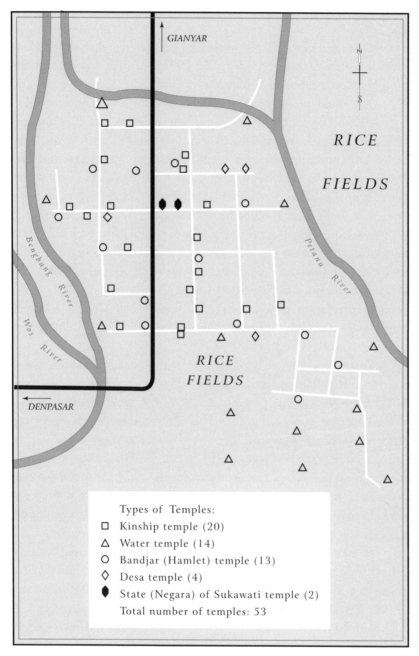

GIANYAR

RICE

FIELDS

Bengbang River

Wos River

Petanu River

DENPASAR

RICE
FIELDS

Types of Temples:

□ Kinship temple (20)

△ Water temple (14)

○ Bandjar (Hamlet) temple (13)

◇ Desa temple (4)

◆ State (Negara) of Sukawati temple (2)

Total number of temples: 53

Temples in Sukawati, a south Balinese town. In this case there is a 'state temple' because Sukawati was once the capital of a small kingdom and is the ancestral home of the present royal family of Ubud. (Source: J. Stephen Lansing, The Three Worlds of Bali, Praeger) a few years ago (see map). No one knows how many temples of all kinds there are on Bali, but if household temples are included the number would certainly run into hundreds of thousands.

One could cite many more examples of Bali's rich array of social organisation. If it seems hard to comprehend, think back to an earlier period in almost everyone's pre-industrial past. For illustration I will take a late nineteenth-century small town in the American Midwest. One would have found that organisations of all kinds were very important. There would have been first and foremost a church, or more likely several of them. There might have been an annual town meeting to vote on issues of local government. There would have been a farmers' association, part of the Grange movement, and in addition there might have been a farmers' cooperative. There would have been a Civil War veterans' association and a variety of civic, business and social organisations (Freemasons, Elks, Knights of Columbus, and so on). Depending on the period and the location, there would have been railroad and other labour unions.

There would have been school boards and local branches of political parties (perhaps only one depending on location). Finally, there would have been ad hoc committees to arrange such important rituals as the Fourth of July celebration. There might also have been organisations based on kinship, like the Daughters of the American Revolution, its members perforce descended from those who fought the struggle for independence, or in areas of heavy Scottish ancestry a clan association or two. Life in such a setting was very different from the kind of atomised existence that many Americans, now overwhelmingly urban, experience today.

There is not that much to distinguish Balinese civic and political culture from this kind of pattern, except the intricacy of detail and the intensity and persistence of such organisational behaviour up to the present day. As in our Midwestern American example, Balinese social organisation includes a variety of categories: professional, religious, civic; some based on place of residence, others on kinship or ancestry. But the kinship-based organisations are far more important in Bali, relatively speaking, than they ever were in Averageville, Indiana.

Civic and professional organisation

The *banjar*, translated as 'hamlet' or 'ward', is the smallest and in many ways most important of Balinese civic entities. The term 'neighbour-hood' would perhaps convey its essence better, except for the vagueness which that word implies to most of us. There are several *banjar* in a village, or *desa*, the next larger unit in the system. Balinese villages are notoriously difficult to define, thanks in part to extensive tinkering by the Dutch and by successive Indonesian regimes. Suffice it to say that the 'customary law village' in a given area, which includes the afore-mentioned trilogy of temples, does not always correspond to the 'administrative village' based on government convenience and/or fiat.

The Balinese *banjar*, unlike a Western neighbourhood, is precise, structured and invariably important. It often owns property, such as a meeting hall, market shed and gamelan orchestra. It may decide who can reside where, it has other rule-making authority, and it is to be taken seriously; if you don't attend your *banjar* meeting, you will be fined. In general, the Balinese seem mildly addicted to organisational rules and fines. Everyone who lives in the *banjar* is a member, including the nobil-ity and even expatriates.

Banjar councils perform many important community functions, such as road upkeep, participation in major funerals and the organisa-tion of quasi-police structures. The '*banjar* system' is credited for much of the Balinese success in implementing government programmes such as family planning and transmigration because it provides an effective mechanism for community discussion and decision making.

Temples and *banjar* are only part of the story, albeit important ones. The Balinese appear at times to verge on compulsive-obsessive when it comes to organisation. If something needs doing they form a club, so to speak, to do it. In 1975 Hildred and Clifford Geertz observed:

*A Balinese village in 1915, showing pottery, bare breasts and mud brick walls
protected by thatch, all of which have disappeared from the Balinese scene.*
(Source: *Royal Tropical Institute, Amsterdam*)

It should be clear by now that the overriding principle in
Balinese social structure as a whole is one of functional
specificity for every group. That is to say, the premise 'an
independent group for every purpose, and only one purpose
per group' is pursued in Bali almost to the limit of its poten-
tialities. Various social functions, which in many traditional
societies are performed by a single coherent set of institutions, are, in Bali, each provided with a separate
autonomous social apparatus.[5]

Among the most important of Balinese organisations is the *subak*,
or irrigation association, which is both civic and professional. No one
who visits south Bali should fail to walk out in the rice fields and experience the beauty and dazzling physical complexity of the canals, ditches,
tunnels and terraces which organise the flow of water to farmers. Due to

steep intervening ravines, water must be tapped high on the mountain slopes to reach lower elevations. The *subak* manages the downstream end of this system, coordinating not only the use of the water, but the planting and harvesting cycles which are extremely important to ensure that each farmer gets water when he needs it and that the agricultural cycle is timed to minimise pest infestations.

The membership of a *subak* is made up of those who own the rice fields within its boundaries; they are co-proprietors, not necessarily, as in the case of the *banjar*, co-residents. The *subak* is religious as well as agricultural in nature; each has its own temple dedicated to the goddess of rice, Dewi Sri, which also serves as a meeting place for members.

A *subak* is relatively small, with one or two hundred members, so it typically depends on one major water source. This requires a hierarchy of irrigation authority above the *subak* level, accomplished partly through temples and temple ceremonies and, for much of south Bali, originating in the two major water temples on the big volcanic lakes. With urbanisation progressing rapidly in south Bali, *subak* have willy-nilly become increasingly involved in broader water-use issues, as tourism and industry compete for what is becoming a scarce resource.

A good place to see a modern quasi-urban *subak* is Ubud, where several of them are bounded by the main street of town, now densely lined with hotels, restaurants and boutiques. In places irrigation water is running under the tourist-laden sidewalks.

The Dutch, who knew a thing or two about water control, were suitably impressed by the hydraulic virtuosity of the Balinese, one small reason why the island came to occupy a special niche in their colonial philosophy.

It is worth mentioning two additional things about Balinese civic culture. First, the Dutch colonial regime significantly altered a number of key institutions, in a partially successful effort to make administration cheaper and more convenient (see Chapter 6). However, the *banjar*, 'the fundamental civil community in Bali',[6] has remained more or less as it was.

Second, for reasons which are anything but clear, the structured and rule-shrouded character of the Balinese community, including the existence of caste, is without counterpart on previously Hindu Java, despite the close historic ties between Bali and its big neighbour. This raises the interesting question, to be discussed later, of whether there is a historical explanation for this contrast.

Kinship-based organisation

Virtually all Balinese belong to kinship-based organisations, some of them local, others island-wide. The most famous are the high-caste groups and royal lineages whose members trace their descent back to Javanese nobles who arrived in the fourteenth century and their Balinese associates. Caste status is of course hereditary, as are the titles that go along with it.

Caste continued to matter in the colonial period because the Dutch exempted the three high castes from community service, less euphemistically described as corvée labour. It still matters, as witness the lopsided proportion of Balinese in senior government positions whose names indicate high-caste origin. Polygamy, concubinage and widespread variations in the written record have always encouraged disputes and claims to higher caste status, which could and still can be litigated. The Gedong Kertya in Singaraja, north Bali, is a library established by the Dutch for the preservation of traditional texts. It is now patronised mainly by Balinese doing genealogical research not out of purely academic interest.

Go back to our Midwestern village with its Daughters of the American Revolution and imagine that membership in this august association determined not just attendance at tea parties, but real political power. Passion to prove that one really did have an ancestor who fought the war for independence might well have reached white heat. Motivation of this kind has long driven Balinese attention to ancestry.

On Bali most genealogical records were copied and recopied on palm-leaf manuscripts which rapidly decayed in the hot, humid climate, and as most of the scribes worked for, or under the influence of, some powerful and not disinterested patron, there is some lively variety in the historical record. The Balinese have been writing history for centuries, in the form of chronicles or *babad*, and it should not be a matter for surprise that accounts written to bolster the prestigious ancestry of individual rulers tend to present multiple and often contradictory versions of key events.

Illustrious ancestry was by no means the sole determinant of political power on Bali, but it mattered a great deal. In the early eighteenth century, one of the first things that the founder of the new Kingdom of Mengwi did was to establish his legitimacy by unveiling, with the help of a priestly advisor, a distinguished family tree (Chapter 4). Indeed, the history of the island has been characterised by constant competition for power legitimised by descent.

Competition among descent groups goes a long way to explain Balinese preoccupation with rank and status, something that has troubled sympathetic Western observers who have difficulty reconciling it with the apparent democracy of local institutions like the *subak* and *banjar*. Such competition has encouraged and envenomed political factionalism throughout Balinese history. It was one factor behind the terrible bloodletting of 1965–66 on the island following the failed communist coup in Jakarta. The spirit of competition on Bali does not stop with kinship-based organisations, and it can have very real positive aspects, as when communities compete for excellence in the arts.

As this book is written, a debate within the Balinese Hindu establishment over the role of high-caste *brahmana* priests resonates because it reflects on the status of important elements in Balinese society. Many Balinese belong to ancient clans, one of the best known being the island-wide metalworker or smith (*pandé*) clan, which have no high caste status but are nonetheless powerful and important. Some of the most significant of these groups are associated with the Bali Aga and

Balinese Hinduism includes Buddhist elements, as illustrated by this 'Buddhist' priest photographed in 1915. (Source: KITLV Archives, Leiden)

date back to the time before the Majapahit conquest. Today these non-caste descent groups are sometimes referred to collectively as *pasek*. Their ceremonial importance has long been recognised. For example, the leader of the major water temple at Lake Batur is a non-caste *pasek* priest. Yet some high-caste Hindus argue that such priests should be subordinate to those with high-caste, Majapahit-derived credentials.

Caste and Hinduism on Bali

According to virtually all writing on the subject, there are three high castes on Bali. The highest, *brahmana*, is the priestly caste, but not all *brahmana* are priests. The *satria* or warrior caste was the caste of most rulers. Note that priests theoretically outranked kings, just as they did in India or mediaeval Europe; in the pre-colonial period, this had about the same limited degree of real-world meaning. Today many *satria* are in business as well as government. The *wesia*, third in status, were merchants in the Indian system, but on Bali they have tended to be minor officials. Together these three groups comprise a kind of gentry known as the *triwangsa*, which now amounts to less than 10 per cent of the population. Since Dutch times, all other Balinese have been lumped together as *sudra* or 'commoners', including members of otherwise prestigious descent groups mentioned above, such as the metalworking or smith clan.

However, Balinese caste differs from the better-known Indian model in fundamental ways. The work-related aspects of caste are much less strict than in the mainstream Indian model, there are fewer ritual restrictions on social contact between people of differing castes and there is nothing resembling the Indian concept of untouchability. These differences are profound, to the point where the term 'caste' is misleading and arguably not appropriate for what are really no more than status distinctions, important to be sure, but similar to those found on Java and elsewhere. I have used the term 'caste' only because it is embedded in the literature about Bali and, despite its Dutch-manufactured aspects, largely accepted by the Balinese themselves.

As early as the twelfth century, inscriptions mention what appear to be caste distinctions, but we know nothing about actual practice at that time. The Balinese themselves believe that caste in its present form was imported from Java by a talented Hindu priest only at the time of the Majapahit conquest in 1343, discussed in Chapter 3.

The Dutch systematically reinforced and rigidified the system of caste, part of a broader effort to bring order out of apparent chaos by reinventing the norms of a centralised Balinese state which, in fact as opposed to legend, may never have existed. But caste certainly was important before the colonial era. For a woman to marry a man of lower caste was a serious offence theoretically punishable by death. For a man to marry a lower-caste woman was, on the other hand, quite acceptable. Semen, like water, the Balinese believed, should flow down-hill.[7] As we shall see, caste was beginning to become more formal and rigid even before Dutch rule.

As in the case of caste, the Balinese version of Hinduism differs in many ways from Indian Hinduism, which of course itself has many local variations in India. Fusion with ancestor worship is particularly prominent on Bali, yet the practice of deifying monarchs as god-kings, customary on Java and elsewhere in Indianised Southeast Asia, seems to have existed only in the Old Bali period, before the fourteenth century.

Much of the physical and aesthetic character of Balinese Hinduism is gloriously unique. Balinese gods include such familiar Hindu deities as Brahma, Shiva and Vishnu, as well as a whole universe of localised gods and spirits, such as the water goddesses who dwell in the big volcanic lakes. This spirit world, the world of the unseen, including ancestral spirits, is far more important in daily life than the Indian-origin pantheon. That is why you will see women putting out offerings at various points around your hotel, and just about everywhere else.

A Balinese temple is a place where the highly mobile gods descend on important festive days. There are no dominating images of particular deities, much less of god-kings. A walled courtyard encloses a number of shrines as well as sheds and other structures necessary for the preparation of offerings. Apart from their distinctive and sometimes monumental gates, most Balinese temples are modest and visibly community oriented, unlike the more massive structures of India, ancient Java or Cambodia.

Buddhist elements are integrated into Balinese Hinduism to the point where the term 'Hinduism' itself is less than wholly satisfactory. One of the prevailing myths about Bali is that it became a repository for Javanese Hinduism after an exodus of refugees from Hindu Java following the Islamic conquest of Majapahit in the early sixteenth century. Assuredly Bali remained Hindu, and many ancient texts and traditions were preserved there and in the Balinese communities on

Lombok, but there may have been little in the way of a physical exodus from Java. The great Hindu epics, *Mahabharata* and *Ramayana*, are extremely important in Balinese culture, although hardly more so than they still are on nominally Muslim Java.

The features of modern Balinese culture thus include those which arrived with Indian civilisation, beginning roughly twelve centuries ago, and those which, like ancestor worship, originated thousands of years before that. The next chapter examines briefly what little we know about Bali's prehistoric period.

2
MOONSET AT PEJENG: GLIMPSES OF BALINESE PREHISTORY

My wife and I were trying to photograph Bali's most notable prehistoric relic, the 'moon' of Pejeng, but we seemed to be too early. This 'moon', the world's biggest bronze kettledrum, remains where it has been for no one knows how long, resting on its side in a brick, wood and thatch tower at the Pura Penataran Sasih, a village temple near Pejeng, only a few minutes' drive from Ubud in south Bali.

We hoped that the late evening sun might illuminate the westward-facing tympanum of the drum, with its star-shaped central design, but the light as the sun set was too harsh, and the drum was more obscured than usual by gold and white cloth decorations. It turned out that in less than a week the real moon would be full, and there would be a big temple and cockfighting festival here. It would draw thousands of hopeful Balinese and their prize birds, not to mention hordes of tourists, and preparations were well underway.

A chatty temple worker showed us around while we waited in vain for the light to improve. The edges of the temple courtyard are lined with eroded fragments of ancient carvings, statues of Hindu gods and other religious relics somewhat haphazardly gathered together. This region was the centre of ancient Bali, where irrigated rice agriculture probably first flourished and where the civilisation we know as Balinese probably began. Our guide, proud of his rudimentary English, pointed out the artefacts, complained that he was not paid for his temple labours, asked if we would like to buy some land, and cadged a tip for his services. The Pejeng moon remained defiantly unphotographable.

This remarkable metal moon was first reported to the western world by G.E. Rumphius in his book *The Ambonese Curiosity Cabinet*, published in 1705. Rumphius, German by birth, was a gifted amateur scholar who served the Dutch East India Company for 40 years on the island of Ambon in the spice-producing region of Indonesia's far east. Although he was blind, Rumphius recorded everything he knew about the natural history of the island world, including prehistoric relics. He never set foot on Bali, but heard about the moon and its legend from a Dutch ship captain who was among the first European visitors to the island.

According to Balinese legend, the Pejeng moon was a wheel of the chariot that pulled the real moon through the night sky. Once upon a time, as it was passing over Pejeng, it became detached and fell into a tree, glowing almost as brightly as the moon itself. The light disturbed a thief at his labours. Annoyed, he climbed the tree and urinated on the drum, paying with his life for this sacrilege. The wheel eventually cooled down, lost its glow, and has been preserved to this day by the local villagers.

The inhabitants of ancient Pejeng zealously guarded the sacred object in its pavilion, and it was not easily approached. Indeed it was not systematically described until 1906 when the itinerant Dutch artist W.O.J. Nieuwenkamp—the same person depicted in a north Balinese temple mural in Balinese dress, riding a bicycle—managed to climb into the pavilion to measure and draw it.

It turned out to be a gigantic bronze kettledrum, over 1.8 metres in height. It is similar in shape to much smaller metal drums made in eastern Indonesia until relatively recently, and to others still being made

29

in New Guinea from perishable materials. Despite its unusual elongated form—the majority of the drums found on Java and elsewhere are squatter in conformation—the Pejeng instrument is clearly in the tradition of the great bronze drums of Southeast Asia which are the hallmark of its bronze–iron age and have been found from southern China to eastern Indonesia.

It could have been used as a musical instrument by hanging it horizontally from one of the big lugs on its side and striking the tympanum. But it was almost certainly more important as a ritual object and, as it still is, a source of magical power to the owners. Recent archaeological discoveries in north Bali, together with the study of hundreds of drums from other areas of Indonesia, suggest that it could be as much as 2000 years old. Although similar but smaller drums were made on Bali, experts tend to believe that, because of its extremely large size, the Pejeng moon was imported, possibly from mainland Asia.

Earliest arrivals: Did Java Man make it to Bali?

Balinese prehistory does not begin with the Pejeng moon; indeed, it is safe to say that the moon arrived very late in the story of human presence on the island, which could stretch back hundreds of thousands of years. Unfortunately, the earliest prehistoric evidence from Bali consists of scattered and therefore undatable finds of artefacts, supplemented by conjecture based on discoveries elsewhere in the region, especially Java. Only relatively recently does the picture begin to clarify somewhat, thanks to linguistic evidence and some systematic excavation of stratified archaeological sites, including finds which are amenable to radiocarbon dating.

Traces of *Homo erectus*, an early hominid precursor of modern man, *Homo sapiens*, have been found elsewhere in Indonesia. The most famous example is Java Man. Dutch palaeontologists found his or her skull fragments near Solo in Central Java; they are now estimated to be as much as 1.5 million years old. These remains are associated with hand axes and other roughly shaped stone tools. While similar Palaeolithic (old stone age) tools have been found on Bali, they have not been excavated from stratified sites and could date from a more recent period. We simply don't know whether Java Man made it to Bali or not.

What we do know is that *Homo sapiens* did not arrive in Indonesia until a much later period. The shallow seas of the Sunda Shelf between Indonesia and the Asian mainland were dry during periods of intense ice-age glaciation, most recently about 18 000 years ago, when the sea was 100 metres or more lower than at present. The resulting expansion of land area presumably facilitated new migrations southward from the Asian mainland, but it was a slow process. While most details remain obscure, prehistorians now believe that by about 40 000 years ago the *Homo sapiens* ancestors of the present-day inhabitants of New Guinea and Australia were already in place.

As part of the same broad process, people related to the Australia and New Guinea-bound migrants settled in Southeast Asia, including Bali. They were eventually absorbed by later arrivals, except for small Negrito and other fragmented populations which have survived in Malaysia, the Philippines and elsewhere.

These early humans—Melanesians, native Australians and Negritos—were for the most part hunters and gatherers, not farmers, although on New Guinea they developed some of the earliest forms of agriculture known anywhere. Their modern descendants speak a diverse collection of languages very different from the Austronesians who followed them.

The Austronesian revolution: Bronze, iron and the development of agriculture

The prehistoric situation clarifies somewhat only at a much more recent date. About 6000 years ago, people speaking Austronesian languages began moving from the Chinese mainland onto Taiwan. Two thousand or so years later this dispersal was continuing southwards through the Philippines and into the Indonesian Archipelago. 'Austronesian' is the currently accepted term for what used to be called 'Malayo-Polynesian'. This great language family is spoken from Vietnam (by the Rhadai and Jarai in the mountains and the Chams in the lowlands) to Taiwan (by the 'aborigines' there), Hawaii, New Zealand and Madagascar. It includes the languages of the vast majority of people in Malaysia, Indonesia and the Philippines today.

Unlike the New Guinea-Australian-Negrito languages, Austronesian languages are remarkably similar to each other. This linguistic similarity is strong evidence of rapid geographic dispersal, attesting to the high seafaring skills and consequent mobility of the Austronesians. But the details of their migrations are a great mystery. For example, no one has a clear idea how, or from where, they got to Madagascar, only about 2000 years ago. And the late Thor Heyerdahl had no trouble, by means of his daring *Kon-Tiki* sea voyage, persuading millions of readers, in the face of compelling linguistic evidence to the contrary, that the Pacific Islanders, or at least some them, had come from Peru.

The Austronesians were cultural revolutionaries, associated with new artistic styles, the development of metalworking and agriculture. The Pejeng moon was probably imported by Austronesian speakers whose language was closely related to modern Balinese, at least as closely as modern English is related to Old English. Drums are not the only ancient bronze artefacts found on Bali. There are also ceremonial axes, although none as gorgeous as the specimens from the Lesser Sunda islands to the east, and anklets and other ornaments. Similar artefacts, featuring spiral patterns, ship motifs, and friezes of humans and animals, are widespread from the Asian mainland to eastern Indonesia. This style seems to have originated between 2500 and 2300 years ago and is known as Dong Son, after a site in northern Vietnam where many of these items were produced and presumably traded into the Indonesian Archipelago.

In addition to metal implements, stone sarcophagi and jars used for burials dating from the same period have been found in large numbers on Bali. There is an excellent, well-displayed collection of them in the antiquities museum in Bedulu, not far from the Pejeng moon. Most have been haphazard finds with the human remains they once contained long vanished, but enough have now been systematically excavated to prove the existence of a highly stratified society with emphasis on burial rites, possibly including human sacrifice, and ancestor worship. The overall pattern is consistent with what we know of similar societies elsewhere in Indonesia, where some bronze–iron age cultures remained largely untouched until the colonial era, most notably in Toraja land (Sulawesi), in the Batak highlands (Sumatra), on Nias off the west coast of Sumatra and in portions of eastern Indonesia.

The introduction of metal tools was among the most important aspects of the Austronesian revolution. Iron and bronze implements, including weapons, appear at the same time, which is why scholars of the region do not refer to a discrete 'bronze age' but rather to a 'bronze–iron' age. This chronology is significant because iron tools would have been necessary—or at least extremely useful—not only for making the most lethal weapons, but also for clearing the forest and for digging irrigation tunnels through volcanic rock. These two activities were essential to the full development of the wet rice agriculture upon which Balinese civilisation would depend. It is not hard to understand why metalworkers and their descent groups were accorded privileged status in early Bali.

We do not know when the Balinese began developing irrigated rice agriculture, leading to the complex irrigation and terracing which exist today. Rice itself has been around for a long time. Archaeologists have found evidence of rice culture on Bali dating to about 2000 years ago, but there is no way to tell whether it was irrigated or not. Efforts to date the older portions of the terraces themselves have not yielded conclusive results thus far.

The question is important, because without the increased production made possible by irrigation, the economic surpluses required to

Bali's magnificently terraced rice fields probably developed gradually, beginning before the arrival of Indian religion. (Source: Robert Pringle)

finance the artistic and ceremonial aspects of Balinese culture would not have been possible. Before irrigated rice, there was of course non-irrigated or dry rice cultivation, still practised throughout the tropics in hilly areas, or where water is not available. But it is not nearly as productive.

Except in swampy areas, non-irrigated cultivation requires the farmer to 'slash and burn' the forest cover. The ash from the burning is an essential source of nutrients, because in most tropical areas without the benefit of recent volcanic fertilisation, soils are notoriously poor, due to leaching by the constant warm rains which prevents organic material from accumulating. As a result, a typical dry rice field can be used once only or twice before the farmer must abandon it and move to a new area, or return to an old one covered with secondary growth and repeat the slash-and-burn process. Irrigation makes possible major increases in productivity and population, because a watery environment around the rice plants creates a nutrient-rich stew which sustains growth, even without fertilisation. Because of this, an irrigated field can be farmed permanently without depleting the soil.

There were two major challenges to be overcome before highly developed irrigated rice cultivation was possible on Bali: clearing the forest and mastering the engineering and social-political management required to channel and distribute water equitably through irrigation systems stretching for many kilometres. Clearing big trees in old-growth forest and above all creating complex waterworks, especially tunnels through rock, required the iron and bronze tools that were both present by 2000 years ago.

References to wet rice agriculture and specifically to irrigation tunnel-building occur in some of the earliest inscriptions found on Bali, dating to the ninth century AD. These inscriptions, written in Indian script, were part of a broader cultural transfer discussed in the next chapter. But there is no reason to believe that irrigation itself depended on technology associated with the adoption of Indian religion and writing. There is equally little reason to assume that today's complex agriculture was created overnight. The Balinese are likely to have initiated it in a rudimentary way in the more easily irrigated areas, with the water tunnels and complex canal systems which now exist evolving only gradually. The Petanu-Pakrisan valleys near the modern Ubud area, the same region where the moon of Pejeng resides, may have been particularly well suited for this evolution because the rainfall is relatively low, and the forest cover for that reason was easier for the Balinese pioneers to clear.[1]

Were there political preconditions for irrigation? None other than Karl Marx concluded that the labour mobilisation required for large-scale water management must have required 'despotic' control by powerful kings. This idea was an important element in his theory of historical evolution, and it led to the concept of 'oriental' or 'hydraulic' despotism. From his cold damp seat in the British Museum, Marx even surmised in 1853 that the Hinduism then being practised on Bali must be similar to that which had supported such 'despotism' in India before British rule.[2]

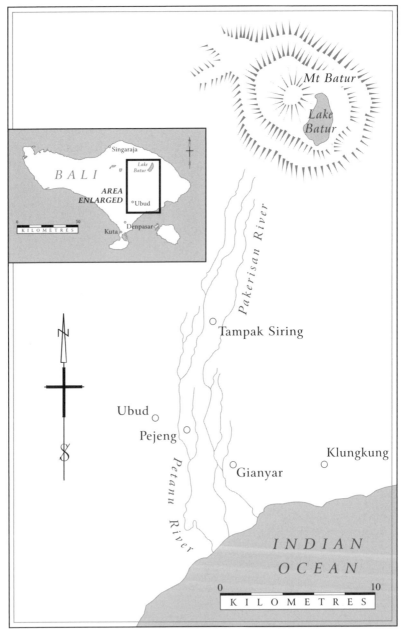

This area between the Petanu and Pakrisan Rivers and the modern towns of Ubud and Gianyar is the heartland of south Bali. The great bronze drum of Pejeng is located here, it is likely that complex irrigated rice culture evolved here, and it was probably the location of the principal royal courts of Old Bali from the ninth to the mid-fourteenth centuries, although scholarly debate continues on the last two points.

More recently, social scientists observing the *subak* cooperatives have gone to the other extreme and stressed the egalitarian community-based nature of Balinese irrigation management. As we shall see, however, the historical record indicates that there was indeed a role for strong kings in the expansion of wet rice agriculture as late as the eighteenth century, even though they were far from being the oriental despots of political theory.

The importance of early trade

Recent archaeology on Bali has underlined the importance of trade as well as agriculture from an early period. Excavations near Gilimanuk in northwest Bali, where the modern ferry arrives from Java, and at an ancient port zone around the villages of Julah, Pacung and Sembiran on the north coast have revealed the existence of trading communities associated with bronze and iron implements and, in the case of Gilimanuk, with stone sarcophagi.

Sembiran, a few kilometres east of Singaraja, is particularly important. There archaeologists working in the early 1990s found fragments of a stone stamp used to decorate moulds for the production of bronze drums. Unlike a similar find from Manuaba in south Bali, this one could be dated and proved to be about 2000 years old. The drums being manufactured in both cases were similar in style to the Pejeng moon, although much smaller; the stamp fragments from south Bali even bear the same human face motif (see page 38), now among the best-known icons of early Southeast Asian art.

From these mould fragments we know that bronze drums were manufactured locally using the lost wax process. Such casting would have required a considerable degree of metallurgical and mechanical skill. Moreover, neither copper nor tin, the components of bronze, is found in quantity on Bali. Hence the raw materials would necessarily have been imported, evidence of long-distance trade with the island by roughly 2000 years ago.

The decorations on the side of the great Pejeng drum, including this famous face motif, are similar to those found on fragments of stone stamps used to decorate bronze drum moulds, which prove that similar but smaller drums were locally made. This drawing was made in 1906 by Dutch artist W.O.J. Nieuwenkamp, the first European to record the drum. (Source: From Van Heekeren, The Bronze-Iron Age of Indonesia, *courtesy of KITLV Press*)

Equally significant, the Sembiran dig also produced quantities of rouletted ware pottery, named for its incised design pattern, which was definitely manufactured in India. This find is fascinating and unusual; it is not typical of other early sites in island Southeast Asia, where evidence of trade with China tends to predominate, mainly in the form of ceramics. We have no idea whether the pottery was brought by Indian traders, or by Indonesian or other middlemen, but direct contact between Bali and India is certainly a possibility.

It should not be assumed that such contact, if it took place, had anything to do with the introduction of Indian religion to Bali. The timing is wrong: it would have predated by several hundred years the first evidence of Hinduism or Buddhism anywhere in Indonesia. More than a thousand years later Islamicisation provides a parallel: Muslims were visiting and trading in Indonesia centuries before widespread conversion to Islam took place.

Bali on the eve of Indianisation

What does all this tell us about the end of prehistory on Bali? It seems clear that by about 1500 years ago, two important types of development were underway: commercial and agricultural. There were trading centres in the west and especially on the north coast, at Gilimanuk, Sembiran and elsewhere. Although the majority of the island remained forested, irrigated agriculture was most likely already in existence in the Petanu-Pakrisan valleys and quite possibly elsewhere. A high and increasingly affluent culture existed which would have looked familiar to a modern inhabitant of Nias, Tanah Toraja, Flores, Roti or any other region in Indonesia where bronze–iron era heritage has remained strong to this day.

There was trade between the Pakrisan-Petanu area in the south and the ports in the north. These ports may have existed initially to conduct beach-based trade in rare woods, rattans, exotic birds, and the forest products used in early medicine. But they would have been increasingly oriented to serve the developing agriculture-based southern settlements, requiring trans-Bali transport routes across the uplands and eventually motivating the southern rulers to exert control over them. Of course, there might have been trade through small ports in south Bali as well, although as yet we have no evidence of it.

We know nothing about the politics of Bali in the immediate pre-Indian period or the names of any of the rulers, who did not possess writing and thus could not leave records. It is unlikely that any of them aspired to rule beyond a limited area, if only because the concept of kingship, of monarchy divinely ordained to rule beyond the limits of extended family, probably arrived only with Indian civilisation. For that reason, the bronze–iron age rulers are best thought of as chiefs, not kings.

But we can assume that by the eighth century at the latest, the high chiefs of the Pakrisan-Petanu area, no doubt including the lord of the Pejeng moon, were increasingly in contact with the commercial north and through it with the outside world. By this time relatively powerful Indianised states existed in central Java. They left great monuments, including the splendid Borobodur temple, with its murals depicting sophisticated ships, testimony to an already well-developed seafaring tradition. The Balinese chiefs would have learned more about conditions beyond Bali as their interest in trade developed. They would have been poised to move beyond ancestor and volcano worship, and to take advantage of the social and technological assets, especially access to literacy, offered by a powerful world religion already being practised elsewhere in Indonesia. In other words, the political foundation for Indianisation was in place.

3
FROM INDIANISATION TO THE MAJAPAHIT EMPIRE (NINTH TO SIXTEENTH CENTURIES)

The three most important features of Balinese history, it could be argued, were the development of irrigated rice agriculture, the adoption of Indian religion and civilisation, and the growth of tourism. But of these three, it is the Hindu religion in its distinctive local variation which famously defines Bali today. How and why did Indian civilisation reach this island, so distant from the Indian subcontinent?

The Indianisation of Bali was far from an isolated process. From approximately the fifth century onwards, major Indianised states developed throughout what we now call Southeast Asia, a term not invented until World War II. Before that, the region was known as 'Further India', and the great island chain of which Bali is part was the 'Indian Archipelago'. Indeed, until modern times 'India' remained more a cultural than a political concept. Some of the greatest Indian art of all time was created on Java, the most famous example being the Borobodur, a Buddhist monument. Indeed, the term 'Hinduisation', although often

41

used, is somewhat misleading in this context. In fact the religions which took root in Indonesia were variants of both Hinduism and Buddhism, often coexisting or intermingled.

During the nineteenth century, Western ethnologists coined the term 'Indonesia'. Later, in the 1920s, the leaders of the new nationalist movement adopted it to name the country they hoped to establish. Like 'the Indies', 'Indonesia' evoked an ancient Indian political heritage. This was compatible with nationalist aspirations because the greatest pre-colonial state, Majapahit, was also the last and most potent of the Indianised states in the archipelago, laying admittedly dubious claim to an area roughly congruous with modern Indonesia. Majapahit's Hindu-Buddhist heritage was moreover useful for a generation of nation-builders struggling to unify a culturally diverse nation and involved in a passionate debate, which continues today, over the role of a more recently arrived religion, Islam.

The summoning of the Brahmans

For years scholars struggled to decide how and why Indian religion spread across Southeast Asia. Early Western visitors, intrigued by the grand monuments they found and unwilling to accept that local populations had been capable of constructing them, assumed that Indian conquest or colonisation must have taken place. Others thought that Indian traders were the most likely vehicle since, as we have seen, they had been in commercial contact with Southeast Asia well before Indianised states developed there.

Today it is generally accepted that the transfer of Indian religion, like most great religious conversions, was primarily a political process. The key agents of change were local rulers who sought not merely a new form of worship, but access to a new social, political and technological world order. Christianity appealed in much the same way to the pagan leaders of Europe in the waning days of the Roman Empire.

Indianisation brought a revolutionary change in political perspective. As noted in the last chapter, bronze–iron age chieftains, no matter how powerful personally, typically had no concept of rule beyond the limits of extended kinship (clan or tribe). But a central feature of the Indian system was the concept of the universal monarch, or *cakravartin*, whose divinely ordained authority extended indefinitely. Indian civilisation conveyed technology of all sorts, from law codes to architectural manuals. It meant access to literacy and to a great tradition full of useful concepts, both secular and divine. Indian religion did not drive out earlier belief patterns such as ancestor worship, but integrated and built around them, much as Christianity has assimilated many pagan beliefs, feast days and stylistic components, from Halloween to Christmas trees.

The key agent in this process was the brahman, who in the ancient Indian system was a priest, but also and more importantly a prestigious advisor to kings. Thus historians speak of the 'summoning of the brahmans' to denote that crucial if hypothetical moment when local rulers decided that they would avail themselves of this powerful new phenomenon.[1]

At first, such conversions may have been motivated by desire to gain advantage over more backward neighbours. Later, for the laggards, it was no doubt a need to catch up with the latest political fashion. Yet, as we have already seen, the process of Indianisation, like the later process of Islamicisation, was slow and never complete, and some peoples of Indonesia retained their prehistoric religions and political systems until modern times.

We do not know the details of how or why Bali became Indianised. The broader theory of Indianisation does not necessarily apply, for the simple reason that Bali, then as now, was a minor political element in a Java-dominated context. Contacts with Java may have been well developed in prehistoric times, and dynastic interrelationships with already Indianised Javanese courts may have played a dominant role in the introduction of the new order, rather than independent decisions by local rulers to summon a brahman or two.

The Dutch, when they completed the conquest of the island in the early twentieth century, were already well embarked on the study of the great Indianised kingdoms of Java. Recognising Bali's importance as a repository of Hindu-Indonesian culture, and entranced by what they found, they began looking in earnest for evidence to reconstruct early Balinese history. This activity picked up pace between the two world wars, when Dutch scholars investigated artefacts, linked them with local traditions, and began training a first generation of Balinese archaeologists.

The oldest physical evidence of Indianisation on Bali is a collection of small sun-dried clay stupas and seals, the latter impressed with Buddhist images and fragments of religious texts (mantras). Many of them were manufactured locally. They are dated to the eighth or ninth centuries and were revealed by a landslide in 1924 near Pejeng, the site of the great bronze drum discussed in Chapter 2. They are significant for three reasons. First, the mantras on them, written in an old north Indian script, are in the tantric tradition, with its strong emphasis on magic. It is a tradition which runs through the subsequent history of Balinese culture, including most famously the phenomenon of trance and the emphasis on witchcraft.

Second, the stupas and seals indicate the existence of links between Bali and the Sailendra empire of Sumatra and Central Java, and with a widespread international religious establishment which led to the movement of clerics and scholars between India and China via Indonesia. Numerous small stupas identical in style have been found in the vicinity of the Borobudur in Central Java.[2] This great monument was probably completed in about 824.

The Borobudur was the product of an already highly developed state, located only a few hundred kilometres from Bali, on an island where Indian religions had been established for more than three centuries. We have seen that trade routes along the north coast, linking Bali with India, existed by approximately 2000 years ago. Thus it is probable that the Balinese were in contact with the Indianised realms on Java and possibly elsewhere well before the first physical evidence of local Indianisation. Indeed, conversion may have started even before the ninth century.

One authority speculates that the absence of royal inscriptions dating to before the late ninth century signifies only that Bali may have been under the control of a Javanese ruler who would not have issued such edicts locally.[3] That ruler would have been the lord of old Mataram, a Hindu kingdom which ruled in Central Java just before the Buddhist Sailendras who constructed the Borobodur. (Old Mataram should not be confused with the much later Muslim Sultanate of Mataram.)

Third, the Pejeng stupas and seals are Mahayana Buddhist, not Hindu. But it is important not to overemphasise this distinction, for there is often no clear division between these two great world religions in early Southeast Asia. Buddhism in this setting was one of many essentially similar Indian-derived cults. Royalty could and did emphasise different cults at different times.

When rulers were personified as deities and worshipped in god-king cults they sometimes fused Hinduism and Buddhism, producing funerary images of themselves as 'Shiva-Buddha', as did the Javanese king, Kertenagara, who invaded Bali in 1284. Hinduism and Buddhism still coexist on Bali where, although the primary emphasis is now on Shiva, certain priests are still associated with Buddha. As we shall see, the court religion of the Majapahit empire, remembered in Balinese tradition as the major source of modern Balinese Hindu culture, was Mahayana Buddhist.

Old Bali

History as opposed to prehistory begins on Bali with the advent of inscriptions written in Indian scripts on stone and on copper plates. For the first time we learn the names of kings and something of their social and political concerns. The very earliest inscription dates to 896, but does not mention the name of the reigning monarch. I have used the term 'Old Balinese' to describe the period from this time up to the conquest of Bali by the Majapahit empire in 1343.

By the tenth century, a clearly Balinese dynasty named Varmadeva was ruling the inhabited area of south Bali, perhaps filling a vacuum left by waning Javanese power. The first ruler of this line erected an inscribed pillar found at Sanur on the south coast, a location which was to figure prominently in later Balinese history. Dated 914, the Sanur pillar is reminiscent of those created by the famous Indian king, Asoka. It is the first inscription to name a ruler, Adhipatih (King) Sri Kesari Varma. It was written in a combination of Old Balinese and Sanskrit languages using two scripts, one of them the north Indian script used for the Pejeng seals, and the other Old Javanese (Kawi). This complex mingling of languages and scripts indicates that the ruler was not primarily interested in communicating with his people. Rather, the inscription served to emphasise his status and supernatural authority.

The Sanur pillar commemorates a successful expedition to conquer settlements which may have been located either on Nusa Penida, visible only a few miles offshore, or, more impressively, in the distant islands of Maluku in eastern Indonesia. The same king left two other inscriptions, at inland locations, which indicate that he was also at war with enemies in the mountainous interior of Bali. Revered locally, the Sanur pillar remains where it was found, in the now urbanised village of Belanjong, just off a busy street serving the modern hotels on Sanur Beach.

Writing of the Sanur inscription and two earlier ones, George Coedès, the great French historian of early Southeast Asia, noted, 'These inscriptions reveal a Hindu-Balinese society, independent of Java, making use of a dialect particular to the island and practising Buddhism and Sivaism at the same time'.[4]

Indianisation brought with it a penchant for jaw-breaking names. Thus in 962 a king of the Varmadeva Dynasty named Chandrabhayasimha Varmadeva constructed a reservoir at the holiest spring on the island, located near Tampaksiring. Known as Tirta Mpul, the ancient bathing place is today frequently visited by foreigners and is still a holy place for Balinese. A commemoration stone kept in a nearby village marks its foundation.

The villagers who preserved this stone could not decipher the ancient lettering on it, but they knew it was important, kept it wrapped in white cloth to protect it from evil spirits, and provided it with regular offerings. In addition they took it to the Tirta Mpul spring in the fourth month of every year at full moon to bathe it in the holy waters. When a Dutch archaeologist deciphered the inscription, it revealed that the founding had indeed taken place in the fourth month at full moon in 962. 'Thus,' he commented, 'the people have kept alive the connection between stone and watering place for almost one thousand years, and have always celebrated its anniversary ceremony on the correct day; but of the true meaning of this connection every recollection was lost.'[5] No one familiar with the intense and enduring Balinese fascination with calendars and everything pertaining to the reckoning of time can be surprised by this engaging story.

A few years later the first truly memorable Balinese monarchs appear. This time they are a royal couple, with the queen in the lead role and the husband acting like a prince consort. Her name was Mahendradatta, or Gunapriyadharmapatni ('spouse of virtue's friend'), and she was the granddaughter of Sindok, a powerful Javanese king. Her consort, Udayana, was a Balinese of the reigning Varmadeva Dynasty and clearly a strong figure in his own right. He is known from a portrait statue with another, later wife, kept at the mist-shrouded Tegeh Koripan temple on the rim of Lake Batur, Bali's highest mountain shrine. Udayana University in Denpasar is named after him, as is the regional military command. But Mahendradatta is always mentioned before Udayana in their joint decrees, and she is credited with a significant increase of Javanese influence at the Balinese court. From this point on, all royal decrees on Bali were written in Old Javanese rather than Old Balinese.

Mahendradatta's marriage to Udayana came to a bad end, with

47

King Airlangga was son of a Balinese king and a Javanese queen who may have been the prototype of the demonic witch Rangda. He became king of Java early in the eleventh century after which his youngest brother ruled Bali. This statue, now in an East Javanese museum, shows him as Vishnu mounted on the supernatural bird Garuda.
(Source: Robert Pringle)

consequences which continue to reverberate in Balinese legend (see below), but not before the birth of a famous son, Airlangga, in 991. Represented as the six-armed Hindu goddess Durga, this memorable queen may be portrayed by a statue in a temple at Kutri, not far from Ubud.

The half-Balinese Airlangga returned to his mother's homeland and came of age in the Javanese capital, where he was probably assigned to administer a province. Catastrophe struck in 1016, when an unknown adversary, perhaps the rival state of Srivijaya, based on Sumatra, killed the reigning Javanese king and sacked the royal palace. In the best Indian tradition foreshadowing future greatness, Prince Airlangga took refuge with holy men in a remote mountain area. But high-ranking brahmans sought him out and begged him to accept the throne. He did so and was crowned king of a much diminished Javanese realm in 1019, with the title (take a deep breath) of Sri Maharaja Rakai Halu Sri Lokesvara Darmavamsa Airlangga Anantavikramottungadeva.

It took Airlangga almost two decades to restore and then expand his kingdom. He may never have lived on Bali, and probably left its affairs to be managed by a sibling. Before his death in 1049 he somewhat inexplicably divided his Javanese realm in two, perhaps because he had no legitimate offspring and wanted to arrange matters so as to avoid squabbling among the offspring of his concubines. His reign was a period which saw a flowering of culture and international trade in Indonesia generally and apparent peace between hitherto antagonistic Javanese and Sumatran kingdoms, with evidence of extensive international trade.

Airlangga was memorialised in East Java at Candi Belahan. A *candi* is a royal funerary monument, maintained as a temple where a deceased monarch is worshipped by later generations. The site was marked by one of the greatest masterpieces of early Indonesian art (later relocated to a nearby museum), a statue of Airlangga as the god Vishnu mounted on the giant mythical bird Garuda, one of modern Indonesia's national symbols. Airlangga was the only native son besides President Sukarno, who was also half-Balinese, ever to rule both Java and Bali, and he is still celebrated in local traditions.

Airlangga was eventually succeeded on Bali by his youngest brother, referred to in inscriptions as Anak Wungsu, which indeed means 'youngest brother', who was nonetheless a powerful king. The same dynasty continued to hold sway over Bali throughout the twelfth and thirteenth centuries, gradually trailing off into obscurity. It is these kings and queens who are memorialised in the tourist-circuit royal monuments at Gunung Kawi. Scholars have found it difficult to determine exactly which monarch goes with which monument because their posthumous names often differed from the names they used while living. There was one more memorable Old Balinese ruler, a bureaucratic whirlwind named Jayapangus, who issued no fewer than 30 inscriptions on a single day in 1181, one of them quoted later in this chapter, but about whom little more is known.

Bali continued to be influenced by the rhythm of politics on Java. Relative independence was typical of times when Java was weak. But in the mid-thirteenth century Airlangga's realm was reunited under a powerful monarch, Kertanegara of Singasari in East Java. Profiting from the decline of the Sumatra-based empire of Srivijaya, he embarked on an aggressive course, expanding his realm to West Java and parts of the Malayan peninsula. In 1284 he invaded Bali, returning to Java with its king as prisoner. But this first Javanese conquest did not last long.

Kertanegara is otherwise famous for addiction to tantric Buddhism, characterised by a mysticism sometimes expressed through erotic and macabre rites. His palace art, often superb, is memorable for garlands of skulls around demonic figures. He had the appealing audacity to insult and possibly mutilate an envoy sent to Java by the Mongol emperor Kublai Khan, an affront which led to a brief and unsuccessful Mongol invasion of Java in 1293. By the time the Mongols arrived Kertanegara was already dead, and a time of turmoil ensued on Java. Eventually the new kingdom of Majapahit was founded. One can imagine why Bali was probably left to its own devices during these action-packed years.

With the exception of Udayana and Airlangga, almost nothing is known about the personal histories or characters of the various Old Balinese kings. But we do know that they were able to accumulate enough wealth to support a complex religious establishment, thanks to the development of irrigated agriculture. And because they left a remarkable variety of inscriptions we know something about their relationship with their people, and even their economic interests.

Many Old Balinese inscriptions, some on stone but most engraved on copper plates, were zealously preserved by villagers in the localities concerned, where they often remain, and new ones are still being discovered. In September 2002, sixteen of them were found under a tree in north Bali, leading to a well-publicised dispute between two villages over which would get to keep them. Written initially in the Old Balinese language, later in Old Javanese, they record important royal decisions, often contractual in nature, which were frequently the product

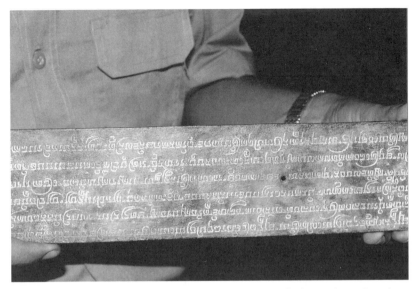

This copper plate inscription recording a royal decree is typical of many dating from the ninth to thirteenth centuries recording decisions by Old Balinese monarchs. Many of them have been preserved in Balinese villages, and new ones are still being discovered.
(Source: *Robert Pringle*)

of negotiation between the king and village communities. They were inscribed on copper to give them permanence, in contrast to the easily decayed palm-leaf manuscripts which were the standard of written communication. They sometimes conclude with hair-raising imprecations aimed at anyone who should attempt to violate the decisions which are recorded.

How far did royal writ extend? The inscriptions confirm that some if not all of the Old Bali monarchs aspired to rule the entire island, whether or not they actually did so. These texts have been unearthed in both north and south Bali, and many of the earliest are from the highland territory of the Bali Aga in the centre of the island. If nothing else, this suggests that the rulers wanted to exert control over both the agricultural south and the commercial north, as well as the trade route between them. Much later, any full-fledged Balinese realm needed a foothold on the seacoast as well as in the uplands for religious and symbolic reasons, in addition to a court located in the symbolic centre of the kingdom.

The leading Balinese scholar and analyst of these texts, I Wayan Ardika, believes that the Old Balinese monarchy was resident primarily in south Bali, in the Pejeng-Bedulu area, although the exact site of the royal court or courts is not known. The location of the Gunung Kawi royal monuments appears to reinforce this theory. In any case, judging from later practice, it is likely that monarchs had to travel constantly to keep their ill-defined realms together.

The inscriptions reveal lively dialogues between Old Balinese rulers and their people. One, dated 1025, records that villagers living on the edge of Lake Batur have successfully petitioned the monarch to be allowed to purchase a tract of land which had hitherto been part of the royal hunting preserve, explaining that the land they had was too dry to support their growing flocks.

A series of six inscriptions dating from 922 to 1181 concerns the port community of Julah in north Bali, near one of the excavation sites dating to prehistoric times mentioned in Chapter 2. By the eleventh century, Julah had a population of 300 families, perhaps 1500 individuals. However small, it was a cosmopolitan trading community probably quite similar to contemporary port towns on the neighbouring north Java coast.

In one of the earlier inscriptions the king spells out regulations and obligations for the inhabitants following an attack by unidentified enemies, perhaps pirates, who had killed or driven away most of the inhabitants. The ruler urges those who fled the town to return and help rebuild it, and grants them relief from taxes. Other edicts mention the special status accorded foreign merchants, who lived in a separate community with their own headman. Some describe salvage regulations similar to those that centuries later were to embroil Balinese rulers in controversy with the Dutch. Proceeds from salvaged cargo were to be devoted to welfare, while any timbers recovered from a shipwreck were to be used to maintain the stockade around the community. The citizens had many duties, including the defence of the port against attackers, and they were subject to some rather intrusive regulations. They were not allowed to pick certain kinds of fruits or tubers, or to abuse certain domestic animals, or to bring wild animals into their houses. Certain kinds of trees with religious or economic significance were protected, such as the spirit-shrouded, shade-giving banyan tree and another used for making red dye, and there was an official in charge of forestry. It is less clear what citizens received from the king in return for their services.

Taxes were a major preoccupation. In the final edict of the series, issued by King Jayapangus in 1181, we learn that the king's tax collectors are tired of complaints and litigation. Royal annoyance, etched in copper, echoes down through the centuries, giving this pronouncement a surprisingly modern flavour. Note the emphasis on the importance of the king's wives (descendants of the moon). The term 'Haji' as used here was an Old Javanese title meaning 'lord' and apparently had no connection with the more familiar Islamic usage. Note also the reference to 'balidwipamandala', translated here as 'the state of Bali'; the literal meaning would be 'Bali-land-network'. The term *mandala*, or network, was drawn from ancient Indian texts on governance. It described a circular pattern of alliances or 'circle of kings',[6] usually unstable and with at best vaguely defined borders, and a ruler claiming sovereignty, in this case Jayapangus, at the centre.

> The Saka year 1103 [1181 AD], the month of July-August, the ninth day of the fifth week, . . . the week of Wayang-wayang.
>   At that time the order of Paduka Haji Sri Maharaja Jayapangus (the descendant of the sun) [the king]
>   And his two wives, Paduka Bhatari Sri Parmeswari (descendant of the moon)

And Paduka Sri Mahadewi (descendant of the moon) is given to all senapatis [state officials]

The order of Paduka Haji [the king] is brought to the assembly particularly to the priests of Shiva and Buddha and the great brahmans.

The reason for the order of Paduka Sri Maharaja to them is that he heard about the villagers of Julah who were worrying about their problems without being able to solve them.

These problems are boring to discuss.

They have had additional taxes imposed on them by the tax collectors. The villages of Julah and Kaduran originally were ruled by Julah itself. This village now has become part of the state of Bali [balidwipamandala].

Paduka Sri Maharaja knows correct procedures and has heard the essence of the book of Manawa Kamandhaka [a legendary Indian law code, The Laws of Manu]. He is striving after virtue and the welfare of the state which he takes care of, as well as the stability of the state.

It is the nature of the supreme ruler/king with his wives to create the stability of the state. Therefore, Paduka Sri Maharaja [Jayapangus] gives an explanation . . .

The king goes on to spell out a resolution of the dispute in great detail.[7]

Indeed, there would seem to have been cause for popular resentment of taxes: there were taxes in money or kind on buildings, ships, making lime or charcoal, on cattle, cockfighting, construction activity and even breeding animals. In one of the later inscriptions the king grants relief from some of the taxes after another attack on the port. There were also many requirements for community services in addition to defence against raiders, including maintenance of monasteries, shrines, bathing places, fish ponds, roads, graves, the harbour stockade, and the supply of provisions for ceremonies.

Statues of Old Balinese royalty are revered in a sanctuary at Mt Penulisan, the highest point on the rim of the volcanic caldera around Lake Batur. This and other evidence suggests that the Bali Aga people who live in this upland area enjoyed a special relationship with the Old Balinese monarchs. (Source: Robert Pringle)

The Old Balinese kings were equally concerned about people, especially skilled workers, no doubt recognising that royal revenue and royal power depended on them. The inscriptions mention more than 20 professions, including metalworkers, lime and charcoal makers, cloth and mat weavers, cloth dyers (including specialists in both red and blue dyeing), specialists in resist dyeing (*ikat*), stonemasons, boat makers, rice millers, musicians (including both singers and gamelan players), dancers and irrigation tunnel diggers. There are references to what were probably village officials and to varieties of weights, measures and coinage.

Smiths or metalworkers were in a separate category. A special official, the supervisor of smiths (*juru pandé*), was responsible for overseeing them, and they were required to live in one place. That they got such close attention from the state is hardly surprising, given that metal-working was associated with magical power and that metal products had strategic as well as economic value. A royal permit was required for the manufacture of wavy-bladed krisses (daggers) and for the crowbars which were used for agriculture as well as, most importantly, for the construction of irrigation tunnels. It is not clear whether the monarch attempted to monopolise trade in such metal items, but it seems likely.

We may assume that warfare was endemic, as it continued to be down to the colonial period, but we know little about the nature of Old Balinese warfare. As the Dutch were to learn, the Balinese were truly a martial people who fought tenaciously and with dangerous guile. Given the terrain, especially in the south, one may imagine a warfare of raids and ambushes. Weapons included bows and arrows, long lances, krisses and blowpipes similar to those still used in forested areas elsewhere in the archipelago. Krisses were often beautifully crafted, imbued with sacred and magical properties, and seen as repositories of power. Javanese literature from the fourteenth century contains what may be a reference to ritual taking of heads, and the custom may have existed on Bali as late as the nineteenth century.[8]

Old Bali did not lack for international contact. Trade with India, China and, of course, with Java undoubtedly continued. As we have seen, the clay seals and stupas of Pejeng bear witness to cosmopolitan religious influences from the beginning of Balinese history. The pace and content of Indianisation, an ongoing process, was influenced by such factors as pilgrims travelling to the holy places of India and by dynastic contacts with Java and beyond.

Old Balinese monarchs were apparently sufficiently prestigious to intermarry with the royal families of major foreign powers elsewhere in Southeast Asia. A Cambodian inscription of the early eleventh century suggests that a Balinese prince named Narapativiravarman was ruling the Angkorian Empire in 1002. It is possible that this prince was none other than the brother of King Udayana, the father of

Airlangga, and that Udayana himself may have held the Angkorian throne for a time under the title of Udayadityavarman I.[9]

Elsewhere in Southeast Asia, including Java, kings were typically associated with specific deities and posthumously worshipped as gods. This most famous aspect of early Southeast Asian statecraft permeates Old Balinese as well as Javanese art. Royal cults facilitated the integration of traditional ancestor worship into the new religious order. Local deities identified with the ancestors were adorned with new Indian-style titles, sometimes with names that sounded like Sanskrit but were actually Sanskritised Balinese names.

There were Hindu and Buddhist priests, no doubt, but there were also folk priests, the successors of village shamans. Indeed, the prehistoric distinction between political/military leaders and religious leaders, which survived in nearby eastern Indonesia, and probably existed on pre-Hindu Bali as well, synchronised neatly with the Indian distinction between *brahmana* priests and *satria* warrior-kings. In general, on Bali as on Java, the earliest Indian art is the closest to classic Indian models, while later art shows a gradual reappearance of ancestor worship and prehistoric style mingled with Indian-derived content. Javanese influence ebbed and flowed, but on balance the degree of interaction and influence from the larger island increased over time.

Today the tone and character of Javanese and Balinese culture often seem far apart, most obviously in the arts, with the Javanese famous for refinement, muted tones in art and music, and languorous understatement, while the Balinese accent falls on bright colour, emphatic rhythm and bold drama. Bali's modern stylistic distinctiveness *vis-à-vis* Java extends to other realms, from the Balinese penchant for highly structured social organisation to the pervasive competition between multiple descent groups.

Some scholars believe that this cultural contrast may be a relatively recent phenomenon resulting from later history: Java's conversion to Islam and its much longer exposure to a brand of Dutch rule which was both harsher and more transforming in its impact. In that case,

Demonic Rangda has descended the temple steps and is now engaged with kris-wielding dancers in a classic contest between the cosmic forces of left and right, or good and evil. Later benevolent Barong will make his entrance, but neither side ever 'wins'. No dance did more to make Bali famous. (Source: Robert Pringle)

the contrast between Old Java and Old Bali may have been less marked than what we see today.

It is also likely that more of what characterises modern Balinese culture dates back to Old Bali, and less to later influence from Majapahit, than is generally believed by the Balinese themselves. In the period just before the Majapahit invasion, Balinese art was already moving away from classical Indian models towards a style which foreshadowed that of modern Bali. Willem Stutterheim saw the trend in a fourteenth-century waterspout found at Pejeng, 'superabundant in form, baroque, wild, flaming'.[10]

One element of Balinese culture present almost from the beginning derived from the tantric system of esoteric practices which occurs in variants of both Hinduism and Buddhism. Tantric Buddhist influence is evident in the inscriptions on the Pejeng stupas and seals, the oldest of all Indian-era relics. It is also visible in the story of Airlangga's mother, Queen Mahendradatta, the Javanese princess who married King Udayana late in the tenth century.

According to legend, the high-born Mahendradatta was a practitioner of occult arts. She is said to have turned against her husband when he broke his pledge not to take another wife. Spurned and then banished, she fled to the forest. There she became the prototype of the demonic, blood-dripping Rangda, meaning 'widow' or 'witch.' In the Calon Arang story and the Barong dance sequence, Rangda still frightens thousands of children and their parents, including tourists, every year. One version of the legend, in which the enraged Rangda visits pestilence on Bali, may be a folk memory of the bubonic plague which was beginning to spread in Asia during Mahendradatta's time.[11]

The Majapahit conquest

In 1343 the Javanese kingdom of Majapahit invaded Bali, unseated the reigning monarch and established some degree of control. Most of what we know about this event is based on a court chronicle in epic poem form, the *Desawarnana*. A Dutch philologist found a copy of it in a Balinese temple on the island of Lombok when he accompanied the military expedition of 1894, described in the next chapter. Much later, Queen Wilhemina returned it to President Soeharto during a visit to Indonesia.

The *Desawarnana* is justifiably famous, portraying as it does the Majapahit Empire, a major precursor of the modern Indonesian state, at the height of its power. It was written by the court poet Rakawi Prapanca in 1365, during the reign of King Rajasanagara, better known as Hayam Wuruk. The king was assisted by a powerful prime minister, Gadjah Mada, renowned as the architect of Majapahit expansion.

There are two sections in the *Desawarnana* that refer to events in Bali, both of them interesting. Canto 49 describes the conquest in eloquent terms:

> Further in the Saka year 'arrows-season-eyes-navel' (1265, AD 1343),
> The King of Bali was evil and base—
> He was attacked by an army, broken and completely crushed;
> Every kind of evildoer was fearful and made off quickly.[12]

The second major reference, concerning royal authority and the organisation of the Buddhist clergy on Bali, comes in Canto 79:

> Among the outer islands Bali conforms with all the customs of Java;
> The status of sanctuaries, hermitages and *kuwu* has been checked and put in order:
> The Buddhist Superintendent in Badahulu, Badaha and Lwa Gajah is not careless,
> He supervises all the Buddhist foundations and is sent out by the King to watch over them.[13]

The poem suggests an ongoing special relationship between Majapahit and Bali, not surprising in view of an already long if uneven history of close relations between rulers of the two islands. It also underscores the importance of Buddhism at the court of Majapahit, suggesting that there might have been friction with a predominately Shivaite and possibly disloyal Balinese religious establishment.

The Majapahit rulers sent Buddhist priests to Bali and the other eastern islands to look after their *dharmas* (domains), which 'were meant to be strongholds of Javanese cultural and dynastic loyalty . . . They seem to have left no clear traces in the country. Perhaps this fact is another indication of the ephemeral existence of Majapahit Court

A demonic figure (once thought to represent an elephant) guards the entrance to Goa Gajah, a cave where Buddhist holy men may have meditated. This site in the Old Bali heartland near Bedulu is mentioned in the Javanese poem Desawarnana written in 1365. An extensive bathing place associated with the sanctuary was not excavated until the 1950s. (Source: Robert Pringle)

Buddhism in Bali'.[14] The third stanza of Canto 79 clearly refers to Bedulu, in the Old Balinese heartland, and to Lwa Gajah, probably today's Goa Gajah or Elephant Cave, as 'principal places', and the next canto goes on to name nine additional Buddhist domains in Bali.

The long list of Majapahit's far-flung possessions claimed in the *Desawarnana* should not be taken literally. The court poet was striving to enhance the reputation of his royal patron, not to write history in the modern sense. But no one doubts that Majapahit invaded nearby Bali, or that it remained under Majapahit rule for some period of time. While the poem indicates that the Majapahit rulers were keenly interested in the patronage of religious establishments, including those on

Bali, the kingdom probably possessed only rudimentary administrative capacity. Like other Indian-style states, Majapahit relied primarily on a combination of alliances, personal charisma, the projection of magical power and occasional displays of military force.

For some period of time, Balinese resistance to the invasion continued in the Bedulu-Pejeng area, the epicentre of Old Balinese strength. According to the Balinese royal chronicle *Babad Dalem*, Gadjah Mada appointed the son of his teacher, a Javanese prince named Kresna Kapakisan, to bring the situation under control. But it was difficult, and before he could finish the job Kapakisan had to appeal to Gajah Mada for help. The minister responded by sending his most powerful regalia, including a kris named Ki Lobar. At the mere sight of this magical weapon, the remaining Balinese rebels fled and peace was restored.

Then, in 1352, Kapakisan established what was to become the Gelgel kingdom, with its capital initially at Samprangan in modern Gianyar. Kapakisan brought with him a number of Javanese nobles who, according to the *Babad Dalem* and other Balinese chronicles, became the progenitors of many prominent Balinese families. Gelgel may have been less than independent at first. A Balinese inscription of 1384, one of the few extant from this period, refers to a King Kudamtra from Wengker in East Java who apparently held vice-regal power on behalf of Majapahit. However, following the death of Hayam Wuruk and his great minister, there were divisions in the Majapahit royal family, and the Javanese state began to weaken.

The fifteenth century was a period of decline for all the great Indianised realms of Southeast Asia, and Islam was waiting in the wings. By this time Malacca, in modern Malaysia, had supplanted Srivijaya, on Sumatra, as the commercial hub of western Indonesia and the dominant power on the Malacca Straits, a major trade route then as now. The founder of Malacca was a Hindu-Buddhist king, who late in his reign, perhaps early in the fifteenth century, converted to Islam. Muslim merchants had been present in the Indian Archipelago for centuries, but only now did Islam gradually become a useful instrument of statecraft for ambitious rulers, an evolution similar to that of Hinduism a thousand years earlier.

The new religion gained increasing strength in reaction to the growing European presence, which commenced early in the sixteenth century. The benchmark event in this process was the fall of by-now Muslim Malacca to the Portuguese in 1511, which threatened the commercial and political interests of Southeast Asian rulers elsewhere, but especially on the north coast of Java. Far from suppressing Islam, the fall of Malacca only served to stimulate its spread.

As Hindu-Buddhist Majapahit declined in the fifteenth century, new Muslim-ruled states formed around the north Java trading centres. Majapahit did not fall beneath the hammer blows of an Islamic rival in some dramatic clash of civilisations, but rather trailed off into obscurity. The final demise of the old regime appears to have occurred between 1513 and 1528; the exact date is not known. A major new player, Muslim Mataram, gradually established hegemony over Central and East Java in the late sixteenth and early seventeenth centuries. Its primary antagonist was to be the Dutch East India Company, which had beaten out Portuguese and English rivals for control of the eastern Indonesian Spice Islands and established its headquarters at Batavia, now Jakarta, in 1619.

Gelgel and the Golden Age

The two centuries following the Majapahit Conquest are a period which the Balinese regard as politically and culturally formative. For later generations of Balinese, 'Majapahit' became a code word for the source of all civilisation. Local tradition has it, for example, that Gunung Agung, which is equated with Mount Meru, pivot of the Hindu cosmos, was brought to Bali from Majapahit Java at this time. To this day, Lord Majapahit is venerated in certain Balinese temples in the guise of a deer's head, as a kind of exemplar of civilisation. Majapahit came to encapsulate an entire cultural legacy and to reinforce the status of those who could assert ties to it.

Certainly many modern assumptions about Majapahit fall in the realm of mythology. As we shall see, the Dutch nurtured their own myth about the Majapahit conquest, namely that an alien, invading Javanese aristocracy had imposed itself over independent Balinese 'village republics' which the colonial rulers liberated and restored. On the other hand, not all Majapahit influence was mythological. The physical resemblance between modern Balinese temples and Majapahit monuments, for example, is striking. The Majapahit state temple, Panataran in East Java, resembles 'an old and gorgeous version of contemporary Balinese temple art'.[15]

It is widely believed that as the Islamic scourge swept through Java there was a physical exodus of refugee Hindu-Buddhist priests and aristocrats from the Majapahit court to Bali. In fact, there may have been a more subtle process of cultural conservation carried out in Balinese courts, temples and hermitages. Certainly, Balinese consciousness of the Majapahit heritage remained strong. In the early eighteenth century, according to contemporary Dutch records, the Balinese on at least three occasions planned and eventually carried out armed expeditions to Java, much in the spirit of the mediaeval European crusades, to capture the sacred site of the old capital, which they believed their ancestors had ruled.

However, the Balinese do not believe that their forebears simply accepted Majapahit institutions and culture as a whole. This would hardly accord with the fact that the state religion of Majapahit was Mahayana Buddhism, which left very few traces on Bali. Rather, the mainstream Balinese version of events accentuates the importance of a golden age under the kingdom, mentioned earlier, established by Kresna Kapakisan in 1352.

This new state got off to a slow start, faltering badly under weak leadership, until it was deemed necessary to move its capital from Samprangan to Gelgel, south of modern Klungkung. The move probably occurred early in the fifteenth century. The next hundred years are largely a blank in Balinese history. Only in the mid-sixteenth century, almost two centuries after the Majapahit conquest, did the Gelgel kingdom suddenly reach its apogee under a great ruler named Batu Renggong. During his reign a Hindu *brahmana* priest and poet, Nirartha, arrived from Java to be his counsellor.

According to the most widely accepted account, Nirartha is credited with refashioning Balinese religion into the form known today, including the caste system. He was the founder of the modern Shivaite priesthood which now dominates Balinese Hinduism and the ancestor of all subsequent Shivaite priests. According to this version of events, it was only through Nirartha's reforms that the heritage of Majapahit civilisation could truly flower on Bali.

The Gelgel rulers transformed a prestigious prehistoric terraced sanctuary in the Besakih complex into their own ancestral temple, reinforcing their legitimacy and making Besakih Bali's primary official temple. At its peak the Gelgel kingdom supposedly ruled over a united Bali which included Blambangan and Pasuruhan in East Java, portions of Lombok and perhaps a foothold on Sumbawa, the island east of Lombok. The golden age faded fast, but Gelgel lingered until the end of the seventeenth century, a life span of more than 300 years.

There is reason to be sceptical about a Gelgelian golden age despite the continuing acceptance of this version of past events, especially among the Balinese upper-caste elite. The story is drawn in large part from the *Babad Dalem*, only one of several major and numerous minor pre-colonial Balinese histories, which rarely agree with each other and which were all written 200 years after the establishment of Gelgel. Independent evidence that might confirm or challenge this establishment narrative is scarce. The post-Majapahit rulers were not in the habit of leaving numerous edicts on copper plates, as their Old Balinese predecessors had been.

Certainly Gelgel, whether or not it controlled the whole island, was not just a myth. The first Dutch visitors arrived on Bali in 1597 and were favourably impressed both by the king, probably Batu Renggong's son, and by what they were told about his state. At Kuta they witnessed an assemblage of troops being sent off to help the king of Blambangan on the nearby eastern salient of Java. As this suggests, the Balinese were beginning to flex a considerable amount of expansionist muscle at this time, intervening on Lombok as well as East Java. Their involvement on Java was to last almost two centuries and to end only because of Dutch intervention. Their presence on Lombok was to prove permanent.

By establishing a foothold in Blambangan, the ruler of Gelgel became an implacable enemy of the rising Muslim sultanate of Mataram, so much so that in 1633 the Dutch East India Company considered forming an alliance with Bali against a state which was still vigorously challenging Dutch control of Java. A few years later Mataram invaded Balinese Blambangan, and this time it was the Balinese who sought Dutch help, but in vain. The increasingly powerful sultanate had driven the Balinese out of Blambangan by 1640, but only temporarily.

The main phases of Balinese expansion to Lombok did not take place until after the fall of Gelgel. When it began is not clear, but by the mid-seventeenth century Balinese were struggling for control of Lombok with Makasarese operating from Sumbawa, the next island to the east. The Balinese won a decisive victory in 1678, and over the next century and a half established themselves throughout the entire island, expelling the Makasarese, subjugating the native Sasak people, who were and remain Muslim, and even gaining a temporary toehold on Sumbawa, east of Lombok. They retained this position until the Sasak rebellion of 1891 which expelled them from east Lombok (see Chapter 6). The Balinese have remained in west Lombok to this day.

This evidence of an ability to project military power is not however, proof positive that Gelgel united Bali. Indeed, it is not clear whether it was Gelgel that accomplished the initial expansions mentioned above. It could have been the other strong Balinese states that were emerging in this period, either separately or in temporary alliances. It was the newer states of Mengwi and Buleleng that regained footholds on Java in the late seventeenth century. The Balinese were

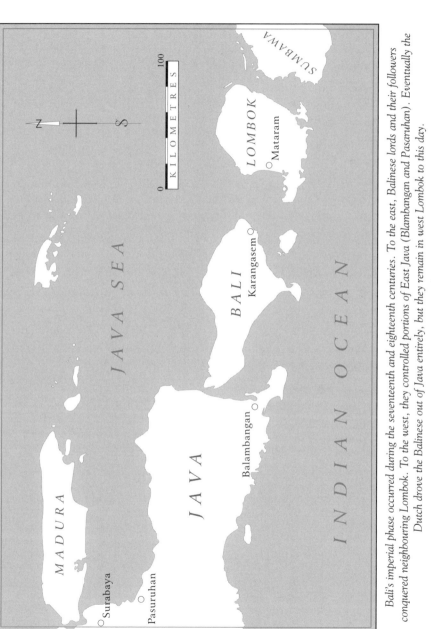

Bali's imperial phase occurred during the seventeenth and eighteenth centuries. To the east, Balinese lords and their followers conquered neighbouring Lombok. To the west, they controlled portions of East Java (Blambangan and Pasaruhan). Eventually the Dutch drove the Balinese out of Java entirely, but they remain in west Lombok to this day.

not finally expelled, this time by the Dutch, until 1771. And it was Karangasem, in eastern Bali, which completed the conquest of Lombok. In the absence of better information, the degree of Gelgelian control over its subordinate rulers, even under Batu Renggong, is impossible to judge, but from what we know about later Balinese statecraft it would likely have been sporadic.

Nirartha, the great brahman, may indeed have been a powerful and creative personage. Probably the most important of his reforms as described in the *Babad Dalem* was the creation of what, after further reinforcement by the Dutch, became the modern Balinese caste system. But the idea that Balinese civilisation in its entirety sprang from Majapahit borrowings as modified by Nirartha is, like the Gelgelian golden age, open to question. Such an interpretation neglects four preceding centuries of Hindu-Buddhist religion and often intense political relationships between Bali and earlier Javanese realms. Why is this view of history so widely accepted by the Balinese?

To understand, it is important to appreciate the political circumstances surrounding the fall of Gelgel. In 1656 Dutch records reported a 'new king' on Bali.[16] The last of the Gelgel rulers had been overthrown by one of his own ministers, Gusti Agung, whose offspring later founded the powerful Kingdom of Mengwi, discussed in the next chapter. By 1696 members of the Gelgel royal family had reclaimed the throne and reestablished themselves at nearby Klungkung, not hitherto the seat of any state.

From this time onwards Klungkung, as the heir of Gelgel and hence of Majapahit, was to retain a theoretical seniority among the Balinese kingdoms, its ruler distinguished from the others by a unique and prestigious title, Dewa Agung or 'great king'. There would be times when this seniority made a difference, notably in the first stages of the struggle against the Dutch.

But in reality Bali became fragmented into 'an acrobat's pyramid of "kingdoms" of varying degrees of substantial autonomy and effective power'.[17] The most serious players were Karangasem in the east,

Buleleng in the north and, in the south, Klungkung, Badung, Tabanan and Mengwi. Bangli, Gianyar and Jembrana completed the pre-colonial constellation of states. Today eight of them remain as districts of the modern province of Bali, the exception being Mengwi, dismembered by its neighbours in 1891, but leaving as a parting gift one of the most beautiful state temples on the island.

Given the conditions of acute division which prevailed after the fall of Gelgel, it was useful, perhaps vital, for aspiring rulers to accentuate the ideal of unity, inspired by the political and cultural model of Majapahit, as modified on Balinese soil by Nirartha. As Clifford Geertz put it, 'Like the myth of The Founding Fathers in the United States, or of The Revolution in Russia, the myth of The Majapahit Conquest became the origin tale by means of which actual relations of command and obedience were explained and justified'.[18] Old Bali was almost forgotten, in part because it seems to have faded from collective memory by the time most of the Balinese chronicles were written, none of them before the mid-sixteenth century.

However, the broader reason for the Balinese downgrading of Old Bali was surely political. While the Majapahit occupation may have been superficial and short-lived, it resulted in the replacement of some Old Balinese elites with new ones, although others, rather like the Saxon gentry of post-Norman Conquest England, were assimilated in the new order. The post-Majapahit Balinese rulers sought legitimacy by identifying themselves with culture-bearing Javanese nobility, and they—the winners—were the ones who wrote the *Babad Dalem* and other histories.

But the 'losers'—those who had lost power or status with the demise of Old Bali—did not go away. Although few of them were integrated into the new high-caste nobility, they and their descendants, some of them associated with the Bali Aga, as well as with the smiths and other non-caste clans, have continued to exert their own claims for seniority and equal status.

69

Why Bali remained Hindu

Why, after the fall of Majapahit, did Bali remain aloof from the archipelagic trend and fail to embrace Islam? Geography is certainly not a sufficient answer: as noted earlier, the narrow, shallow Bali Strait, which separates the island from Java, has never been a serious obstacle to change. Of course there were cultural barriers to Islamic penetration—fondness for pork is the one most frequently cited—but the same barriers existed on Java, where conversion to Islam was virtually, if often nominally, universal. The Balinese had never been markedly anti-Islamic. Muslim communities continued to exist around the post-Majapahit Balinese courts, and the Balinese rulers continued to welcome Muslims as traders and to hire them as soldiers.

Timing gave Hindu Bali political breathing room. There was no strong Islamic state on Java until the rise of Mataram, which began in the late sixteenth century, almost a hundred years after the fall of Majapahit. While Mataram was able to expel the Balinese temporarily from Blambangan, Gelgel and its successor states remained vigorous enough to make an invasion of Bali difficult, with or without support from the Dutch. In any case, Mataram, preoccupied first with rivals on Java and later with the Dutch, was apparently not tempted by notions of proselytising with fire and sword among the innumerable pockets of unbelievers along the island chain east of Java.

Later, Dutch expansion threw Mataram on the defensive. As the power of the Dutch grew, eventually enabling them to overwhelm their last serious Indonesian rival, any political advantage which the Balinese rulers might have gained through conversion to Islam diminished and finally vanished altogether.

4
THE BALINESE STATE TO THE EVE OF DUTCH CONTROL (SEVENTEENTH TO NINETEENTH CENTURIES)

Following the fall of Gelgel, nine independent states emerged on Bali. In time, each of these mini-kingdoms would have its own chronicle recording its royal genealogies and much more. Each could easily be the subject of a book, and several have been. These states were to interact with each other and with Dutch colonial rulers with momentous consequences for the people of Bali. We will be looking at that process in a later chapter, but in order to do so it is necessary to understand the nature of these realms.

The mass of factual material available pertinent to all nine kingdoms is daunting. Fortunately, however, historian Henk Schulte Nordholt has written a superb account of one of them, the Kingdom of

Mengwi, which was broadly typical of the entire constellation. Drawing on both Dutch and Balinese sources, Nordholt tells the story of Mengwi from its beginnings around 1690 to its demise in 1891. I have attempted here to summarise the main points of his book, *The Spell of Power: A History of Balinese Politics*, and to review, with only minor additions, the conclusions he draws about Balinese statecraft generally.

There was no such thing as a precise or static 'pre-colonial' Balinese political model. In addition to the differences among the nine states, each of them was deeply affected by indirect European influences for two and a half centuries before Dutch conquest, which itself occurred in fits and starts over a 60-year period, from 1849 to 1908.

Mengwi is located in the west of south Bali, north and a little west of Denpasar. According to one of its chronicles, the founder of the state, Agung Anom (lived approximately 1690–1722), was descended from Gusti Agung, the minister of Gelgel who had overthrown its last king in the mid-seventeenth century. In his youth, Agung Anom endured defeat and exile, following which he fought his way to regional prominence. Then he married a princess of the already powerful northern Balinese kingdom of Buleleng, daughter of a famous ruler named Panji Sakti (literally, Prince of Supernatural Power).

Agung Anom used this alliance in combination with his own military skill to make his new state one of the strongest on Bali, extending Balinese rule once again to Blambangan, the nearby extremity of eastern Java. As soon as his political base was established, according to the Mengwi chronicle, he asked his senior *brahmana* priest to determine and narrate his genealogy, in order to tie his lineage to one of the nobles who had accompanied the first king of Gelgel from Java as prime minister, and whose descendants had served in this same capacity for later kings of Gelgel.

With their prestigious ancestry thus firmly grounded, this king and his successor nonetheless had to struggle constantly to maintain control over Mengwi's satellites ('possessions' is too strong a word), notably

The Kingdom of Mengwi was gobbled up in 1891 by its neighbours, leaving a rich history as well as its state temple, the wonderful Pura Taman Ayun, originally built in the mid-eighteenth century. (Source: Robert Pringle)

Buleleng and Blambangan. The Buleleng connection allowed Mengwi to profit from the ancient international trade route which skirted the north coast. Even so, by the late eighteenth century both these realms had broken away—in the case of Blambangan, thanks largely to Dutch intervention—and Mengwi was reduced to a narrow wedge of territory stretching about 50 kilometres from the volcanic heights of Bali to its south coast, with a population of about 85 000 in the late nineteenth century, the earliest period for which an estimate is available.

Partly due to this loss of territory and prestige, Mengwi declined into a state of weakness and was almost totally dismembered by its neighbours in 1823. But the kingdom bounced back and enjoyed a second apogee in the mid-nineteenth century before its final decline and extinction in 1891.

Mengwi had much in common not only with the other little Balinese states, but with small-scale Indianised realms throughout Southeast Asia. As noted earlier, the post-Majapahit Balinese kings, unlike their Old Balinese forebears, were not regarded as gods while living, although they might have been seen to have supernatural attributes. They were, however, responsible for the suitable conduct of royal ancestor worship, and this was one of several vital religious functions upon which a ruler's reputation, and hence power, depended.

It was up to the king, for example, to make sure that a ritual axis between the royal centre, the mountain temple and the sea temple was maintained, and securing the territory to make this possible sometimes required the use of armed force. A king could not be a king without a prestigious *brahmana* priest in his service, and the *brahmana* was of higher caste than his *satria* (warrior caste) monarch. Palace (*puri*) was always in theory subordinate to temple (*pura*). Brahmans were not always priests. They could also form warrior bands, reminiscent of the battling clerical orders of the European Middle Ages.

The Balinese lord ruled above all by attracting and holding followers. He did so through personal authority established by valour in battle, a commanding presence, high reputation and the ability to control both natural and supernatural forces. The realm was composed of shifting concentric circles of lesser rulers, each a lord in his own right, around the royal centre.

Geographic borders were equally fluid, unlike today's fixed district borders approximating those of the old kingdoms. The king had constantly to reinforce his personal alliances, both within his own realm and beyond it with other realms. He did this partly through marriages and adoptions, but primarily by demonstrating ability to protect and reward subordinates. A strong king would attract both fugitives and upwardly mobile opportunists from other kingdoms.

Written treaties between realms were common but, as the Dutch discovered, the Balinese felt they meant nothing unless reinforced by constant personal contact. Throughout this period, Klungkung under its Dewa Agung remained theoretical overlord of the island. Its actual power fluctuated considerably, but was never extinguished until it fell to the Dutch in 1908.

Bali in the eighteenth and nineteenth centuries was a dangerous place, constantly at risk from wars, plagues, famines and volcanic eruptions, most of which the Balinese believed to be the result of supernatural forces. For example, there were smallpox epidemics in south Bali in 1850, 1861, 1863–64, 1871–73, 1883 and 1885. The 1871 outbreak alone killed from 15 000 to 18 000 people. To combat omnipresent danger, a ruler needed to be able to rally followers, to wage war, and also to organise and deploy ritual.

The Mengwi rulers did have functionaries—one category (*mekel*) to mobilise manpower to service the palace; another (*sedahan*) to manage irrigation systems and collect taxes on irrigated land. But in general there was nothing like a regularised bureaucracy, and the king's officers had limited powers beyond his own immediate territory. Like other Indian-model states, the Balinese kingdoms lacked the well-defined pattern of reciprocal obligations between king and vassal which typified, at least in theory, the mediaeval European model.

Striking personalities and real leaders abounded among Balinese royalty. The first and second kings of Mengwi both attempted armed pilgrimages to Java, rather like crusades, to find the site of Majapahit. According to Dutch records as well as Balinese accounts, the second king succeeded in reaching Mount Semeru, the highest peak on Java and by legend a fragment of the cosmic central mountain of Hindu mythology imported by Java's first Hindus. He held a royal wedding on its slopes, attended by the Dewa Agung of Klungkung among others, and obtained a sacred kris from the resident Hindu priest.

There were palpable villains as well as heroes scattered through Mengwi's history. In the early nineteenth century a weak king met his demise after becoming infatuated with a group of *gandrung* (bisexual dancers). That was not so bad, but then he made one of them his crown prince, which was definitely beyond acceptable. In following chapters we will meet a number of memorable Balinese rulers, including Gusti Ketut Jelantik, prime minister of Buleleng, whose fiery defiance led to war with the Dutch in 1846.

Twice Mengwi was ruled by queens, in both cases widowed senior wives (*padmi*). Senior wives were often powerful personalities with important regional followings. Usually partners in dynastic alliances, they often brought their own property and followers and retained control over them. While senior widow succession was permissible, it was not possible for a royal daughter, no matter how high born, to accede to the throne in her own right. The first and most famous of the two royal widows, Ayu Oka, ruled Mengwi from the 1770s until 1807 and seems to have done a good job. But then she fell in love with the ruler of Gianyar, gave him valuable dynastic heirlooms, and failed to respond when he attacked two of Mengwi's satellites, with unfortunate consequences.

War was serious business. Nordholt observes that '. . . a warring nobility did not leave the people untouched. War was no knightly sport, it was a scourge that deeply scarred local life'.[1] Real battles caused hundreds of casualties and widespread property destruction. In the eighteenth century, a warrior prince born of Mengwi's dynastic alliance with Buleleng died in pitched battle with rebel forces. Even after the end of the Mengwi kingdom, a war in 1898 between would-be successor factions left trenches which are still visible today. Always aware of the strategic importance of water, Balinese rulers did not hesitate to dam streams and then release destructive floods on the fields of downstream enemies.

The king could reward warriors of low status by giving them titles and high caste status, especially in the early days. At one time the Mengwi king was served by an extended family of shock troops, or 'raiders', who were allocated special quarters near the palace. '. . . violence mastered by the leader lay at the root of the hierarchical system on Bali,' Nordholt observes.[2]

Surrounded by potentially predatory neighbours, the state was inherently unstable. Weakness at the centre would result in immediate challenges from the stronger satellite realms, while lesser satellites would

Strong rulers could emerge rapidly in nineteenth century Bali. Cokorde Gde Sukawati of Ubud, shown here in 1915, was a classic example. He led his family to political dominance in the kingdom of Gianyar and persuaded its ruler, his nominal overlord, to accept Dutch 'protection' in 1900. But rivalry persisted between the Ubud and Gianyar ruling families and they quarrelled during the Indonesian Revolution, with tragic consequences. (Source: Royal Tropical Institute, Amsterdam)

seek new protectors and defect when they found them. Ambitious young rulers were always ready to advance their own fortunes at the expense of failing superiors. 'On Bali, intrigue is a transcendental art,' observed a perceptive Dutch agent stationed at Kuta to buy slaves for service in the colonial army in 1828.[3] Frequently, as in the case of nineteenth-century Badung, established lineages were in more or less routine competition for control of the state. Charismatic new leaders could quickly gain recognition and power within old states, as happened on the eve of Dutch control when the founder of the modern Sukawati family first put Ubud on the political map within the kingdom of Gianyar.

In theory, succession passed to the eldest son of the chief queen. In fact, this does not seem to have happened even once in the entire history of Mengwi. Of the nine recorded successions from 1700 to 1891, only the second was uncontested. Polygamy and constant intermarriage among the nobility produced royal kinship patterns of unbelievable complexity and virtually guaranteed the existence of rival lineages competing for royal succession. No wonder that the manipulation of genealogies to reinforce claims to status and power is a constant theme of Balinese history.

The character of the Mengwi state changed significantly over its 200 year history. In the early years of the eighteenth century, Mengwi was aggressively expansive, with the king always on the move to keep his restive and far-flung subordinates in line, but there were to be no more adventures on Java or in north Bali after the middle of the century. Instead, the second and third rulers were heavily involved in bringing new irrigated rice lands into cultivation in the vicinity of Mengwi itself.

There was still much forested or otherwise uncultivated land on Bali, and it took royal leadership of the highest order to initiate the building of main dams, canals and irrigation tunnels. Not until the water supply had been secured was it possible for the *subak* irrigation societies to operate in the cooperative autonomous manner which is today accepted as 'traditional'. Indeed, one of the king's more important means of attracting followers was his ability to give them newly created, or sometimes newly conquered, irrigated rice land. (Of course, he had the option to keep the best land for himself.) But this pioneer aspect of the Mengwi state had ended by the mid-nineteenth century, primarily due to the exhaustion of suitable land.

Rulers were always concerned to secure economic power beyond irrigated rice agriculture, but the way they did so altered over time. The king made money from the sale of slaves, and slave trade revenue became increasingly important under the indirect stimulus of colonial markets in Batavia and elsewhere. The slave trade encouraged warfare because prisoners could be sold into slavery. It encouraged royal patronage of gambling and harsh judgments in the royal courts, because debtors and convicts faced the same fate.

Yet the Balinese monarchs were not hidden from their subjects. Princes mingled with those of lesser rank in the crowded marketplaces outside the palace gate. It was apparently quite acceptable, if somewhat hazardous, to gamble or chat with the king, as long as you did not insult him, for example by using the wrong level of language. The flavour of such intercourse is captured by a Balinese poem of advice to rulers:

> Let your discourse be enlightening,
> do not hide your meaning;
> consult with your underlings,
> and you will touch their hearts . . .
> Permit no insolence among your subjects,
> they would hold you in low esteem.
> Be alert to equality and difference;
> let their speech be seemly,
> their words sincere, courteous, clear and friendly.
> All this will prompt them to behave properly,
> instill obedience, and they spring no surprises on you.[4]

Still, such familiarity, however guarded, was quite a contrast to the extremes of royal isolation common in larger Asian courts.

Just as the regional European presence stimulated the slave trade, so its gradual abolition in the early nineteenth century, initially by the British, changed the economic base of Mengwi and the other Balinese states. A new trade pattern developed, centred on Singapore, and the Balinese kings turned to cash crops, especially coffee. Again the royal family of Mengwi was involved, this time in opening lands for coffee cultivation in hitherto marginal upland areas. In some cases the Balinese nobility, especially women, actively engaged in trade, but more royal revenue derived from protecting Chinese traders, granting them monopolies, and levying tolls and fees on them.

Rulers granted Chinese and other foreigners exclusive rights to collect harbour taxes, in return for a share of the profits. The same system was applied to opium, which became increasingly important up to the end of Balinese independence and thereafter. Opium was not produced on Bali; it was imported from India, primarily through Singapore. The rulers smoked it in gold-encrusted pipes, but it was also used by the common people for its medicinal (or pain-deadening) value, and soldiers employed it as a courage-raising stimulant before going into battle. In the latter half of the eighteenth century, Chinese merchants on Bali were a major source of the opium being smuggled into Java, and Dutch desire to control and profit from the trade themselves was one reason for their final intervention in 1906 to end what was left of Balinese independence.

European technology was spreading long before the Dutch achieved direct control over all Bali. During a contest with neighbouring Badung in the early nineteenth century, Mengwi purchased arms from Batavia. Mengwi's army, in turn, was later almost extinguished by a Badung force spearheaded by Buginese riflemen, Muslim natives of Sulawesi who had been recruited by the Badung monarch primarily to conduct trade but also to be employed as mercenaries.

The political character of Mengwi changed as well. As the state became less expansive, its rulers moved around less and became more formal. Fewer commoners were ennobled in return for services rendered. 'Gone were the times,' Nordholt writes, 'when in the heat of a battle a leader would shout "If you fight with me I will make you a Gusti".'[5] Bali's nobility had proliferated to the point where there was less need to recruit commoners. Rules on dress, house decoration and marriage were more strictly enforced, and in general the line between noble and commoner was more tightly adhered to. This trend would continue under the Dutch, with their encouragement. By the mid-nineteenth century Balinese power was already severely, if indirectly, circumscribed by British and especially Dutch expansion in the region. The waning power of the rulers may have contributed to the increasing formalism of their courts.

From study focused primarily on late nineteenth-century Bali, anthropologist Clifford Geertz concluded that the Balinese realm was less a government than a 'theatre state' where the primary objective of government was ritual display. Geertz based this conclusion partly on the consideration that, despite endemic warfare, a Balinese king had rather little governing to do, since most important functions were carried out by non-state actors, from irrigation associations to Chinese traders. Beginning his analysis at an earler period than Geertz, Nordholt presents a very different and more persuasive picture of kings recruiting followers, initiating irrigation systems and, above all, engaging in a constant struggle to maintain political primacy by every means possible under conditions of constant instability. Ritual was important as a manifestation of powerful kingship, but to succeed a Balinese king had to be a warrior, a commanding personality, and above all a successful patron, politician and protector.

Such was the situation on Bali prior to the establishment of colonial rule. It was a complex setting, replete with regional variations, charismatic individuals and constant political change. Pre-colonial Bali bore little resemblance to the idyllic vision of later European visitors. Warfare, disease and natural disaster were all commonplace. Slavery and drug addiction were among the less savoury customary practices. The Dutch were to be initially shocked by the force of Balinese resistance, then charmed by the positive aspects of Balinese civilisation. Their stay was to be short, but their impact profound.

5
THE DUTCH ARRIVE: FROM FIRST CONTACT TO FINAL CONQUEST (1597–1908)

The Dutch first visited Bali in 1597. They did not control the whole island until 1908, more than three centuries later. During those 300 years Bali was increasingly affected by European influences on all sides but, unlike Java, remained largely untouched by the most intrusive aspects of colonial rule. In that respect the Balinese were lucky.

In 1597 three ships under the command of Cornelis de Houtman arrived off Bali. It was not the first Western visit. Magellan's expedition may have sighted Bali almost 70 years previously. It is possible but not confirmed that the Portuguese explorer Mendez de Pinto visited in about 1546. British freebooter Sir Francis Drake called briefly in 1580, and Thomas Cavendish in 1585, but apparently neither recorded his impressions. In 1585 a Portuguese ship from Malacca attempting to open a trading post foundered off the coast and five survivors made it to shore. The king of Gelgel treated them kindly but would not let them return to Malacca, and at least one of them was still there to meet de Houtman twelve years later.

Two of de Houtman's sailors jumped ship and remained on the island, leading to the pretty hypothesis, convenient for tourism promotion in later years, that Dutch contact had begun 'not with a shot, but a seduction'.[1] It is not totally clear whether the young Dutch sailors were seduced or abducted, although both remained and took Balinese wives.

However, in general the visit went well. De Houtman's expedition produced the first detailed Western report on the island, which was complimentary about the ruler, the son of Batu Renggong, the powerful monarch who had brought Gelgel to its apogee. The Dutch were impressed by his lavish court, which included a troupe of malformed dwarfs, by his abundance of wives and concubines, and by his regalia, which included a magnificent kris. The king's emissary claimed that he ruled the entire island, and the Dutch believed him. They saw Gelgelian troops on their way to Blambangan to aid Bali's ally there against the Muslim sultanate of Mataram.

De Houtman took due note of Bali's substantial population of 300 000 and its lively commerce. He even decided to name the island 'Young Holland'. But there were also, not surprisingly, undercurrents of tension: both sides took hostages for the duration of the visit, there was bickering over gift exchange, and the mission did not accomplish anything in the way of trade. Bali, of course, had no spices comparable to the cloves and nutmeg grown further east, which had already initiated a century of conflict among Portuguese, Dutch and English.

It was this absence of major commercial prospects which allowed Bali to escape serious Dutch attention for the next two and a half centuries. At first the Dutch had no interest in acquiring territory, beyond the strong points needed to control trade. Initially they established fortified outposts in the spice-producing islands of eastern Indonesia. In 1619 they founded Batavia (today Jakarta) as a stronghold on Java and eventual capital. In 1652 they built the twin of Batavia's fort in Cape Town to anchor and provision the long sea route to Holland.

They ruled through a quasi-state trading organisation, the Dutch East India Company, for almost two centuries, initially with the sole aim of making money. In the early years the Company had its hands full subduing or co-opting potential Indonesian rivals for control of Java. It did not get a firm grasp on all Java until early in the nineteenth century, and the more remote or commercially valueless areas of the Outer Islands beyond Java remained independent even after that. The Company's territories became known as the Dutch East Indies.

The Company may have tried to open a trading post on Bali around 1620, but if so it didn't last. Bali developed a reputation as a distant curiosity, populated by fierce and intractable kings, of interest mainly as a source of slaves and, since the Balinese rulers were more than happy to sell slaves to the Dutch, hardly worth the trouble of occupying. As we have seen, both the Dutch and the king of Gelgel toyed with the idea of enlisting each other's assistance against a common Javanese enemy, Muslim Mataram, without results. But after that, chronic political instability helped to dissuade Dutch or other European interest in Bali.

Slavery and merchant adventure

Sad to say, slavery was for many years the most important factor in Dutch-Balinese relations. From the mid-seventeenth century onwards, slaves were Bali's 'most lucrative cash crop'.[2] Balinese slaves came from several sources. Rulers were obligated by custom to enslave anyone who was indigent or otherwise became a charge on public welfare. Criminals, the wives and children of executed felons, and illegitimate children could be enslaved. The justice system was skewed to produce slaves because it inflicted higher fines for the same crime on offenders of low caste than on those of high caste, and when offenders couldn't pay they could be sold into slavery.

These slaves, one of them a Papuan, belonged to the Raja of Buleleng, North Bali, where they were photographed in 1865. Most slaves on Bali were Balinese and the Papuan was probably considered an exotic rarity. (Source: KITLV Archives, Leiden)

Prisoners of war were enslaved, and the slave trade undoubtedly provided a new economic motivation for endemic warfare. The chief minister of Karangasem remarked in 1808: 'We wage war upon the others when we, lords, lack money; at such times we swoop down on the weakest of our neighbors, and all prisoners and their entire families are sold for slaves so that we . . . have money to buy opium.'[3]

There was also debt slavery, common in Southeast Asia at the time. Individuals often pawned themselves to powerful patrons to obtain money and protection, which meant they could then be sold by the owner for any offence, however trivial. The rulers, who of course were the major slave owners, encouraged debt slavery by organising large-scale cockfights and obliging their subjects to participate. Those who gambled on the outcome and lost could become slaves if they could not pay their debts. Since slavery was hereditary, the children of slaves added to the pool.

Bali exported an estimated total of 150 000 slaves of both sexes between 1650 and 1830, generating an estimated 4.5 million silver dollars.[4] The Balinese rulers controlled the trade, utilising Chinese, Buginese and Europeans as intermediaries. They used the proceeds to buy opium, luxury goods and arms to give them a competitive edge over their Balinese rivals.

The Dutch East India Company was the primary market for slaves, relying on them for labour of all sorts. By the mid-seventeenth century Batavia had a total population of around 30 000, of whom about half were slaves; of these, from 8 000 to 10 000 may have been Balinese. Including freed slaves, Balinese may have been the largest ethnic component in the population.[5] They were numerous enough to leave a permanent Balinese imprint on the dialect of Malay (Indonesian) spoken in the future national capital of Indonesia. There is to this day a community in Jakarta known as the 'Depok Dutch', descended in part from Balinese slaves.

In this commerce, young Balinese women were much in demand for their beauty. They were also popular with Chinese buyers because, not being Muslim, they did not object to cooking pork. But Balinese men, often recent prisoners of war and not inclined to be submissive, had a reputation for being hard to control.

Selling slaves was discouraged in Batavia itself, so they were often freed upon the deaths of their masters. Many of the resulting population of free Balinese found employment in the Company's army. Some ex-slaves prospered, becoming large landowners around Batavia, and some Balinese may even have gone to Batavia voluntarily to advance themselves. Other slaves escaped and formed bands of rebels in the nearby Priangan hills. Thereby hangs the extraordinary tale of Surapati, among the most renowned Balinese in Indonesian history.

According to Javanese accounts, Surapati was the son of a Javanese prince who had lived on Bali, although evidence from Company records affirms he was Balinese. After many adventures he was sold into slavery in Batavia and served initially as a soldier for the Company. Later, offended by the Dutch, he deserted and took up with a band of brigands. In 1684 he joined Javanese forces opposing the Dutch. He rapidly emerged as a leader and military genius and became 'the most hated of all the Company's Indonesian enemies'.[6]

As the struggle continued, Surapati fled to East Java and established a domain which he and his descendants were to rule for almost a century. It was at this period that he allied with Balinese elements who were still operating in the Blambangan salient, and with whom he fought furious battles against the Dutch. Surapati was killed in 1706, but his descendants and followers remained at large until the Company successfully ended local resistance in 1771–72. When the dust settled, the Dutch required those native Blambangan leaders who were still Hindu to convert to Islam, which the Dutch feared greatly elsewhere. They did so to lessen the prospects for further mischief-making, as they saw it, by the Hindu Balinese. Surapati is remembered as a heroic proto-nationalist, and a park in Jakarta is named after him.

The nature of the Balinese slave trade shifted over time. Many Balinese slaves were sent to the Company's maritime way station at Cape Town, to work in its fort and ship-provisioning facilities. There the Balinese, along with other Indonesians, gradually merged into the polygot, Dutch-speaking population which is today known as Coloured or, in the case of a minority who are Muslim, Cape Malay. Later Balinese slaves were shipped to the sugar plantations of Reunion and Mauritius. The British outlawed the slave trade in 1807 throughout their empire and tried to end it in the Dutch East Indies in 1810, at the beginning of their Napoleonic-era occupation, but it persisted for decades longer.

The Balinese did not take kindly to being exported from Bali, all the more so because of their belief that the gods lived only there. Fear of slave rebellions, of which at least two were recorded in the early nineteenth century, led slavers to make liberal use of chains and of informers planted among their human cargo. A shocking vignette of the trade was left by an Arab emissary in the service of the Dutch who visited Bali in 1824:

> On the 17th [of August 1824] we sailed along the coast of Bali and at three in the afternoon we saw a two-masted schooner lying anchored in the roads of Buleleng . . . It was the schooner *Victorie* commanded by Captain Moesie [Monsieur?] James Diviled, equipped with six iron eight-pounders and with a crew of twenty-five Frenchmen . . . The schooner had no merchandise aboard, only Spanish dollars to buy slaves with . . . One day the Raja of Buleleng sold the French Captain a woman and her two children. The woman was old, about 40 years of age, while her children, a girl and a boy, were about nine and six respectively . . . The Captain did not want to take the woman on account of her age—he only wanted the children. When the three slaves arrived at the beach, the Captain ordered the children to be led away. But the children did not want to be separated from their mother and held her around the neck. The mother too did not want to let go of her children and they embraced each other, crying loudly . . . The Captain became very angry and ordered two European sailors to lead the children away from their mother—one sailor held the mother and the other the children and they violently separated them. The two sailors dragged the children in the boat and rowed to the schooner. The mother fell down on the beach and lay as if dead for over an hour. When night came she cried and screamed for her children . . . She remained in this condition for several days . . . but the hearts of those who had brought her into this state were harder than iron.[7]

Napoleon, Raffles and Singapore put Bali on the map

The slave trade aside, Bali continued to experience 'the priceless bene-fits of European neglect'[8] until the mid-nineteenth century. The island was spared the tumultuous strife between the Company and local rulers which was endemic on Java, as well as the forced production of cash crops, coffee and later sugar, which after 1830 developed into the highly profitable but socially disastrous Culture System, a tax in kind on the relentlessly ground-down peasantry.

Oddly enough it was the Napoleonic Wars which began the end of Bali's isolation. When Bonaparte made his brother King of Holland in 1806, the East Indies became part of his empire. Determined that these valuable islands should not fall into the hands of the British, the French ruler sent a vigorous military governor to fortify Java as a base against them. In response the British, who had kept a fleet off Batavia since 1795, conquered it and appointed Thomas Stamford Raffles Lieutenant Gover-nor of Java and, by extension, the rest of the Dutch East Indies.

Raffles fell madly in love with the Indies and dreamed of retain-ing them in the British Empire. In addition to being an energetic, reforming governor, he wrote a remarkable two-volume *History of Java* largely to promote this ambition, to no avail. Holland was a traditional British ally and London was uninterested in acquiring more Asian terri-tory, feeling that India was more than enough. In 1816 the British restored the territories of the Dutch East India Company, by now defunct, to the direct control of the Dutch government.

Deeply disappointed, Raffles languished for a brief time in Bengkulu, a marginal British outpost on the wrong side of Sumatra, far from the vital Malacca Straits. Then in 1819 he achieved enduring fame by founding Singapore, at that time no more than a village but ideally located to become a major international port, which, under British rule, it did with amazing speed.

During his tour as Lieutenant Governor of Java, nearby Bali predictably attracted Raffles' wide-ranging interest, but his other duties left him time for only one short visit. It took place in 1815 by accident when his ship, bound for a destination in East Java, was blown off course. His subordinate and intellectual rival, John Crawfurd, had visited a short time before. Both men were fascinated by Bali's Hindu culture, and both published accounts exaggerating similarities with Hinduism in India.

Raffles was among the first to conclude that 'the present state of Bali may be considered . . . as a kind of commentary on the ancient conditions of the natives of Java',[9] a theme later to be much emphasised by the Dutch. Oversimplifying greatly, he observed the prevalence of private landholding on Bali, in contrast to Java. He pronounced the Balinese to be 'active and enterprising, and free from that listlessness and indolence which are observable in the inhabitants of Java'.[10] Raffles' comments were often inaccurate, hardly surprising given the brevity of his visit, but they helped to flag the island as a place worthy of further attention.

It might have been expected that Britain's decision to return the Indies to Dutch rule in 1816 would diminish traditional Dutch anxiety about British encroachment—but it did nothing of the kind. Instead, the rapid commercial growth of Singapore resulted in a proliferation of new players in the region—British, Asians and others—which aggravated Dutch concern. In 1824 the Dutch and British signed a treaty intended to prevent the British from trading in Dutch territory and vice versa. It did not work, if only because Dutch control over the Outer Islands around Java was as yet spotty and ill defined.

The Lombok Straits, bounded on both sides by squabbling Balinese states, developed new strategic importance as a way station and provisioning point between Singapore and Australia. The Dutch began to fear that the British would attempt to establish a new Singapore on Bali or Lombok. More importantly, perhaps, the entire nature of international colonialism was changing. European overlords, no longer solely concerned with trade, were becoming more interested in other forms of economic exploitation and in the orderly administration of territory and the sea lanes. Marginal realms left in the hands of 'barbaric' native rulers were beginning to seem anachronistic as well as dangerously attractive to European competitors.

No sooner had the British formally relinquished control of Java in 1816 than the new post-Company regime in Batavia sent a Dutch envoy to Bali to urge its rulers to accept 'contracts', or treaties, which in effect would surrender independence to the Governor General in Batavia. It soon became clear that Dutch and Balinese understanding of what treaties were about differed almost as profoundly as their objectives.

The Balinese rulers were not illiterate savages; they knew about written treaties. They habitually concluded treaties among themselves to cover many aspects of interstate relations. But for the Balinese, treaties were primarily ceremonial in nature, and they lost significance if not constantly reinforced by personal contact. For the Dutch, on the other hand, treaties were supposed to be valid indefinitely or until revoked by mutual consent.

The Dutch were rebuffed in their first attempt to peddle treaties. The Balinese rulers were looking for military aid against each other, while the Dutch wanted submission, not useless political alliances. Wandering Arabs were common in the archipelago at this time, and in 1824 the Dutch enlisted one of them, Pangeran (Prince) Said Hasan al Habashi, as an envoy. Al Habashi, the same individual quoted earlier about slavery, was no more successful than his Dutch predecessor at the treaty game, although he did pick up valuable intelligence about pirates using Balinese ports, enabling the Dutch to send warships to evict them. In 1826 another Dutch envoy opened a trading post at Kuta, then the port of Badung, in time to become the gaudiest of tourist enclaves. But the post didn't prosper and in 1831 it closed down, temporarily as things turned out.

Enter the convivial Dane

The tale of Mads Lange encapsulates everything about this proto-colonial era that was beginning to seem outrageously messy to a new generation of proconsuls in Batavia. Lange, 'more . . . the bold Viking than prudent trader',[11] was an independent Danish operator who in 1834 installed himself with his brothers at Ampenan, a large harbour in western Lombok, under the protection of its Balinese ruler. He built a thriving trade exporting local rice from Lombok to China and importing Chinese copper coins with square holes, strings of which served as currency on Bali. He also imported textiles, opium and weapons.

Lange was a generous and gregarious character, who soon became known as the 'White Raja of Ampenan'. This happy state of affairs didn't last long. The ruler of Karangasem died, leaving a large progeny quarrelling over his domains: one state on Bali and a divided state on Lombok. The result was civil war, with Lange eventually backing one ruler on Lombok and an English trader, George Pocock King, backing the other. Unfortunately Lange picked the loser, who fled and later committed ritual suicide, or *puputan*, a phenomenon which would assume major importance in the final stages of the Dutch conquest of Bali.

Lange survived this debacle, but lost most of his trading fleet except for the *Venus*, a little schooner on which he fled to Bali. He went into business at Kuta in 1839 at about the same time that the Dutch tried to reestablish themselves there. Once again they failed and closed the post. In 1844 the Dutch tried a different tack and appointed Lange to be their agent at Kuta. But his real patron was the most powerful of several would-be rulers of Badung at the time, Gusti Ngurah Gede Kesiman, based in nearby Denpasar, for whom Lange became harbourmaster and trade agent.

Near modern Kuta Beach, Lange established a large compound for a warehouse, marketplace and dwelling. Here he lived with his brothers, his Chinese and Balinese wives, his children (one of whom later married the Sultan of Johore in Malaya), a large and multinational crew of servants, and his dalmatians, whose descendants still roam the back streets of the town.

Here he entertained a succession of Dutch officials, scholars and adventurers, especially after he became the official Dutch representative. After dinner he and his brothers would entertain their guests with piano and violin recitals and Danish folk music. The convivial Dane henceforth played three roles: commercial broker between the Balinese, the Dutch and international traders; information conduit and source of intelligence for both sides, and agent of political reconciliation between colonial officials and local rulers.

Lange's arrival in Kuta coincided with significant changes in Balinese trade patterns. Raffles had initiated a gradual halt to the slave trade. This had destroyed a major source of revenue for the rulers, so they had begun to produce rice, pigs, cattle hides, coconuts, coffee and tobacco for sale and export, demonstrating no small measure of entrepreneurial appetite and skill.

At this time Bali was recovering from the massive 1815 eruption of the Tambora volcano on Sumbawa, east of Lombok. The Tambora blow-out, more violent by far than the better-known 1883 eruption of Krakatoa in West Java, had a global impact on climate. It laid down ash deposits on Bali which initially ruined crops, but over time enhanced soil fertility and agricultural production. Due to this coincidence of geologic and economic circumstances, some of the rulers now passed beyond rustic affluence and became downright rich.

Lange organised an inter-island trade system centered on Kuta to gather produce. He bought from Chinese merchants and Balinese noblewomen, ladies of status who were aggressive and competitive traders. Always wary of provoking friction with his Balinese patron, he did not allow Europeans to participate in the inland portion of the trade. Ever the diplomat, he would sometimes buy more than he needed rather than disappoint an eager and possibly influential Balinese vendor.

Dutch interest in Bali continued to increase. Late in 1838 Batavia sent an envoy who promised a rhinoceros to the Dewa Agung of Klungkung, supposedly lord of all Bali, which he wanted for a very special state ceremony. The rhinoceros has not in historic times been native to Bali, although it is found on Java and Sumatra, and it was the rarest thing the ambitious ruler could imagine. The hapless beast was eventually delivered by the officer who reopened the Dutch post at Kuta in 1839 and sacrificed at Klungkung with enormous pomp. The ritual was sufficiently memorable to become the subject of a Balinese epic poem. It describes how thousands of celebrants high on opium attended, and how pickpockets worked the unruly crowd. Men and women groped each other 'accidentally', leading to profanity. The poet did not approve.

> The followers (of kings) came in scores
> flowing from the north, flowing from the east,
> filling the streets to watch,
> like a swarm of wasps;
> there were probably more than 100 000
> people in Klungkung
> crowding and jostling each other.
> Not knowing who was noble and who was not
> they jostled each other
> Uncertain of the way . . .
> Everyone went out of their way to follow whatever
> pleased them . . .
> they forgot about how such wrong actions made slaves of
> them as they daily dared to take a ball of opium.
> So they didn't know what was right or wrong
> and it made them confused
> because they thought only of the moment.[12]

In 1840 the Dutch sent another official, H.J. Huskus Koopman, to push the Balinese to accept 'contracts'. He succeeded on Lombok, where the

Balinese raja who had won the 1839 civil war signed up. Irony of ironies, Koopman appointed this ruler's hired hand, George Pocock King, once considered to personify the British menace, as Dutch agent. The Lombok state was to be a critical source of support for the Dutch in their coming campaign against the recalcitrant rulers of north Bali.

In south Bali a new factor came into play, the problem of 'reef rights'. According to Balinese tradition, ships which ran aground on Bali's numerous fringing coral reefs were gifts from the sea god, and rulers had the right to plunder them. To the Dutch this quaint custom fell into the same category of barbarous Balinese habits as 'widow burning', also known as *suttee* (from the Sanskrit *sati*), the ritual sacrifice of women on the funeral pyres of their deceased husbands. As commerce flourished, both 'reef rights' and 'widow burning' became increasingly important sources of friction.

In 1840, coinciding with the beginning of Koopman's treaty-seeking mission, the Dutch frigate *Overijssel* ran aground off Kuta, spilling its heavy iron cargo, a complete sugar mill destined for Java, onto the reef. The Balinese pillaged the wreck while the crew was entertained by Mads Lange on shore, one result being the arrival of the first European child born on Bali. Koopman demanded compensation and used the affair to pressure Lange's patron, Raja Kesiman of Badung, to accept a treaty. Thanks to mediation by the Dane, he finally did. Soon afterwards the rulers of Klungkung, Buleleng and Karangasem also signed treaties with the Dutch, followed in the next two years by Tabanan and Lombok. Koopman had already returned to Batavia.

At the very least the Balinese rulers did not understand what they were signing, and they were probably deliberately deceived. As the Dutch were aware, the Balinese knew enough about Dutch rule on Java to be particularly wary of insistence that they yield sovereignty. So to make the treaties acceptable, Koopman presented a more palatable text in Malay than in Dutch, which of course the Balinese could not read. The Dutch soon attempted to enforce these dubious agreements by military force. The campaign which followed nearly taught them 'no end of a lesson', as Kipling said about the British and the Boer War.

Conquest: The first stage

Hostilities began after another ship-plundering episode near Buleleng in 1845. The Dutch had no agent resident there, so they named a senior official in nearby East Java 'Commissioner for Bali', and sent him to protest. Arriving on a big warship with an impressive entourage, he got a brusque reception. The Raja and his prime minister, Gusti Ktut Jelantik, denied the existence of a treaty, probably assuming it had lapsed when Koopman left Bali after 1843. The best they would offer was friendly relations.

Jelantik, a firebrand and natural leader who was to emerge as the Balinese hero of the coming war, had already insulted the honour of the Netherlands by spitting betel juice on a Dutch passport. His angry words to the visiting Dutch Commissioner were prophetic:

> Never while I live shall the state recognize the sovereignty
> of the Netherlands in the sense which you interpret it.
> After my death the Radja may do as he chooses. Not by a
> mere scrap of paper shall any man become the master of
> another's lands. Rather let the *kris* decide.[13]

The Balinese further shocked the emissary by their brazenly impudent behaviour, such a contrast to the polite, subservient Javanese nobility to whom the Dutch were by now accustomed:

> From time to time the Gusti [Ketut Jelantik] turned to one
> of his followers close to him in rank, a fat man whose face
> shone with oil and whose features expressed stupidity . . .
> [The Gusti] would say something, the words impossible for

us to catch, with a scornful twitch of the mouth and a contemptuous glance in our direction, whereupon the fat one would lead the others in a round of guffaws and loud, jeering laughter.[14]

It would be interesting to know what the hot-tempered prince was saying to his followers. It may not have been political in nature. We know that while the Balinese were impressed by the ornate uniforms worn by nineteenth-century Dutch envoys, they also noticed their foul breath.[15]

By now the Dutch were convinced that this challenge to their honour and authority could only be resolved by force. The result was three punitive expeditions against Buleleng. Several things about the political context need to be kept in mind. The Balinese states of Buleleng and Karangasem were ruled by brothers, making them natural allies against the Dutch. But the ruler of Lombok, now advised by George Pocock King, had been a bitter opponent of the ruler of Karangasem in the 1839 civil war, so was now a natural (and as it turned out decisive) ally of the Dutch. Finally Klungkung, the spiritual heir of Gelgel, continued to exercise an ill-defined but sometimes critical influence as theoretical overlord of all Bali. The three expeditions may be summarised as follows:

The first Dutch invasion fleet arrives off Buleleng in late June, 1846: two frigates, four steamships, twelve schooners, 40 smaller craft, an army of 1700 including 400 Europeans, and 230 artillery pieces. Jelantik and his men have prepared heavily fortified defences around the port, which the Dutch frigates bombard. The Dutch land and destroy the royal palace at Singaraja, taking few casualties. The defenders retreat to heavily fortified positions at Jagaraga, eight kilometres inland from Singaraja. Then George Pocock King appears on the scene and negotiates an apparent settlement in which the Balinese agree to abide by the treaties, pay the costs of the expedition, and accept a garrison. The Dutch jubilantly return to Java, leaving behind only a small force. But the Balinese fail to pay anything, while Jelantik travels around Bali stirring up opposition to the Dutch.

In 1848 the Dutch send a more powerful expedition under one of their most distinguished colonial soldiers. The land force consists of 2400 men, of whom about one-third are European, the rest mainly Javanese and Madurese. There is also a company of Africans, probably recruited at one of the Dutch trading stations in what is now Ghana. On 7 May the Dutch force lands without heavy opposition. As in 1846, the Balinese withdraw to their fortified positions at Jagaraga. In a classic display of colonial arrogance, the Dutch frontally attack a vastly superior force of 16 000 Balinese, about 1500 of them with firearms, in tropical midday heat. The Balinese counter-attack and rout the Dutch, who lose about 200 dead and wounded and retreat to their ships. More than 2000 Balinese die in the fighting.

After this humiliating rebuff the Dutch send a third and even bigger expedition. It appears off Buleleng in April 1849, this time with 5000 troops of whom the majority are Dutch. After inconclusive negotiations with the ruler and his prime minister, the invaders besiege and capture Jagaraga, this time avoiding a frontal assault. They lose 34 dead, the Balinese thousands, including the wife of Jelantik and other highborn ladies who commit ritual suicide (*puputan*) by advancing into the Dutch lines. However, Jelantik himself and the ruler of Buleleng escape to allied Karangasem. The Dutch, wary of following the Balinese overland, decide to shift their campaign to the south.

The Dutch re-embark on their ships and land in south Bali near Padang Bai. At first they are not sure whether to pursue arch-rebel Jelantik at Karangasem, or to attack Klungkung, the theoretical overlord, which has emerged as an important source of support for Jelantik. The issue is decided after the Balinese ruler of Lombok enters the war on the Dutch side and sends troops, transported by the Dutch, to attack his old enemy and relative in Karangasem. Both Jelantik and his patron, the ruler of Buleleng, are killed in this campaign, while the ruler of Karangasem commits ritual suicide. The exact circumstances of Gusti

Ketut Jelantik's death are not known. After independence, he will be designated an Indonesian National Hero, one of only two Balinese ever to be so honoured.

With Jelantik out of the way the Dutch advance westward along the coast into Klungkung, capturing the ancient holy site at Goa Lawah (better known to modern tourists as the Bat Cave) against heated resistance, and then occupying the port town of Kusamba. Already weakened by fighting in the north, the colonial troops are now smitten by an epidemic of dysentery. Before they can recover, the sister of the old and frail Dewa Agung of Klungkung and her ally the ruler of Gianyar stage a surprise night-time raid on the Dutch camp, mortally wounding the elderly Dutch commander, Major General Michiels. According to Balinese accounts this is accomplished with a gun possessing magical power, whose bullets can look for the enemy, a Balinese equivalent of today's 'smart bombs'.

General Michiels' deputy orders the force to retreat to its ships and await the arrival of a new commander. At this point the situation is extremely tense, with over 33 000 Balinese troops from Badung, Gianyar, Tabanan and Klungkung in a position to attack the Dutch. But the intervention of Mads Lange and his powerful patron, Raja Kesiman of Badung, saves the day. Lange's business is being ruined by the war and he desperately wants peace, while Kesiman is hoping to advance his political ambitions in south Bali with Dutch support. Lange persuades the Dutch to stop advancing, and Kesiman persuades Klungkung to eschew further resistance. The war is over.

The subsequent peace talks were held with great ceremony in July 1849 at Mads Lange's compound in Kuta, where Raja Kesiman took centre stage as official host while Lange covered the costs of entertaining at least 30 000 Balinese guests. The Dutch brought in a German duke who happened to be in command of their colonial army, Duke Hertog Bernard von Saksen Weimar Eisenach, so the rulers would feel they were dealing with someone of sufficiently exalted rank. On 15 July, the

Balinese once again signed treaties more or less identical to the old ones. The Dutch obtained the right to station representatives in Bali, but promised not to interfere in the states' internal affairs.

The two sides left Kuta nursing parallel illusions. The Balinese thought, or hoped, that the Dutch would once again go away, and things would get back to normal. The Dutch thought, or hoped, that the Balinese would now honour the treaties, and that the unruly states of south Bali could be left to their own devices. They rewarded the ruler of Lombok, Gusti Ngurah Ketut Karangasem, for his decisive assistance by installing him as ruler of Karangasem in place of the ruler of Buleleng's deceased brother. They punished Buleleng, whose ruler had also been killed in the war, by splitting it in two. One part, Jembrana, was set up as an independent state, while the other was given to Bangli, an arrangement which did not last.

One consequence of the 1846–49 war was the end of Mads Lange's little empire in Kuta and the ruin of the southern economy. The fighting had badly disrupted trade, and with the return of peace it gravitated away from Kuta to Dutch-controlled Buleleng in the north. Bigger ships were coming into service and the reef-fringed anchorage at Kuta was no longer adequate. As modern colonialism spread, the day of freelance merchant-adventurer-diplomats like Mads Lange and Rajah James Brooke of Sarawak was coming to an end.

Lange died in 1856 at age 49, allegedly poisoned by a Balinese rival of his patron, Raja Kesiman. He and several of his relatives were buried in Kuta, where his grave, refurbished by his relatives in Denmark, may be seen on a back street not far from today's tourist strip. He turned what was left of the business over to his son and nephew, but it did not long survive his death. Deprived of its economic base, Badung never achieved the dominance in southern Balinese politics which in 1849 had seemed likely. Instead the region degenerated into half a century of normalcy, or anarchy, depending on one's point of view.

In the north, the victorious Dutch soon felt it necessary to assert greater control, placing the first resident expatriate official there in

1854. Following the pattern established on Java, a member of the Bule-leng ruling family was appointed as regent, paralleled by an aptly-named Dutch *controleur*, similar to a district officer in British practice. Things did not go smoothly at first, mainly because the Balinese did not take kindly to the Dutch-dictated selection of district chiefs. In 1858 and again in 1868 Batavia had to send military expeditions to put down local uprisings. The second expedition led to the Banjar War, named after the district where it took place, and resulted in about 20 Dutch soldiers killed. In 1872 a troublesome regent had to be exiled to Sumatra. In 1882 Batavia finally imposed direct rule on north Bali, installing a Dutch resident.

The crisis which precipitated the final stage of Dutch conquest began in 1891 as a result of continuing unrest in south Bali. The specific cause was an effort by the ruler of Lombok to help his relative, the ruler of Karangasem, in a war against Klungkung. Simplifying more than somewhat, the story runs as follows:

Lombok's Balinese overlords sent an expeditionary force to Bali consist-ing mainly of Sasaks, Muslim natives of Lombok who were habitually exploited by their Hindu Balinese rulers. This caused a Sasak rebellion on Lombok.

Both sides in the ensuing struggle appealed to the Dutch for help, without success. Lombok's Balinese ruler, no longer the same prince who had supported the Dutch in 1849, had employed a wealthy Singa-porean Armenian as his harbourmaster, the same job once held by George Pocock King. Through this man he now sought British assis-tance, which greatly upset the Dutch, while the Sasaks continued to bombard Batavia with complaints about what today would be termed human rights violations perpetrated by their Balinese lord.

Throughout this period the Dutch were preoccupied with a decades-long struggle to subjugate Aceh, the northernmost state of Sumatra. In 1894 they thought the Aceh War was winding down, incor-rectly as things turned out, and therefore felt free to intervene in

I Gusti Gde Jelantik was installed by the Dutch as ruler of Karangasem with the title of stedehouder after the Lombok War. On his left is his nephew, I Gusti Bagus Jelantik, who succeeded him in 1908, reading a palm-leaf (lontar) text. I Gusti Bagus Jelantik was the father of Dr. A.A.M. Djelantik, medical doctor, public servant and author of a lively memoir of his eventful career. (Source: KITLV Archives, Leiden)

Lombok. They sent its ruler an ultimatum, followed by a punitive expedition manned by tough veterans of the Aceh campaign. The expedition began well, with the Balinese ruler of Lombok paying some of the indemnity which the Dutch demanded. Then on 25 August the Balinese launched a surprise attack and expelled the Dutch from Lombok with heavy casualties. Once again the Dutch commanding general was among those killed.

Outraged by what they saw as treachery, the Dutch returned with a much heavier force which shelled and razed the capital, Mataram (not to be confused with the Javanese kingdoms of the same name). From its treasury they took a variety of plunder including 1000 pounds of gold and 6000 pounds of silver, more than sufficient to cover the expenses of the Lombok War. It was impressive testimony to the wealth of the Balinese ruling classes. Following their victory the Dutch exiled the raja and immediately established direct rule over Lombok. They appointed the least culpable prince of the Karangasem-Lombok royal house, I Gusti Gede Jelantik, as governor (*stedehouder*) of Karangasem in southeastern Bali, a title implying more autonomy than 'regent'. His subsequent performance was entirely satisfactory to Batavia.

The finishing

The Lombok War left the southern Balinese states of Bangli, Badung, Gianyar, Klungkung and Tabanan as the only ones more or less outside Dutch control, but not for long. Klungkung's theoretical suzerainty was by now truly meaningless, while the once ascendant Badung remained impoverished. Mengwi had been snuffed out of existence in 1891, and Gianyar narrowly avoided a similar fate.

In 1899 Gianyar's relatively weak ruler, Dewa Gede Raka, embroiled in warfare with his Balinese neighbours, sought Dutch protection. He was encouraged to do so by his much more powerful subordinate, Cokorde Gede Sukawati, the ruler of Ubud. The Dutch finally agreed the next year, giving Raka the same title (*stedehouder*) held by the ruler of Karangasem. At about the same time they appointed a capable official, H.J.E.F. Schwartz, as their envoy to south Bali. The Dutch presence in the south had started in earnest. Coincidentally the stage was set for bitter rivalry between the palaces of Gianyar and Ubud in later years, most notably during the Indonesian Revolution.

By 1904 the Aceh War was finally smouldering to a conclusion, and the Dutch were ready to end the anomalous situation in southern Bali. In May 1904 they got their chance when the *Sri Kumala*, a Borneo-based Chinese trading vessel, ran aground on the massive fringing coral reef off Sanur and was plundered. The Dutch sent a bill to the ruler of Badung who, backed by Klungkung and Tabanan, refused to pay. The Dutch then blockaded the coast and on 14 September landed troops, including cavalry and artillery, at Sanur. They advanced slowly toward Denpasar, the capital of Badung, where on 20 September they found the palace in flames, accompanied by a wild beating of drums. To quote one account:

> As they drew closer, they observed a strange, silent procession emerging from the main gate of the *puri*. It was led by the Radja himself, seated in his state palanquin carried by four bearers, dressed in white cremation garments but splendidly bejeweled and armed with a magnificent kris. The Radja was followed by the officials of his court, the armed guards, the priests, his wives, his children and his retainers, likewise dressed in white, flowers in their hair . . . One hundred paces from the startled Dutch, the Radja halted his bearers, stepped from his palanquin, gave the signal, and the ghastly ceremony began. A priest plunged his dagger into the Radja's breast, and others of the company began turning their daggers upon themselves or upon one another. The Dutch troops, startled into action by a stray gunshot and reacting to attack by lance and spear, directed rifle and even artillery fire into the surging crowd. Some of the women mockingly threw jewels and gold coins to the soldiers, and as more and more people kept emerging from the palace gate, the mounds of corpses rose higher and higher. Soon to the scene of carnage was added the spectacle of looting as the soldiers stripped the valuables from the corpses and then set themselves to sacking the palace ruins.[16]

A similar encounter took place that evening in nearby Pemecutan, part of Badung.

In the neighbouring state of Tabanan the rulers were not only implicated in the recent ship plunder, they had also allowed two aged widows of a deceased ruler to sacrifice themselves on his funeral pyre, in spite of warnings from the Dutch not to do so. Their disobedience had personally offended the governor-general of the Indies, who even offered to resign over his failure to prevent this barbarity. The Tabanan raja and his senior son now sought terms from the Dutch, but were threatened with exile and jailed in Denpasar. They promptly committed suicide in prison.

Klungkung was the final act. Its rulers initially accepted a Dutch ultimatum, but friction soon erupted in nearby Gelgel, the seat of the illustrious sixteenth-century state of the same name. It happened because the Dutch, already worrying about revenue, were determined to open branches of their official opium monopoly even before they had achieved political control. But first they had to abolish the Balinese ruler's opium monopoly, exercised through a Chinese merchant. Under the old system the drug was eventually sold freely on the market, but now (as the Balinese were aware) consumers would have to buy it from official outlets staffed by Javanese. The result was anti-Dutch riots which soon got out of hand.

A by now familiar sequence of events ensued. The Dutch bombarded both Klungkung and Gelgel, and sent in troops and artillery. On 28 April 1908, the Klungkung royalty staged another dramatic self-sacrifice. About 400 Balinese were killed and there were few survivors, although some of the Klungkung aristocrats were exiled to Lombok. The palace was destroyed, leaving only a magnificent gate still standing near the Hall of Justice with its painted ceiling, familiar to modern visitors.

Of this last episode Clifford Geertz wrote, '. . . the king and court again paraded, half entranced, half dazed with opium, out of the palace into the reluctant fire of the by now thoroughly bewildered Dutch troops. It was quite literally the death of the old order. It expired as it had lived: absorbed in a pageant'.[17]

The meaning of *puputan*

A total of about 1100 Balinese died in the 1906–08 ritual suicides, or *puputan*.[18] What were these extraordinary spectacles, almost without parallel in the history of warfare? Were they just lethal pageantry, or was something more political or even strategic going on?

The Balinese term *puputan* comes from the root *puput*, meaning 'finishing' or 'ending'. Western accounts frequently suggest that the *puputan* were stimulated by opium use and/or by a cultural affinity for spontaneous violence, the tradition of *amok* (an Indonesian word) found throughout the Malay world, from which the English expression 'running amuck' is derived.

But not all *puputan* were the same. They were not all staged against colonial armies. There are several recorded instances of Balinese forces resorting to them against other Balinese, as in the case of the Lombok civil war of 1839. Nor were all *puputan* suicidal. The original meaning seems to have been a last desperate attack against a numerically superior enemy. In at least one conflict between Balinese antagonists, a *puputan* succeeded, resulting in victory for those who launched it.[19]

Of course times had changed by 1906. The military advantage of the Dutch had grown overwhelming and obvious, and many Balinese realised that physical resistance would be futile. Some rulers may well have been seeking death, fearing that colonial conquest would deprive them of everything it meant to be a lord, a humiliation too profound to be borne.

For them perhaps, the *puputan* was indeed more symbolic than strategic, the last act of a tragic dance-drama, natural for a people whose genius for theatre is unsurpassed. In most cases the participants, unlike Japanese kamikaze pilots or Palestinian suicide bombers, were apparently not even trying to defeat a military adversary. If they had been, they surely would have retreated to the interior and carried on the war, as Patih Jelantik had done in 1846.

This monument in Denpasar's central square commemorates suicidal Balinese resistance to heavily armed Dutch troops which took place nearby on 20 September 1906.
(Source: *Robert Pringle*)

But there is another dimension to the story. The best analysis of a *puputan* suggests that the Klungkung event may have been intended as an ultimate act of sacrifice whereby the king, powerless to avoid a hopeless situation on earth, could in death join forces with the supernatural to help his people.[20] Seen from this Balinese perspective, the *puputan* was an effort to mobilise immediate support from magical power (*sakti*) against superior force. Thus, on 28 April 1908, the doomed ruler of Klungkung sank his sacred kris in the ground, hoping that it would open and swallow up the advancing Dutch force. Magical weaponry had been credited with the dramatic death of a Dutch general, also in Klungkung, in 1849. There are other instances from around the world where traditional societies faced with overwhelming colonial firepower have appealed to the supernatural in final desperate efforts to avoid subjugation. One thinks of the Mahdi in Sudan, or of the Sioux at Wounded Knee.

Today the *puputan* are remembered by Balinese and other Indonesians as part of a national heritage of fierce anti-colonial resistance. In this spirit, the near-annihilation of a Balinese guerrilla unit by the Dutch in November 1946 is remembered as a *puputan*, a heroic last stand, even though it was surely not intended to be suicidal in nature. The Balinese recall this episode and those of 1906–08 with pride, and commemorate them with museums, monuments and periodic celebrations.

Whatever their motivation, the political impact of the *puputan* on the evolving colonial order was significant. They were a huge embarrassment to the Dutch, who were hard put to explain why European troops armed with artillery and other modern weapons were justified in inflicting such slaughter on people engaged in suicide, not serious resistance. The Dutch were supposedly imposing their rule to do away with barbarities such as slavery and widow burning, and now they had been caught up in a pattern of massacre.

There was a considerable uproar in Holland, followed by acute twinges of guilt. This reaction to events on Bali played into the development of a new 'Ethical Policy', which sought to emphasise a more socially responsible approach to governing the Indies. It referred to a 'debt of honour' to the people of the Indies who, through their labour, had made Holland rich. Seen from this perspective, those who went through a 'finishing' did not die in vain. Their heroic sacrifice not only inspired later nationalists, it also helped to produce immediate improvements in the motivation and quality of Dutch rule, both on Bali and throughout what was to become Indonesia.

6
PAX AND POVERTY NEERLANDICA (1908–1942)

Now began 34 years of Dutch peace, relatively speaking. There were to be no more major political changes on Bali until 1942, when the Japanese arrived. In considering the impact of Dutch rule on Bali, it is important to remember that this rule was quite brief, considerably shorter than the period that has elapsed since Indonesian independence in 1949. The Dutch saw themselves as still engaged in a work in progress when Greater East Asian Co-Prosperity so rudely intervened.

The results of colonialism were mixed. The Dutch brought peace to Bali, introduced a modicum of education and health care, and built harbours, roads and eventually an airport. By resorting to indirect rule through the old aristocracy, they reinforced its position in Balinese society. They increased and regularised land taxes, contributing to growing landlessness. They subjected peasants to an onerous forced labour (corvée) service. They strengthened and stiffened the caste system. For a mixture of economic and political motives, they began the modern tourism industry. They tried quite successfully to save Bali from the full impact of capitalism and cultural disruption of the kind

The 'barbaric' Balinese custom of 'suttee' or 'widow burning' was one of several pretexts for Dutch intervention in south Bali. This depiction, from a Balinese version of the Indian epic Mahabharata, *is among those commissioned by the Dutch–Chinese lexicographer Hermann Neubronner van der Tuuk in the 1870s to help him compile the first dictionary of the Balinese language. (Source: University of Leiden Oriental Collection)*

they had visited on Java. But their policies also aggravated social tensions which simmered under the surface, to re-emerge with lethal force after World War II.

Bali's new rulers were driven by complex and contradictory motives. On the one hand they were committed to the idealistic standards of the new Ethical Policy, with its emphasis on popular welfare. On the other hand, they still felt compelled to meet a fundamental requirement for any colonial administration anywhere—to show a surplus of revenue over expenditure wherever possible. Like British, French and American colonialists, the Dutch saw themselves as running a branch of government in the interests of their state, not a foreign aid programme. Despite the new focus on welfare, they enforced strict limits on social services and maintained high taxes even when the result impeded development and increased poverty. When motives conflicted, administrative convenience and the imperative of revenue usually trumped ethics.

At first the Dutch concentrated on the maintenance of peace and order, the elimination of 'barbaric' practices, such as widow burning, and the integration of Bali into an Indies-wide system and philosophy of administration. True to this priority, they ended the endemic warfare which had plagued Bali in the past. Some Dutch administrators were fond of talking about a *Pax Neerlandica*, or Dutch peace, a play on the *Pax Romana* of the Roman Empire. Although there were episodes of localised political unrest in the early years, they had run their course by the 1920s and surprisingly did not recur even during the Great Depression, when Bali was increasingly and severely distressed by poverty and landlessness.

The Dutch knew that uncritical reliance on the Balinese rulers could lead to abuse and scandal, as had been notoriously the case on Java. But in order to avoid losing money on an island with few productive resources, they needed to minimise an expensive Dutch presence, which as a result never exceeded more than a few dozen officers and technicians. They also brought to Bali a few Javanese and other Indonesian clerks and teachers, one of whom married a Balinese and in 1901 became the father of Indonesia's first President, Sukarno.

The obvious solution to the administrative cost versus ethics problem was to govern through the existing ruling class, but to mingle this indirect rule with reform. Soon the Dutch conceived a 'macro-legend' to justify such an approach.[1] It asserted, quite without basis in fact, that the Majapahit invasion of 1343 had destroyed a pre-existing system of independent 'village republics' by superimposing a layer of 'alien' Javanese despotism. The trick was to strip away the allegedly despotic elements and retain the best in Balinese culture without at the same time abandoning a virtually cost-free instrument of local government.

An official reception in Denpasar in about 1925. The photo shows a mingling of Dutch and Balinese notables, including the Raja of Karangasem, his wife and children; Balinese district officials (on the left) and priests (on the right); and, in the middle, V.E. Korn, the Dutch scholar-bureaucrat who codified Balinese customary law (adat) for administrative use. (Source: KITLV Archives, Leiden)

Based on the legend, a strategy of maintaining a sanitised 'living museum' of Hindu-Balinese culture emerged. The germ of the idea was in place as early as 1902, when Henri Hubert van Kol, a reform-minded member of the Dutch parliament, visited Gianyar and observed the very first Dutch administrator in the south at work.

In a book entitled *From Our Colonies* he wrote:

> We grant the radja self-rule and we permit the people to observe their ancient laws and customs. We remove abuses and those which remain, will yet disappear. The rule of the radja replaces that of the *punggawa* [district rulers] who

are concerned only with their private satisfactions. The position of the once powerful *punggawa* is now reduced, as it should be, to that of the servant of the radja, under our watchful supervision . . . We have brought law and order.[2]

The concept was aesthetically, ethically and administratively appealing. However, the colonial administration soon found itself trapped in a contradiction which led to heated internal debate. If the idea was to eliminate the 'alien' despots and restore pristine village democracy, how could increasing reliance on these same despotic rulers be justified? One explanation was to assume that the Balinese rulers had indeed been rapidly reformed to meet Dutch standards. Another, no more credible, was to assert that the rajas had never had much power at the village level anyway.

In truth, despite all the talk about village-level democracy, the Dutch administrators were sorely vexed by the absence of island-wide institutions of strong central rule. While the bolstering of 'tradition' was appealing, real Balinese tradition was fluid, inconsistent from one region to another, and indeed verged on what looked like anarchy. Bali's 'great failing', one administrator admitted, was 'the lack of a powerful government over the whole realm'.[3] To deal with this problem, the Dutch were forced to reform 'tradition', and even to create new tradition wholesale.

In the early years the Dutch differentiated between directly and indirectly ruled principalities. The five states which had been least cooperative in the process of conquest (Badung, Buleleng, Jembrana, Klungkung and Tabanan) were directly ruled by Dutch officials. The royal houses were not formally recognised, and backsliding or recalcitrant leaders were frequently exiled. In the three states which were indirectly ruled, Bangli, Karangasem and Gianyar, the ruler assumed a dual status. As a *stedehouder* or a regent in the Dutch system, he was responsible to the local *controleur*, to the resident in Singaraja and his deputy in Denpasar, and eventually to the governor general in Batavia.

In 1938 the Dutch held a great ceremony at the Besakih mother temple to inaugurate the rajas of Badung, Bangli, Buleleng, Karangasem, Gianyar, Jembrana, Klungkung and Tabanan, all shown here, as theoretically autonomous rulers under the Dutch queen. It was the climax of a broader effort to reinforce, or in some cases to reinvent, Balinese 'tradition'. (Source: KILTV Archives, Leiden)

As raja he was solely responsible only for such seemingly innocuous duties as the maintenance of temples and the proper execution of state ceremonies.

Once the few troublemakers had been dealt with, the Dutch realised that the Balinese aristocrats were natural allies, all the more valuable as nationalism and communism began to emerge elsewhere in the Indies. Beginning in the late 1920s, Batavia began a more formal policy of support for the traditional rulers. This eventually resulted in the official restoration of indirect rule everywhere on Bali and the recognition of eight royal houses in a grand ceremony held at the Besakih mother temple in 1938. It was a colourful display of Balinese tradition brought up to date, Dutch style: 'The robes of state were half-Balinese/half Western, the oath of loyalty [to the Dutch queen] was in Balinese, but the speeches in Malay [Indonesian]; Western were the official photographs, to say nothing of the champagne.'[4]

Economic and social impact

Dutch colonialism was least admirable in its economic and social aspects. Opium was the most glaring example of revenue trumping ethics. We have already seen that Dutch eagerness to replace the ruler's traditional monopoly in Klungkung with their own led directly to perhaps avoidable slaughter in 1908. The drug remained a money-maker, producing a substantial proportion of administrative revenue on Bali.

The Dutch tried to put a reform-oriented face on their opium policy. As early as 1870 they persuaded the Raja of Klungkung to kick his habit. Pronouncing himself cured, the dean of Balinese royalty sent his silver opium pipe to the Dutch governor general, receiving in return a fine damascene sword. The Indies-wide Dutch opium monopoly subsequently imposed on all Bali was supposed to control mass consumption. But opium became increasingly popular among the Balinese people, encouraged by the official sale of smaller doses affordable to the average person. In a peculiar twist, adult users who failed to make their habitual purchase from the Dutch monopoly were fined for presumably buying opium on the black market, a tacit acknowledgment that the state was in fact supporting addiction.

Opium revenue was, however, far from sufficient to meet the needs of the state, and over time the colonial administration introduced a bewildering host of new taxes, from levies on cockfights to road tolls. Between 1917 and 1930 total government revenues from Bali more than doubled and the authorities collected 37 million guilders more than they spent on the island. At least until the Great Depression, Bali did not lose money for Batavia.

Most importantly, the Dutch regularised land registration and eventually more than doubled the land tax, to the point where it was among the heaviest in the Netherlands Indies. In most cases—the impact varied from place to place—the burden of the land tax fell on increasingly impoverished tenant farmers. By 1923 tenants were allowed to keep only as little as one-third of their crop, and things were to get worse. The Great Depression hammered Bali hard. Prices for Balinese cash crops plummeted, yet farmers were by this time required to pay the land tax in Dutch currency, in effect at an increasingly unfavourable rate of exchange. Economic depression coincided with growing population, resulting in a surge of landlessness and increasing concentration of land in the hands of the rulers, their families and other aristocrats.

A few of the more perceptive Dutch administrators realised what was going on. One of them wrote in 1932: 'Whoever gets to know the situation of the common man in Bali from close only then discovers what a drab, poverty stricken mass of people inhabit this beautiful island. And the poverty is on the increase . . .'[5] Another noted that 'a great many people consider themselves lucky if they manage to eat one decent meal a day'.[6]

Forced labour for the state was another element of Balinese tradition which the new rulers found useful. Lower caste Balinese (*sudra*), over 90 per cent of the population, had traditionally owed service to the ruler, mainly for temple upkeep, irrigation system repair and other services of immediate benefit to the local community. The Dutch regularised the practice and called it 'feudal service' (*herrendienst*). They used it to build roads, harbours and bridges, and put it under the supervision of local Balinese functionaries. When there was work to be done, the *controleur* would get the raja to 'call up the farmers'.[7] The result was admirable progress on public works and an added burden on the hard-pressed poor.

When the Dutch introduced corvée it led to some episodes of local unrest, at least in part because villagers no longer perceived any benefit to themselves from the new kinds of work being performed. In 1917

Villagers are shown at work on a road in about 1920. The Dutch converted the traditional practice of community service owed to Balinese rulers into a system of compulsory labour for the colonial state. (Source: KITLV Archives, Leiden)

peasants in Gianyar refused to perform the service as urged by their raja. At the climax of the episode the rebellious leaders appeared dressed in white and armed with krisses, an ominous evocation of the ritual suicides of a decade earlier. Armed police fired on the crowd, killing five and seriously wounding eleven. Popular resentment in this and other cases was directed against the raja, not against the Dutch, proving the effectiveness of their indirect rule strategy.

Dutch restructuring of village administration, allegedly to restore the traditional order, was designed in part to achieve units which could supply 200 men each for corvée service. The exemption of high-caste Balinese from such service resulted in many low-caste Balinese litigating to establish their aristocratic credentials, and a rash of so-called 'paper *satria*', *satria* being the rulers' caste.

There was modest progress on health. The Dutch introduced vaccination in North Bali as early as 1881 and established a few clinics. The system gradually expanded, and real progress was made against common diseases. The flu epidemic of 1918 nonetheless killed more than 22 000 Balinese. A 1935 government report noted a generally poor state of health, with high levels of malnutrition, tuberculosis and venereal disease.

A similar pattern of minimal progress held true for education. A few local schools were built, and children of the senior rulers were encouraged to attend Dutch schools. Javanese teachers arrived on Bali, and some Balinese aristocrats continued their education on Java. One unintended consequence was that a small group learned about and began to sympathise with the nascent Indonesian nationalist movement.

By the 1890s schools on Bali were enrolling around 600 pupils. It was not a major effort, and a greater number were probably still becoming literate through informally learning Old Javanese from temple priests. In 1910, when the Dutch made over 1 million guilders from the opium monopoly on Bali, they spent less than 20 000 guilders on education, a discrepancy which greatly distressed Henri van Kol, the parliamentarian who had been so enthusiastic about the prospects for Dutch rule on his first visit in 1902. He urged an immediate expansion of the education programme, which did occur, but slowly and not always under colonial sponsorship.[8] In the 1930s a network of private, nationalist-oriented schools, part of the Indonesia-wide *Taman Siswa* system, was established on Bali. However, by 1940 only six Balinese had attended university.[9]

The colonial rulers rapidly became fascinated with Balinese culture and over time applied substantial scholarly resources to its study. They knew that successful administration under the banner of reform required knowledge of local customs. Scholarship was also a useful counter to critics of colonialism. As tourism developed, scholarship became economically relevant as well. The effort began as early as 1873 when the Dutch hired a part-Malay linguist, Herman Neubronner van der Tuuk, who compiled a Balinese dictionary.

The Dutch set up a library for traditional manuscripts in Singaraja in 1928, named after van der Tuuk and still in existence. To the dismay of private merchants, they established the Bali Museum in 1932 to encourage excellence in Balinese art through both sales and collection. The colonial archaeological service excavated and deciphered inscriptions that began to reveal an almost forgotten Balinese past. A number of Dutch administrators assiduously studied traditional law and government, to extract from it whatever might be useful. Preservation of the best in Balinese culture, whatever that might be, became a central objective of Dutch rule.

This effort was related to a remarkable and unique aspect of Dutch policy. Throughout the Indies the Dutch recognised customary law, invented a name for it (*adat*, taken from Arabic) and established a prestigious department at the University of Leiden to study and help administer it. The colony was divided into nineteen *adat* law regions, and for each a scholarly 'guide' to *adat* was compiled, the one for Bali (*Het adatrecht van Bali*, by V.E. Korn) being published in 1924. Dutch scholars were well aware that customary law was at heart oral and that it changed over time, hence could not be codified in writing without distortion, but a compulsion to be orderly drove them to write it down anyway.

One of the more amusing examples of the Dutch effort to impose order on chaos came in the management of currency. The traditional Balinese system of coinage was unwieldy strings or 'loops' of Chinese copper coins (*kepeng*), but the type of coins used varied from kingdom to kingdom, and even from village to village. At first the Balinese refused to use paper money and were dubious about silver coins, a wide variety of which were in circulation, from Singapore dollars to Portuguese pieces-of-eight. They particularly did not like the silver coin bearing the image of King William II which the Dutch proudly attempted to promote. They called it 'the dollar of the king with a long neck', and would not accept it at its full value in silver. For the Balinese, coinage irregularities were just another excuse for amusing litigation, but they drove systematic bureaucrats nearly distracted. In the end, of course, colonial pressure for standardisation prevailed.[10]

Inventing tradition

In fact, the Dutch were in a real dilemma on the matter of 'tradition', and nothing illustrates it better than their approach to village administration. They claimed to be basing their policy on a restoration of traditional village-level democracy, but they also felt it essential to have consistent standards of administration, which, of course, had never existed on Bali. The key player on this issue was F.A. Liefrinck, who served as *controleur* and later resident in north Bali in the 1880s. He was a keen student of land tenure and village administration, and a founding father of *adat* law studies.

Liefrinck's detailed research in the north later served as the basis for Dutch administration in the south, although previous practice there had been neither uniform nor similar to that in the north. The result was to regularise what had been a highly fragmented and regionally varied political order and to increase the power of the aristocracy at the local level.

This served the need for administrative convenience but had negative aspects as well. Previously, for example, farmers had utilised complex networks of lords and their followers as multiple intermediaries between court and village. Now there could be only one government-appointed Balinese official (*perbekel*) in each village. Villagers became more dependent on their rulers, backed by the Dutch, than they had ever been in the violent past, when they could always move to the protection of a competing lord.

The problem extended to the very top of the system, where the eight officially recognised rajas, many of them big landowners, had much more real power over their subjects than the Dutch system envisioned. Increasingly desk-bound by paperwork, the handful of *controleurs* were sometimes aware that they didn't know everything that was going on in their districts. But, having just restored the monarchs to royal status, the Dutch were reluctant to punish them for abuse of power. 'Well, now,' sighed one officer, '. . . you had to keep up a working relationship [with the local raja]. If you were to go and investigate some such rumor about extortion, then you had no idea of what else might come to light.'[11]

The most serious criticism of indirect rule goes well beyond individual royal peccadilloes. It argues that by hiding behind a façade of princes, the Dutch were able to escape accountability for the inequities of their flawed stewardship, especially the growth of landlessness and the strengthened caste system. Instead of blaming the Dutch, the Balinese blamed each other, and the resulting tensions in Balinese society aggravated post-war unrest up to and including the killings of 1965–66 (see Chapter 8). But it is not a foregone conclusion that direct rule by Dutch officials would have had a happier ending, certainly not without much greater expenditures on education and social welfare plus a forthright Indies-wide policy of preparation for independence. In the context of the times, that would have been too much to expect.

In time the preservationist 'living museum' philosophy got out of hand. By the 1920s it had resulted in an official policy of 'Bali-isation' (*Baliseering*) which tried to mandate the use of traditional dress, traditional architecture and the Balinese language. Use of Malay (or Indonesian), which the Dutch had initially promoted everywhere in the Indies, was eventually made a punishable offence on Bali. While this was done in the name of preservation, it really happened because Malay had become the lingua franca of the feared nationalist movement.

'Traditional' architecture was protected, despite the fact that Balinese buildings, often built from soft volcanic stone, are by nature impermanent, and the real tradition was one of constant decay and renovation. But now the colonial government required a permit to change anything that appeared more than 50 years old. After the great earthquake of 1917 the Dutch supervised the restoration of destroyed temples, enforcing adherence to 'pure' Balinese style. Funny statues of big-nosed Europeans were no longer permitted as temple guardians.[12] Fortunately, quite a few earlier ones have survived.

Dutch colonial policy increasingly emphasised the preservation of Balinese 'tradition', interpreted with un-Balinese rigidity. The restoration of temples required official architectural review and the practice of using statues of big-nosed Europeans as guardian figures (such as this one in Klungklung) was no longer allowed. (Source: Robert Pringle)

The Dutch established courts of customary law whose members had to be 'ordained' Hindu priests and were supposed to rely on ancient Balinese texts, usually written in Old Javanese, which even they could not always understand. In order to fix this problem, administrators authorised translations into Balinese and Malay. Historian Geoffrey Robinson notes, 'There is perhaps no more striking example of the way in which Balinese "tradition" was manufactured by the Dutch colonial state'.[13]

Dubious reworking of 'tradition' was most significant in the matter of caste. Once the Dutch had lost their fear of the old ruling class, and come to depend on it as an essential element in the political system, they put caste high on their list of desirable traditions. In 1910 they made an official decision to uphold the system, defining it as the three high castes (*triwangsa*) plus one low caste (*sudra*) for the remaining nine-tenths of the population. As with the preservationist policy in general,

Dutch objectives were unabashedly political. 'We shall, before all else, have to uphold the caste system,' wrote one official in 1921, 'otherwise the [Balinese Hindu] religion is done for, and there is a chance for the Muslims'.[14] Typically, the reworked system went well beyond the flexibility and imprecision of previous practice. Most seriously, there was no place in it for the various important non-caste groups such as the smiths (*pandé*), who were simply demoted to the new, uniform low-caste category. Since the three higher castes were exempt from corvée, and since *sudra* were not eligible for government jobs, the change generated tension and litigation which was fought out in the similarly retraditionalised customary law courts.

The new caste policy annoyed the man who wrote the book on Balinese customary law, V.E. Korn, who noted that the old system was more supple, sometimes for good reason. For example, rulers could authorise cross-caste marriages, which the Dutch now forbade, and often did so to encourage bonding across social lines. The new formalisation of caste was especially offensive to educated Balinese of lower caste, resulting in a heated debate in the local press in the 1920s on the merits or lack thereof of 'retraditionalisation'. This controversy has never really stopped, and 80 years later it is still fuelling a schism in Bali's Hindu establishment over caste qualifications for the priesthood.

Despite significant failings and contradictions, the colonial emphasis on preservation was on balance good policy. It bolstered those who wanted to save Bali from the kind of foreign economic domination and massive development of commercial agriculture so prevalent on Java. Most 'foreign' economic activity remained in the hands of local Chinese, usually with Balinese wives, who specialised in shop-keeping, money lending, real estate, local produce, and import-export activities. In time Shell Oil and the state-run Dutch shipping firm KPM opened offices in Singaraja. That was about it.

A similar dynamic prevailed in the case of Christian missionary activity, which the Dutch also succeeded in minimising. It had got off to a bad start in 1866 in north Bali, when the first serious evangelist, Reverend R. van Eck of the Utrecht Missionary Society, succeeded in converting only his own servant, who he claimed was a prince. In 1881 the convert, who had been threatened with Balinese damnation by his unconverted people, murdered one of van Eck's successors. Dutch officials seized on this fiasco to support their own anti-missionary sentiments. Protestant missionaries, together with evangelists from Java, were nonetheless able to return and make a few converts. Roman Catholics also gained a foothold following the arrival of the first European priest in 1935.

There ensued a lively argument over whether Christianity should be encouraged as a safeguard against the possible encroachment of Islam and/or nationalism. Bali's foremost official culture maven, Roelof Goris of the Antiquities Bureau, reacted with alarm. He argued that Christianity would destroy Balinese civilisation, and that 'Calvinism is an enemy of art'.[15] Goris got strong support from expatriate artists-in-residence like Miguel Covarrubias, who included ten pages of anti-missionary argument in his 1937 bestseller, *Island of Bali*. In response, pro-missionary forces jeered at efforts to preserve the 'Bali Reservation'.[16] In the end, preservationist sentiment prevailed. It had been nicely summarised in 1924 by the Resident of Bali and Lombok, H.T. Damste, in an article on the missionary issue:

> Let the Balinese live their own beautiful native life as undisturbed as possible! Their agriculture, their village life, their own form of worship, their religious art, their own literature—all bear witness to an autonomous native civilization of rare versatility and richness. No railroads on Bali, no Western coffee plantations; and especially no sugar factories! But also no proselytizing, neither Mohammedan (by zealous natives from other parts of the Indies) nor Protestant nor Roman Catholic. Let the colonial administration, with the strong backing of the Netherlands government,

treat the island of Bali as a rare jewel that we must protect and whose virginity must remain intact.[17]

The year before Damste penned this purple passage, the Dutch steamship company began passenger service to Singaraja. The age of commercial tourism on Bali was about to begin.

7
THE WORLD
DISCOVERS BALI
(1902–1942)

Then it starts suddenly, like a storm, stronger and stronger,
more and more terrible, bolts of lightning, thunderclaps—
all the iron bodies of the *gamelans* are seized by a powerful
trembling, until everything suddenly breaks off in a cry
of anguish—breathtaking silence! and taking up again
fortissimo with chaotic gestures, hissing, splashing! . . .
> – *Walter Spies, letter from Ubud describing*
> *a new form of gamelan, September 1927.*[1]

Today almost everybody has heard of Bali.
> – *Miguel Covarrubias,* Island of Bali, *1937.*[2]

The 1930s saw the beginning of tourism on Bali, if only on a very modest
scale compared to what has happened since 1966. As Bali became better
known it attracted an extraordinary collection of artists, social scientists
and what might be termed pre-jetsetters. The presence of this varie-
gated foreign community coincided with the intrusion of other external

influences, including foreign goods and Western-style media, which today would be lumped together under the rubric of 'globalisation'.

All this plus the demands of a new cash economy and colonial taxation stimulated talented Balinese to develop new forms of music, painting and sculpture which today still define much of Bali's culture to the outside world. The foreigners did not unilaterally transplant new standards and techniques to the Balinese; innovation was always a two-way street. Nor was it simply a question of poor Balinese seeking new income through selling carvings and paintings to tourists, although money was certainly a factor.

Especially at first, the Dutch authorities were ambivalent about the growth of tourism. On the positive side, it generated revenue and put a smiling face on colonialism. It justified an emphasis on cultural preservation which, they hoped, would help counter such disparate threats as radical Islam, communism and Indonesian nationalism. On the other hand they—and just about everyone else—were concerned almost from the beginning that too much tourism would kill the goose that laid the golden eggs of Balinese culture. Thus began an apparently endless policy debate.

The first tourists

A tourist is someone who travels for pleasure, however he or she may define pleasure—aesthetic, intellectual, culinary, carnal or whatever—not for religion, business or conquest. In the West, tourism existed at least as early as Roman times. In Bali it was a by-product of Dutch control after 1908, the end of chronic warfare, and the integration of Bali into the colonial transport and communications network.

This is not to say that earlier visitors to the island did not enjoy themselves. The two Dutch sailors who jumped ship in 1597 must have been attracted by something, unless they were simply repelled by the daunting prospect of a long voyage back to chilly, wind-swept Holland.

However that may be, it would be an exaggeration to say they were Bali's first Western tourists. Of course we have no idea how many Chinese, Arabs or other Indonesians had visited for trade or pilgrimage during previous centuries of external contact.

On Bali the first whiff of something like tourism came with Mads Lange, the personable Danish trader, sometime diplomat, cultural broker and proto-hotelier who went into business at Kuta in 1839. Lange received a stream of visiting officials and globetrotting scholars and scientists, including Alfred Russel Wallace, co-formulator (with Darwin) of evolution theory; R.H.Th. Friederich, a German scholar of Sanskrit who wrote the earliest detailed account of Balinese Hinduism, and many others. Although Lange was hardly in the tourist business as we know it, his guests began a process of publicising Bali which would in time reverse its reputation as a dangerous and barbaric place.

The laurel of 'first tourist' should probably go to Dutch parliamentarian H. van Kol, despite the fact that he was also a professional politician and critic of colonial policy.[3] Van Kol first visited Bali in 1902, before the Dutch had completely subjugated the south. At his first stop he got an amazing reception from the Raja of Karangasem, I Gusti Gede Jelantik, installed by the Dutch as *stedehouder* in 1896 for his helpful role during the Lombok War. Van Kol was lodged in quarters splendidly furnished with gifts from the Dutch queen in return for the 20 000 guilder birthday gift Jelantik had sent her. Along with the splendid furnishings came muddy drinking water and no toilet facilities at all—at least none recognisable to van Kol.

Indeed, life for the early tourist was a far cry from what it later became. A *laisser-passer* was required from the nearest Dutch *controleur*. Since roads were non-existent, the traveller needed a full panoply of servants, horses, pack animals, food, bedding and whatever other Western amenities were deemed essential:

> Roads, trails and pathways were certain to be either rocky
> and dusty or muddy and slippery; ascents and descents were

frequent and treacherous; bridges were likely to give way and apparently shallow fords to prove bottomless. Lodgings were almost always stifling, filthy, vermin-ridden, and stained with betel nut spittle ... Visits to radjas and other dignitaries had to be timed to correspond to the brief intervals between their sorties to patronize cockfights and their seclusion to smoke opium.[4]

Despite all this, as van Kol discovered, the experience was enthralling, and he visited every Balinese kingdom except dry and still largely unpopulated Jembrana in the west. Van Kol was a serious observer, the first European to notice a problem which would get much worse in the years ahead. Karangasem, he wrote in *From Our Colonies*, was seriously overpopulated and could not grow enough rice to support its population, which was already beginning to migrate elsewhere.

With the consolidation of Dutch control in 1908, a trickle of visitors began to arrive as passengers on the freighters which now served the new colonial headquarters at Singaraja, where they took on cargoes of coffee, cattle and especially pigs, which non-Muslim Bali produced in abundance. A few more visitors arrived on Dutch warships at Padang Bai, the small port in southeastern Bali which is still frequented by colourful fishing canoes, inter-island trade craft and the occasional cruise ship. The Dutch soon established a string of rest houses, primarily for official travellers but also available to tourists.

Within a decade Batavia was gearing up for an Indies-wide tourist business which was significant for the times, if microscopic by today's standards. In 1914 the first tourist brochure to include images of Bali appeared. In 1923 Dutch passenger ships began serving Singaraja, and in 1928 the government guest house in Denpasar was upgraded and reopened as the Bali Hotel, the island's first and for many years its only real hotel. Newly restored, it is still in business.

Soon there were five-day excursions with large American touring cars, usually Packards, serving as the standard conveyance. Amenities

*European tourists being robbed, from a north Balinese temple relief as recorded by
Mexican artist Miguel Covarrubias about seventy years ago. The relief itself was pure
whimsy, or maybe wishful thinking, since there is no evidence that any plundering of
tourists ever took place on Balinese roads.* (Source: Miguel Covarrubias, Island of Bali,
Alfred A. Knopf)

remained simple—while on the road, the sanitary protocol was still 'the
rice paddies for the ladies, the coconut trees for the gentlemen',[5] and
of course there was nothing like air conditioning.

Artists and writers began to discover Bali, and two of the earliest
deserve mention even in this abbreviated account. Wijnand Otto Jan
Nieuwenkamp was a freelance journalist and artist who witnessed the
puputan of 1906 at Denpasar. He was shocked but prudently confined
his criticism to family letters. He later travelled widely around Bali
drawing local scenes, wrote several books, and gave us the first detailed
drawings of the Pejeng 'moon'.

Nieuwenkamp is supposed to be the subject of a well-known temple
relief at Meduwe Karang in north Bali, showing a European in Balinese
dress riding a bicycle with flowers for wheels. A member of the Karangasem royal family who attended medical school in Holland on the
eve of World War II recounts in his memoirs how he learned about his
own homeland from reading books by Nieuwenkamp which he found
in a second-hand book store in Amsterdam.[6]

Gregor Krause was a German doctor, photographer and author
who came to Bali as a medical officer in the Dutch army before World
War I and lived in Indonesia for many years. His work on Bali, first

Three young Balinese women pose informally for an unknown foreign photographer, possibly a visiting Dutch official, in the 1920s. Within a decade, more carefully posed and costumed Balinese maidens enhanced a growing volume of tourist brochures.
(Source: *KITLV Archives, Leiden*)

published in 1920, included serious discussion of the island's culture. But it was his photographs which attracted the most attention, in part because they were among the first to focus on Balinese feminine allure. To quote Krause, brandishing his medical credentials, 'the always powerful great chest muscle provides the most favorable foundation for beautifully formed breasts . . . clothing cannot enhance this beauty but it has the merit of not diminishing it'.[7]

In fairness, in addition to its mildly prurient appeal, Krause's photography covered a wide range of fascinating and important subject matter. While his photographs are grainy and primitive by later standards, they, like Nieuwenkamp's drawings, remain an invaluable record of Bali before the impact of modernity. Fortunately, published examples of the work of both men are still widely available.

Word of the island's natural beauty and cultural appeal began to spread. Bali gradually became a fashionable destination for Western artists and intellectuals with a taste for the exotic, and a small but memorable expatriate community came into being. Important changes in the character of Balinese art, drama and music took place at the same time.

This emergence of new styles remains difficult to define or label. It was certainly not a renaissance or even a renewal; Balinese culture was never in need of rebirth. It was not simply a matter of foreign artists teaching Balinese new techniques; in some cases the change was entirely home-grown, while in others the foreign element was marginal. Nor was it exclusively a response to market forces, although as the Balinese discovered that their art was saleable, the Depression-driven need for cash played a part.

Neither was it the product of a calculated public relations effort by commercial interests—they barely existed at the time—much less by a colonial government, which, as mentioned above, was initially conflicted about tourism. It cannot even be said that the change was unparalleled in Balinese history. We know very little about the history of Balinese art, music and dance before the colonial period, but it is unlikely that the selective eagerness for change which marked the 1930s was new.

The pivotal personality

The spirit of one man, a German painter and musician, infuses the cultural history of Bali at this critical period. Walter Spies was born in Moscow in 1895 to a wealthy and cultured German merchant-diplomat family. He inherited a taste for the arts, becoming a talented musician and painter. In the 1920s he visited the Dutch East Indies and found employment as bandmaster to the Sultan of Jogjakarta in Central Java. Although hired to produce European music and play the piano,

Spies became much more interested in the royal Javanese gamelan orchestra.

Then he visited Bali, and soon decided it was an even more appealing venue. Invited by the ruler of Ubud, Cocorde Gede Raka Sukawati, he moved there in 1927 and built a house on what was then the edge of the village, where two streams join. The place is named Campuhan, meaning 'the confluence of two rivers', and it could serve as a metaphor for Spies' life work.

Spies was a painter and photographer as well as a musician and amateur naturalist; indeed he seems to have been interested in just about everything. His enthusiasm is well conveyed by his commentary on *kebiar*, a new form of gamelan music evolving at this time, quoted at the head of this chapter. Indeed, it may well be that his lively and expressive personality endeared him more than anything else to the Balinese and was the primary source of his influence.

Spies was not dogmatically dedicated to the preservation of old styles, realising that the dynamism of Balinese art was essential to its vitality. He was, however, concerned that commercialisation would in time reduce the Balinese to producing anything that would sell. Thus he helped to establish the Bali Museum in Denpasar in 1932 and served as its curator. The primary mission of the museum was to collect and conserve examples of the best Balinese art from the past. But in addition it encouraged, through purchase, the best new art. It was a first step, but Spies and others wanted to go further and develop a more intensive, collaborative effort with the artists themselves.

Changing styles in painting ...

There had been some Western influence on Balinese art before Dutch rule. Mads Lange had his portrait painted by a Balinese artist during his mid-nineteenth century reign in Kuta. When the linguist van der Tuuk commissioned sketches at the turn of the century, the artists were already experimenting with non-traditional techniques and materials such as paper.

Prior to tourism, painting had been among the less important of Balinese art forms. The most significant was dance-drama, central to much religious observance, followed by music, architecture, carving and painting. Painting was used mostly for temple and palace wall decorations, in a restricted palette of colours obtainable from natural sources. Painted cloths, from either fabric or bark, were used for costumes and festive decoration. Black line drawings were used to illustrate religious and other texts on palm leaves (*lontar*). There was no such thing as modern paints, or frames.

Imported materials now began to appear on the market, and foreign artists including Spies enjoyed introducing them to the Balinese. If they admired something the foreign artists were doing, they might incorporate it in their own work. This tendency has of course continued down to the present, and there are now many Balinese artists who paint in international styles.

But this is getting ahead of the story. There is no doubt that the combination of world depression and heavy Dutch taxation, discussed in the preceding chapter, created a need for cash beyond anything experienced in the old, largely subsistence economy. Painting (or carving, or dancing) for tourists was one way to meet it. By the 1930s, visitors familiar with Bali were remarking that, especially in the Ubud-Gianyar area, everybody seemed to be painting.

Spies could have done nothing without the help of Balinese princes and artists who understood and shared his concerns. In 1936 he joined forces with several other individuals to found the painting cooperative Pita Maha, meaning 'Grand Ancestors' in Old Javanese, the literary language of Bali. The name was intended to evoke the forces of creativity and continuity in Balinese religion.

In 1929 Raka Sukawati had invited another foreign artist, Rudolf Bonnet, to live in Ubud. Bonnet was Dutch, a more traditional artist than Spies and, most would agree, less talented. But he loved Bali and

Dutch artist Rudolf Bonnet is shown with one of his most famous Balinese colleagues, Anak Agung Gede Sobrat, perhaps the best-known practitioner of the Ubud Style. This photo was taken when Bonnet returned to Bali after Indonesian independence in 1949. (Source: *KITLV Archives, Leiden*)

obviously got along very well with the people, although by most accounts he was more inclined to attempt to teach them what and how to paint than was Spies. Bonnet, not Spies, was apparently the prime mover behind the founding of Pita Maha. The vigorous participation and sponsorship of the Ubud Royal family, in the person of Raka's younger brother and eventual successor, Cokorde Gede Agung Sukawati, was essential to the success of the initiative. Another Pita Maha co-founder was I Gusti Nyoman Lempad, whose work is discussed below. Lempad, the son of an architect and artist, had been in effect the court architect of Ubud when, in his sixties, he became one of the most talented painters of the era.

With about 150 artist-members, Pita Maha was organised along the lines of a traditional temple or irrigation association, which made it comfortable and comprehensible to its Balinese membership. It met weekly in the palace office of the Cokorde Agung or in Spies' house to discuss and pass judgment on paintings which the artists themselves brought in from the region around Ubud.

Pita Maha did its job with admirable effectiveness, but its selections were mainly earmarked for export and foreign display, in an effort to promote the quality of Balinese art abroad. Following World War II, Rudolf Bonnet returned to Bali and, with Cokorde Agung Sukawati, established a local art museum, the Puri Lukisan, which opened in 1957, to ensure that quality art was displayed in Ubud as well.

Important as Pita Maha was, two anecdotes illustrate more subtle but perhaps more powerful ways in which Spies influenced Balinese artists. The first concerns I Gusti Nyoman Lempad, the co-founder of Pita Maha. Lempad, famous as an architect, carver and master builder, had apparently never painted when he designed a house for Spies at Campuhan. Spies gave him some paper, and an illustrious new career was launched.

Lempad worked in his own variant of the traditional style used for palm-leaf manuscript illustrations. He is most famous for ink drawings flecked with red and gold highlights with vigorously individualistic subject matter. He sometimes depicted explicitly sexual subjects, indicating, given his talent and status, that such work was not necessarily a corruption of Balinese culture by tourist influence. Lempad died in 1978, reportedly at the age of 116.

The second story concerns an occasion when Spies gave a long piece of high-quality wood to a young Balinese and asked him to make two carvings. The artist returned with one carving because he could not bear to damage the spirit of the wood by cutting it in two. Spies was thoroughly delighted, praised the artist, and may have encouraged the development of the long, attenuated carving style for which Bali became famous.

Then there is the question of Spies' own style. His Bali paintings were often based on local folk tales and featured attenuated figures and strong use of silhouette, suggesting that he, and to a lesser extent

Top: *The Sukawati brothers, Cokorde Gede Raka and his younger sibling Cokorde Gede Agung (shown here), were instrumental in making Ubud a cultural centre in the 1930s by extending royal patronage both to foreign visitors like Spies and Bonnet, and to Balinese artists.* (Source: *Puri Saren, Ubud*) Left: *Walter Spies with his cockatoo and pet monkey at Campuan, Ubud.* (Source: *The Horniman Museum, London*) Right: *I Gusti Nyoman Lempad was among the most renowned Balinese artists of the 1930s. He died in 1978 at the age of 116.* (Source: *Neka Art Museum, Ubud*)

Mexican artist Miguel Covarrubias, were both influencing Balinese artists and being influenced by them.

There were other foreign artists in Bali in the late 1930s besides Spies and Bonnet. Some of them, including the Belgian Jean Le Mayeur and the Dutch Willem Hofker, were popular with Westerners (both specialised in lush, bare-breasted Balinese maidens), but none appears to have had any impact on Balinese styles.

Due to the work of Pita Maha and other factors, several new regional and stylistic categories of Balinese art emerged in the 1930s and remain important today, albeit increasingly commercialised. They include three main styles.

The Ubud style, with emphasis on bucolic rural and village scenes of cockfights, temple festivals and farming activities, was influenced by Bonnet's orthodox approach to anatomical style, and for many Westerners came to typify Balinese art. Its best-known practitioner, a favourite of Bonnet's, was Anak Agung Gede Sobrat.

The Batuan style, from a village only ten kilometres from Ubud, featured sombre colours (often black and white), a penchant for the sinister side of Balinese religion (scenes of sorceresses and evil spirits), and finely detailed miniatures.

The Sanur style, the least prolific of the new schools, was the only one including marine subjects, probably inspired by the nearby aquarium and ready access to a beach-going tourist clientele.

In the postwar years these three were joined by the bright, colourful, relatively simple 'Young Artists' style centred in Penestanan, which began under the influence of the Dutch artist Ari Smit in 1960.

Finally, 'traditional' painting, including both palm-leaf and palace decoration, remained alive and important. It usually depicted scenes from Indian-origin religion and mythology, leavened with Balinese folklore. The village of Kamasan was the best-known centre for traditional painting. The style was languishing when, in the 1920s, the Dutch commissioned Kamasan painters to decorate restored portions of the palace in Klungkung, which had been destroyed during the Dutch assault in 1908. The result included the famous ceiling paintings in the Klungkung Hall of Justice.

...and other art forms

Wood-carving underwent its own evolution. The impact of a growing international market for Balinese art was obviously a major driving force in this case. The attenuated style mentioned above rapidly gained favour. It may have been additionally stimulated by the admiration of Spies and Covarrubias for the decorative panels, or *lamak*, which the Balinese use for festival decoration. They are typically adorned with *cili*, stylised feminine figures representing the rice goddess Dewi Sri.

Much later the famous carver Ida Bagus Njana, in the village of Mas, introduced a new style of squat, compressed figures reminiscent of Japanese *netsuke*. And some carvers, inspired by natural forms and pure whimsy, produced a volume of cheap but appealing work for tourists, and some works of genius. The carvings of I Tjokot of Jati fall in the latter category. One of his specialties was to carve an entire tree with intricate designs out to the limits of its extremities, the result often weighing hundreds of pounds, hardly the sort of thing a tourist could carry back to Chicago or Tokyo.

In the realm of music, parallel changes were taking place, without evidence of more than marginal influence from foreigners. During this period the style of gamelan music known as *kebiar* first appeared. Its distinctive rhythms, alternately explosive and languorous, have come to epitomise Balinese music for most non-Balinese. The flavour of *kebiar*, which means a 'sudden outburst of flames', or 'to flash',[8] is well conveyed by the Spies quotation that begins this chapter. It stands in ultimate contrast to the slow tempo and dreamy mood of the Javanese gamelan.

Kebiar originated in north Bali and spread almost as fast as its restless pace. By 1928, when the first recordings of Balinese music were made, it was only beginning to appear in the south. But only three years later, when musicologist Colin McPhee arrived, the new style was already widespread there.

Spies was enthusiastic about the new genre. For him it evoked the passion of German composers of the expressionist period, and he welcomed its innovative style. In 1939, from the jail in Surabaya where he was imprisoned on a morals charge (see below), he wrote to a friend and musical scholar: 'You must come to Bali for a longer stay, there are such fantastic new kinds of music here which you will enjoy incredibly.'[9]

McPhee, more of a classicist, was initially intrigued by the new music but became concerned when it began to supplant older styles, leading to the melting down and recasting of antique gamelans which had been the mainstay of village ritual in the past. McPhee came to regard *kebiar* as the negation of everything classic. He worried that it was superficial, and hinted that it might represent a kind of Balinese identity crisis.

Today, for better or worse, *kebiar* style suffuses most Balinese music, although older styles have survived. *Kebiar* was certainly a hit with tourists, but it seems clear that its appeal to the Balinese themselves was the main cause of its popularity.

Drama was also in a state of flux. Indeed, no other medium better demonstrates the Balinese flair for adaptation and innovation or the rapidity with which styles can change. A famous dancer named Mario (I Ketut Maria), frequently mentioned in the books of the period, invented a *kebiar* dance to accompany the new music. Performed with upper body and arm movements while seated in a cross-legged position, it was wildly popular throughout Bali for a time, but went out of fashion after World War II. Other forms, including *arja* and *janger*, incorporated modern elements, to the mingled dismay and amusement of the expatriate intellectuals.

In 1930, Mexican artist Miguel Covarrubias arrived on a honeymoon trip. He and his wife Rosa, a Mexican-American dancer, attended a *janger* performance staged for tourists. He noted that it was then the 'inevitable sight for the newly arrived tourist'. Boys and girls were

Mentioned in almost every book about Bali in the 1930s, Mario (I Ketut Maria) was the dancer who invented a kebiar *dance to accompany the newly evolved gamelan music of the same name. The photo was taken by pioneer hotelier Robert Koke.*
(Source: *Neka Art Museum, Ubud*)

arranged in a square with a dance master in the centre; the participants wore orthodox Balinese dress, and plot was classic in style. Covarrubias felt the performance was worthy but 'somehow it did not ring true'.[10]

But on their first evening out, wandering on the outskirts of Denpasar, the couple came across something startlingly different—a street performance of *janger* for a Balinese audience, where the costumes were mock European (including mustachios). It included a wild *kecak* (monkey dance) chorus, and the whole was riddled with slapstick humour. This kind of *janger* was then popular in various forms all over Bali, but in the decades after World War II it completely disappeared.

The modern form of *kecak,* now seen by virtually every tourist, was also created at this time. A smaller version of the hissing, chattering male chorus had previously been part of a ritual purification dance form known as *sanghyang.* In 1931 Spies was serving as technical advisor for *Island of the Demons,* a German-made film about a village threatened with destruction by Rangda, the witch. One of his Balinese assistants had the idea of expanding the *kecak* chorus and combining it with a plot drawn from the *Ramayana,* creating what is now the standard version. The result was a purely secular dance quite different from anything in the previous Balinese repertory. As we have seen, *kecak* was also being incorporated into *janger* dancing at this time, and it is clearly an oversimplification to conclude that Spies personally invented modern *kecak.*

Tourism takes root

The resident expatriate community continued to grow in size and variety, reaching a total of several hundred by World War II. In addition to Dutch officials and commercial representatives, still primarily in the north, it included anthropologists, artists, dancers and students of dance, writers and film makers. Musicologist Colin McPhee was married to the anthropologist Jane Belo, and both wrote books of lasting value.

After their honeymoon stay, Miguel and Rosa Covarrubias came back in 1933 for a second long visit and together produced *Island of Bali,* a detailed and affectionate account of Balinese culture. Published in 1937, it was an instant bestseller in the USA. Both the illustrations and the portion of the text on Balinese courtship were quite exciting to a pre-*Playboy* generation of adolescents browsing in their parents' libraries, but the book also introduced them to the notion that alien cultures could produce high-quality art and attractive lifestyles. *Island of Bali* has deservedly remained standard fare for visitors.

Commercial tourism was growing, if slowly. The German Neuhaus

'Every Night is a Festival in Bali' by Mexican artist Miguel Covarrubias epitomises the thirties image of Bali as a romantic paradise remote from the anxieties of the Depression and a looming world war. The painting was published in *Life* magazine in 1937, at about the same time as Covarrubias' book *Island of Bali*.

Top left:
Bali's 'mother temple', where all Balinese Hindus regardless of status may worship, began as a bronze-iron age sanctuary probably used for a combination of volcano and ancestor worship before the coming of Indian-origin religion. Gunung Agung is in the background. (Photo Francine Brinkgreve)

Bottom left:
It was *Patih* (prime minister) Jelantik of Buleleng who said 'Let the kris decide', precipitating the bitter 1846–49 war with the Dutch which ended with the imposition of colonial rule on North Bali. Jelantik, an Indonesian national hero, is depicted in a modern painting in the Gedung Kirtya Museum in Singaraja. (Gedung Kritya Museum, Singaraja)

Top:
A fanciful view of the Indonesian Revolution on Bali by artist I Wayan Bendi, complete with a terrifying jet and kris-wielding revolutionaries fighting Dutch soldiers as photographers record the action. Temple festivals and other village activities proceed all around the action.
(Courtesy Neka Art Museum, Ubud)

Bottom:
The Moon of Pejeng, Bali's great bronze kettledrum, rests on its side in a busy temple not far from Ubud, where it has been for many centuries. (From A.J. Bernet Kempers, *Monumental Bali*, Periplus, 1981)

Top:
This painting by I Made Budi of Batuan shows President and Mrs Soeharto on a 1987 visit to Bali. The First Lady seems to be greeting giant frogs, which are, in fact, dancers (see the foot protruding from under one of the costumes). Armed security guards prowl around, photographers capture the scene and reporters interview farmers while uptight officials witness the ceremony. (Neka Art Museum)

Bottom:
Ogoh-ogoh are papier maché demons and monsters paraded in mardi gras-like celebrations the night before Nyepi, an important holiday when evil spirits are exorcised and no activity of any kind is allowed. To the distress of some religious authorities *ogoh-ogoh* often reflect the tastes of modern Balinese youth (in this case punk-rockers) rather than classical Hindu-Bali themes. (Photo Iskandar from *Latitudes* magazine)

brothers established an aquarium at Sanur, along with an art gallery which became a local outlet for Pita Maha-approved paintings. Tourist numbers increased from around 100 a month in the 1920s to more than double that by World War II. In 1936 an American couple, Robert and Louise Koke, established the Kuta Beach Hotel in partnership with Vaneen Walker, an English-American woman who, inspired by the film *Island of the Demons*, had originally come to Bali to learn painting. Walker, better known by her Balinese name, Ktut Tantri, later quarrelled with the Kokes and started a hotel of her own. She is said to have frequented the lobby of the rather stuffy Bali Hotel in Denpasar to lure guests to her more interesting beach-front location in Kuta. She was imprisoned by the Japanese and later supported the Indonesian Revolution as a propaganda broadcaster known to those who disapproved of her as 'Surabaya Sue'. Her autobiography, *Revolt in Paradise*, is perennially popular.

Louise Koke also wrote a book, *Our Hotel in Bali*, a charming account of Balinese tourism in its infancy. Neither woman mentioned the other in their respective accounts. Both hotels were destroyed during the war, but Kuta itself survived and flourished beyond the wildest imaginings of its pioneer hotel-keepers.

Transportation facilities slowly improved. South Bali already had a network of small roads built with corvée labour, narrow but adequate for big touring cars not in a hurry. In the 1930s a pair of Germans opened the first ferry between Java and Bali at Gilimanuk, and the Dutch assistant resident at Denpasar built a road of sorts linking his town with the ferry, through thinly populated country where tigers were still occasionally seen at night.

In 1932 the Dutch had scratched out a landing strip on the Bukit peninsula south of Denpasar, but after a trial flight crashed it was deemed too dangerous, even though there were no casualties. Regular air services began in 1938, thanks to a more adequate facility at Tuban, near the site of the present airport, and Bali became a stop on Dutch commercial flights to Australia and Makasar. But air travel did not displace shipping as the primary means of transport to Bali until after World War II.

Walter Spies remained an essential first point of reference for scholars and well-connected visitors. He introduced such visitors as Covarrubias and Margaret Mead to Bali, usually helped them find accommodation, and often influenced their initial thinking about what and where to study. He did the same for German novelist and Hollywood screenwriter Vicki Baum, who wrote the novel *A Tale from Bali*, still in print, in which she pretends to draw on the papers of a deceased Dutch doctor who knew everything there was to know about the place. In fact, one of her sources was Walter Spies; another was a local Dutch official.

For years Spies got along well with the colonial authorities, especially the more intellectually inclined, including archaeologist Willem Stutterheim, his American companion, dancer and later art historian Claire Holt, and Roelof Goris who, like Stutterheim, worked for the antiquities service. Even the most orthodox officials saw Spies as a valued advisor on matters cultural, which were increasingly recognised as exceptionally important for Bali.

Spies was a friend of the first director of the state tourist agency, helped organise Bali's contribution to the Paris Colonial Exposition of 1931, which included a dance troupe, and arranged lavish entertainment for the governor general of the Indies when he visited in 1935. He took care of other famous visitors ranging from Charlie Chaplin to Leopold Stokowski. Indeed, Spies became so distracted by his 'host with the most' role that in 1937 he built a small house at Iseh, a remote location on the slopes of Gunung Agung, where he hoped to find occasional peace and get on with his art.

Spies usually lived well. He did not paint much, perhaps in part because one painting made enough money for him to live for a year. In 1928 he traded two paintings to a German friend for a car. 'It is a beautiful car', he wrote his mother, 'Very strong and climbs the mountains like nothing else. I am learning to drive now'.[11] Later he used the proceeds of a painting sale to American millionaire Barbara Hutton to pay for a small swimming pool at his residence in Campuhan, in addition to a house for her which she never used. But his income was sporadic and sometimes, especially during the Depression, he was hard up. What put Bali in the international limelight at this point in time? The beauty of the natural setting and the virtuosity of Balinese art and culture were, of course, the primary reasons. Now, thanks to Dutch roads and modern shipping, the island was suddenly accessible, albeit only to wealthy or highly motivated tourists. Films and other publicity, such as Covarrubias' series of articles in *Vanity Fair*, pitched Bali into prominence as the latest trendy international destination. Bali's reputation for harmony, however exaggerated in the light of social and historic reality, made it increasingly appealing to a generation of Westerners seeking escape from the dismal realities of the Depression and the looming threat of another world war.

The more discerning visitors considered themselves lucky, with some reason, to have witnessed such a treasure before it was subjected to large-scale development and change. The rich or famous were often able to meet some of the Balinese rulers in the throes of cultural transition, their prosperity enhanced by increasing Dutch emphasis on indirect rule. A more colourful spectacle can hardly be imagined. Here is Willard Hanna's vignette of the Raja of Gianyar, Ide Anak Agung Ngurah Agung, with his automobile in the 1930s:

> One of Gianyar's greatest triumphs was his Fiat Grand Phaeton, which he had had refitted to suit his tastes and his station. This was one of the very first motor vehicles to be seen in Bali and what it lacked in power it more than compensated for in panache. The Radja had the windshield so heavily bordered in gold that the driver had to peer around rather than through it; even at that he had difficulty seeing over the radiator ornament, which was almost a life-size Garuda cast in pure gold. The Fiat had power

enough to proceed at a stately pace on level ground, but the royal subjects were summoned to push when it ventured uphill and were well advised to flee when it sped down.[12]

Within a few years Balinese princes were investing in automobiles to the point where Margaret Mead complained that cars were supplanting patronage of the arts as a royal status symbol. But some rulers, notably those of Gianyar and Ubud, continued to patronise art, as we have seen. The rajas were also sending their children to colonial schools, producing leaders who would in some cases fight against the Dutch in 1945–49, and in other cases go on to hold positions of great importance at both provincial and national levels.

For some visitors, visions of bare breasts or Balinese acceptance of homosexuality had something to do with the island's attraction, just as the discos and 'cowboys' of Kuta do today, but one can overdo this point. It is often suggested that Bali's tolerance of homosexuality (or more accurately bisexuality) attracted Walter Spies, but if that had been the case he could as well have stayed on Java, where a similar tolerance is equally traditional. As recently as the 1970s, long before gay rights became acceptable in the West, the Indonesian Marine Corps general who was mayor of Jakarta presided over transvestite beauty contests in the nation's capital and no Indonesian thought twice about it.

Few of the resident expatriates or tourists who relished their time on the island were very interested in the moral or political issues posed by colonialism. Most of them simply accepted it as inevitable. Others regarded Dutch rule on Bali, benign by comparison with its counterparts elsewhere, as essentially progressive, and even as contributing to preparation for independence, whenever that might arrive. There was, it seemed, plenty of time.

Even the scholars rarely commented on the obvious economic problems, such as widespread poverty and growing land shortage, hardly unusual in Asia at the time, or the inequities of such practices as corvée labour (which, after all, resulted in excellent roads that all of them used), or onerous taxation, or scant attention to education except for the ruling families. In some cases the expatriates may have been reluctant to offend the colonial authorities who were friendly and hospitable to them. For example, Margaret Mead, critical of Dutch inattention to public health in a private letter, made approving comments about it in her published research results.[13]

The growing reputation of Balinese performing arts attracted a scattering of film makers, actors and musicians. The most famous was Charlie Chaplin who, together with Noel Coward, visited in the early 1930s. Coward scribbled a ditty in the Bali Hotel complaints book, later widely quoted:

> As I said this morning to Charlie
> There is *far* too much music in Bali,
> And although as a place it's entrancing,
> There is also a *thought* too much dancing.
> It appears that each Balinese native,
> From the womb to the tomb is creative,
> And although the results are quite clever,
> There is too much artistic endeavor.[14]

Ambrosia to the anthropologists

If some found Bali's culture a little exhausting, it was nectar and ambrosia to the anthropologists. Margaret Mead worked in Bali with her third husband and fellow anthropologist, Gregory Bateson, from 1936 to 1938. Mead was already a rising star, thanks mainly to *Coming of Age in Samoa*, published eight years previously, which had suggested to an admiring popular audience that Western societies had something to learn from other cultures about more relaxed and enlightened attitudes toward adolescent sex.

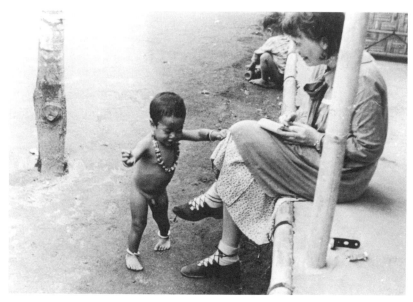

Margaret Mead with a young Balinese informant in the highland village of Bayunggede.
(Source: *Library of Congress, Margaret Mead Collection*)

Mead was also a veteran field worker with plenty of experience in New Guinea locales where both living conditions and access to ceremonies were infinitely more difficult than in Bali. She and Bateson, a less famous but extremely capable social scientist, were entranced by their research assistant, I Made Kaler, recruited for them by Spies. Kaler spoke five languages and did everything from running the household to taking notes on ceremonies. He was 'just about the nearest thing to perfection that God ever made,' she wrote home.[15]

Above all, the sheer volume and variety of Balinese ceremonial life was entrancing. The island, Mead later wrote, 'teemed with expressive ritual'.[16] This was still the springtime of social science, with the accent on science. Its practitioners fervently believed that enough research could systematically unlock the mysteries of human behaviour. It followed that both volume and variety of data was important.

Because the Balinese saw most of their ceremonial acts as offerings to the gods, they were quite willing to stage performances for foreigners who would pay the minor expense involved. 'Only those who have worked in societies where money has no power to persuade people who do not, at the moment, feel like doing something can realize what a paradise Bali was for us. Ceremonies every day—if not in this village, then in another only a short distance away,' Mead wrote.[17] Moreover, Bali's good roads made it easy to observe a great deal: '. . . an anthropologist is presented with an unprecedented situation—quick, easy transport between dozens of versions of the culture. A journey that would take three days in New Guinea—and more than that to prepare for and recover from—is made here in an hour.'[18]

On arrival Mead and Bateson were, like so many others, assisted by Spies. Initially they lived near him in Ubud, but they soon decided to move to a remote and much poorer mountain village, Bayunggede, near Kintamani. Here, among the Bali Aga, they believed they had found Balinese culture stripped to its essentials; a place where they could in only one year understand the 'ground plan of the culture'.[19]

From time to time they would return to the lowlands and mingle with the other expatriates, including Spies and his colleague, Beryl de Zoete, McPhee and Belo, and the American dancer Katharane Mershon with her husband Jack. When Bateson's mother visited, they rented part of a palace owned by the ruler of Bangli for nine dollars a month; elsewhere they paid for an elaborate musical performance. 'It gives one a fine feeling of being a patron of the arts and lord of the manor combined to be able to order an opera.'[20] Of Spies, Mead wrote early in her stay:

Walter is a perfectly delightful person, an artist and a musician, who has lived in Bali for some eight years and has welcomed and entertained all the interesting people who have come here. He has done a great deal to stimulate modern Balinese painting and has painted Bali himself and in general has worked out a most perfect relationship

between himself, the island, its people and its traditions . . .
Our only other neighbor is a mild, responsible, only a little
twinkling Dutch artist [Bonnet] who supplies system and
bookkeeping in Walter's attempts to protect and encourage the Balinese artists to resist the tourists and do good
work.[21]

Mead and Bateson applied Freudian theory to Balinese culture, hoping
thereby to learn about universally applicable aspects of schizophrenia.
In order to test the potential of film to capture large amounts of behav-
ioural data they took more than 25 000 still photos and 22 000 feet of
movie film at Bayunggede. The result was *Balinese Character: A Photographic Analysis*, a rather dry book with large numbers of small pictures,
without much popular appeal at the time and never a huge scientific
success either. But their work remains of great value, even though its
Freudian emphasis may strike the modern reader as quaint. In contrast
to the widely held notion that Bali was a land of harmony, Mead and
Bateson emphasised the role of fear in the Balinese character: 'It is a
character based upon fear which, because it is learned in the mother's
arms, is a value as well as a threat.'[22]

Bateson and Mead were fascinated by a variation on the *legong*
dance in which young maidens impersonate the demonic sorceress
Rangda. Having observed that Balinese mothers enjoyed teasing male
children by, among other things, pulling their penises, they concluded
that the terrifying Rangda represented the mother in Balinese society.
'The dance sums up the besetting fear, the final knowledge of each
Balinese male that he will, after all, no matter how hard he seeks to
find the lovely and unknown beyond the confines of his familiar
village, marry the Witch, marry a woman whose attitude toward human
relations will be exactly that of his own mother.'[23] Freudian anthropology soon went out of fashion and, perhaps surprisingly, no one has
ever suggested that Mead's theory of pervasive fear in Balinese culture
could help to explain the bloodletting of 1966.

During the same period, Spies was doing a very different book on Balinese dance and drama with his British friend and colleague, Beryl de Zoete. Spies, thirty-nine, was homosexual; de Zoete, fifteen years older and often described as a fringe member of the Bloomsbury set, was platonically married to the much older Arthur Waley, a renowned sinologist. De Zoete was an accomplished student and critic of dance and a talented writer. She was the principal author of the book that resulted; Spies was the ideas man and photographer.

De Zoete had an acerbic streak, and could not resist sniping at what struck her as Mead's and Bateson's pretensions to calculated scientific method. She satirised this kind of approach in a series of photos entitled 'anthropology in Bali', featuring an assistant measuring skulls, a clock to synchronise field notes, and a canine presence to represent Pavlov's dog. The plot thickened when another anthropologist, Jane Belo, although a good friend of Bateson and Mead, was initially critical of their 'cold and analytical procedures'. Mead noted in her autobiography: 'Beryl, who had an acid tongue and a gift for destructive criticism, satirized this conflict between science and art, and I identified her with the witch, a prevailing Balinese figure.'[24]

Mead and Bateson also collected art, especially from Batuan, one of the new style centres. They liked the dark hues and sometimes macabre subject matter of the Batuan artists and asked at least one of them to illustrate his dreams. They left Bali in 1938, having decided to return to New Guinea to gather additional material to compare with their Bali findings. I Made Kaler, their talented research assistant, commissioned a farewell painting from one of the Batuan artists with whom the Meads had worked. It shows them in an outrigger canoe paddling away from the island. On the shore behind them Balinese weep, and volcanoes spout smoke letters reading, in English, 'Good Bye, Good Luck'. Before them is an island covered with welcoming, frizzy-haired Melanesians. The artist, I Ketut Ngendon, was later killed in the revolutionary struggle; his story is briefly told in the following chapter.

This superb photograph first appeared in Spies and de Zoete, Dance and Drama in Bali
*(1938), where it was captioned 'Djegog at Djembrana. Old Dance'. The authors lamented
the 'decay' of this form, and especially the great bamboo orchestra which accompanied it.
Today, thanks to the stimulus of tourism, jegog has been revived.*
(Source: *The Horniman Museum, London*)

Meanwhile Spies and de Zoete completed their masterpiece, *Dance
and Drama in Bali*, published in 1938. The book combined profound
knowledge of Balinese drama, elegant prose and dramatic photographs,
and recorded a wealth of material much of which might otherwise have
been lost. In an introductory essay de Zoete lamented the encroachment of cheap cloth, tin roofs and a few missionaries, then wrote:

> Bali is neither a last nor a lost paradise, but the home of a
> peculiarly gifted people of mixed race, endowed with a great
> sense of humour and a great sense of style, where their own
> creations are concerned; and with a suppleness of mind
> which has enabled them to take what they want of the

alien civilizations which have been reaching them for centuries and to leave the rest. And in spite of the few exceptions mentioned above they seem to have left the rest very successfully.[25]

She went on:

The Balinese are always building new temples, always using new motives for their temples and sculptures; whatever comes to hand, whatever amuses them at the moment. Why may they not make new dances? Obviously it would never occur to the uninitiated that they might not. But certain Europeans dread lest anything so awful should happen to the Balinese as to modify what they are pleased to call the Balinese tradition. Yet the great and ineradicable charm of the Balinese is that their tradition is at once so sure and so flexible.[26]

Of course, Spies and de Zoete did not see all change as admirable. Unlike Covarrubias, for example, they did not know quite what to make of the new rage for *janger* dancing. They wrote that despite having 'as respectable a religious origin as any dance in Bali', *janger* had become a vehicle for popular 'Malay opera', or *stamboel*, sometimes in the form of a play within a play, featuring grotesque European characters and 'Malayo-American' music. It was, they concluded, 'fascinating in its absurdity', repellent in some respects, but also a nice caricature of things foreign as seen through Balinese eyes.[27]

The curtain drops

Time was running out, however. By the end of 1938 everyone knew that war was likely. Apprehension, if not panic, was in the air. For reasons

Anthropologists Mead and Bateson are shown leaving Bali for New Guinea in 1938, while Balinese weep, Melanesians in the foreground gather to welcome their new guests, and backdrop volcanoes spout 'Good bye, Good luck' in English. The artist, I Ketut Ngendon, died in the turmoil of the Indonesian struggle for independence.
(Source: *Institute for Intercultural Studies Inc, New York*)

still not fully understood, Dutch officialdom suddenly launched an Indies-wide crackdown on homosexuality. On 31 December 1938, Spies was arrested for violating a law forbidding sex with a minor. His friend Roelof Goris was arrested on a similar charge. Spies' other friends tried to defend him. Margaret Mead, back in Bali on a return visit, explained to the court the difficulty of determining the age of a Balinese youth and delivered a lecture on narrow-minded attitudes toward homosexuality, but in vain.

Spies went to jail in Surabaya where he remained until September 1939, when he was released and returned to Bali. There he tried to resume his old life. He did some exquisite coloured drawings of insects and sea creatures, which he gathered on Bali's reef flats, for the colonial zoological service. But after the outbreak of war in 1940 he was re-arrested and sent with other enemy aliens to internment in Sumatra.

By early 1942 the Japanese were threatening Sumatra, and the German detainees, including Spies, were loaded on the Dutch freighter *Van Imhoff*, bound for Ceylon. On the way the Japanese bombed the vessel and it began to sink. The crew abandoned ship, but the captain felt he could not unlock the hatches without authorisation from higher authority, and Spies and most of the other prisoners on board were trapped and drowned.

He was fondly remembered by the Balinese who felt that, unlike many, he had given more than he took away. One of them said, 'He deepened the colour of our dreams.'[28]

Well before war intervened, Western commentators were beginning to wax pessimistic about the future of Bali. As early as May 1932, an article in *Vanity Fair* intoned, 'Let us hasten to talk of Bali, for tomorrow it will be only a memory, so true is it that men always kill what they wish to love'.[29] A 1939 traveller warned, 'Hasten dear reader, and visit Bali if you want to see the last flicker of unsophisticated native life before modern sophistication drowns it all'.[30] While more knowledgeable observers knew full well that Bali was anything but unsophisticated, and recognised an underlying resilience, even they could not help worrying about the cumulative impact of tourists, missionaries and international commerce.

In the end the enduring contribution of the expatriate intelligentsia was to give Bali a global reputation as a place of extraordinary cultural value. It was important that this recognition should be well established and communicated to other Indonesians, as in time it was. Indonesia's first president, the half-Balinese Sukarno, could credibly claim Bali as an exemplar of Indonesian culture, a matter for national pride and foreign admiration. Other Indonesians came to agree, despite their occasional irritation at foreigners who jetted into Bali with only minimal awareness of the rest of the country.

As their economic circumstances permitted, Indonesian tourists would join the foreigners in coming to Bali. And after the troubled times that lay ahead, tourism would make Bali prosper and eventually replace agriculture as the island's primary source of livelihood. It was to be a development success story on a scale, and with attendant risks and costs, beyond anything foreseen at its inception.

8
OCCUPATION, REVOLUTION AND BLOODBATH (1942–1966)

The *Pax Neerlandica* was over. Bali was to be in political turmoil for the next quarter of a century, a time which included periods of widespread violence associated with the final stage of the Japanese occupation, the Indonesian Revolution (1945–49) and the attempted coup d'état of September 1965. While events on Bali were of marginal national importance compared to what was going on in Java, the human costs were high, and the killing in early 1966 was at least as bad as anything elsewhere in Indonesia. In one sense Bali was reverting to form, to the endemic warfare of the pre-colonial era, but now conflict was sharpened by the new generation of tensions which had accumulated behind the misleadingly tranquil façade of Dutch rule, including growing landlessness and an urge to settle old scores.

Japanese occupation

The Japanese landed at Sanur on 18 February 1942. Under their occupation, Indonesia was divided between army and navy zones of administration. The army was initially in charge of Bali and quickly gained a reputation for harshness, but in May 1942 it was replaced by a more compatible navy regime.

In general, the Japanese found Dutch colonial institutions quite acceptable, and the initial reaction of the Balinese to their new political masters was positive. Most of the rulers had no trouble coexisting with the Japanese, although one senior sovereign, the Raja of Gianyar, whose Fiat Phaeton had been the talk of Bali before the war, was exiled for difficult behaviour. He was succeeded by his son, the western-educated Anak Agung Gede Agung, later prominent in both local and national politics. The Japanese assigned to Bali no doubt congratulated themselves on their good fortune at ending up in such an attractive spot, and some of them became genuinely interested in Balinese culture.

However, as the Japanese began to lose the war, their regime, on Bali as elsewhere, turned increasingly oppressive until it became a hell of hunger, forced labour, and the compulsory production of rice and other commodities. Balinese were pressed into work battalions, the Romusha Corps, and sent to unknown destinations, most of them never to return. Those who remained endured real hardship.

Nonetheless, on Bali as on Java, Japanese rule opened up new political vistas for youth in particular. Both administrative regions, north and south, were now headed by a Balinese. The Japanese expanded education and by 1944 there were 50 000 students on Bali, compared with 26 000 in 1942. They made education available to low-caste Balinese for the first time. They founded paramilitary organisations and martial arts clubs. They peddled their own brand of fiery rhetoric to support the imperial war effort.

On Bali as on Java there soon emerged a distinction between older, often aristocratic nationalists and more radical youth (*pemuda*) who saw themselves, in many cases justifiably, as the vanguard of revolution. The Dutch had established the nucleus of a Balinese military organisation, the Prayoda Corps, in 1938, drawing mostly on recruits from the aristocracy. The Japanese enlisted its members and used its old training ground in Singaraja to form a Balinese unit of their Indonesia-wide militia, Peta (an acronym for 'Protectors of the Fatherland'). Peta was to become the core of the post-occupation Indonesian army.

Throughout Indonesia, Peta and its counterparts provided a heady immersion in military affairs which accorded well with nationalist aspirations. Thus the stage was set for bitter conflict when the Dutch, refusing to recognise that their prestige had been irreparably damaged, attempted to return after World War II.

The Dutch and the French would never have been able to reoccupy their Southeast Asian possessions had it not been for the support of their wartime allies. In the case of the Dutch East Indies, that unhappy responsibility fell to the British. In October 1945, employing British Indian troops, they stumbled into a costly battle with Indonesian Republican (nationalist) forces in the East Java port of Surabaya, and their commanding general was killed. More than preoccupied on Java, the British wanted to move slowly in facilitating Dutch re-entry elsewhere in the archipelago.

Thus the Dutch did not return to Bali until March 1946, when they accepted the surrender of Japanese troops at Sanur, the same location where they had landed in 1906, and where the Japanese had come ashore in 1942. But the Indonesian Republicans had beaten them to it.

The Indonesian Revolution on Bali

The Japanese accepted Allied surrender terms on 14 August 1945. On 17 August the Indonesian nationalists declared independence and proclaimed a Republic under President Sukarno. Less than a week later, Sukarno appointed as governor of the Lesser Sundas (including Bali)

A Dutch army patrol somewhere in south Bali in 1946, during the Indonesian Revolution.
Like many independence struggles, this one was also a civil war. About 2000 Balinese
died, approximately one-third of them fighting on the Dutch side.
(Source: *KITLV Archives, Leiden*)

I Gusti Ketut Puja, who had served as the administrator of north Bali
for the Japanese. Now he returned to Bali from Java to organise a Republican presence before the Dutch could return. At first the Japanese, who
were understandably confused about what to do next, cooperated with
the Republicans. In October they turned civil government over to
Governor Puja and the local branch of the Indonesian National
Committee which he had established. In the same month a small Dutch
naval party attempted to land at Singaraja, resulting in the death of
I Ketut Merta, Bali's first revolutionary martyr.

But by January 1946 it was clear that the Dutch were going to
return with Allied support, and the Japanese authorities on Bali changed
course. They temporarily arrested Puja and his senior supporters, and
remaining nationalist forces moved into the hills to launch armed resistance. In late January, a few weeks before the Dutch landed, what was
left of the Indonesian National Committee turned over power to the

Paruman Agung, a conservative council of Balinese rulers originally set up by the Dutch in 1938.

Once the Dutch were back on Bali their armed forces used tough tactics against the nationalists, re-arresting Governor Puja and harassing the Republican guerillas. On at least one occasion they deployed modest air power, including a B-25 bomber and a Piper Cub, to strafe villages. The poorly equipped Republican forces, initially numbering about 1500, eventually decided on a 'Long March' from their base camp in the mountains between Tabanan and Buleleng to the slopes of Gunung Agung, rather than adopting the dispersed guerilla tactics favoured by the more radical youth. They may have intended to draw the Dutch military away from the west coast of Bali, where it was hoped, in vain, that Republican forces from Java were going to land.

The Balinese forces were constantly harassed by the Dutch military. On 20 November 1946, I Gusti Ngurah Rai, a veteran of the pre-war Dutch militia, led them in a disastrous engagement near the village of Marga in Tabanan, in which they were trapped and overwhelmed by Dutch forces using airplanes. Ninety-six Republicans died along with their leader. Balinese writers have characterised the Battle of Marga as a *puputan* similar in spirit to those of 1906–08, a last heroic stand by ill-equipped nationalists against a better armed colonial force. The engagement is celebrated in at least two Balinese poems in classical style, and by many quasi-religious monuments. After the Revolution the martyred commander, Ngurah Rai, was designated a National Hero, and the modern airport serving Bali is named after him. He is the only Balinese National Hero besides Patih Jelantik, the protagonist of the 1846–49 war. The Battle of Marga coincided with a period of aggressively tough tactics on the part of the Dutch elsewhere in Indonesia, including a notorious campaign of terror against the Republicans on the island of Sulawesi, which resulted in at least 3000 deaths over a three-month period.

Throughout the Indonesian Revolution, the struggle on Bali moved in rhythm with the war on Java and with the erratic progress of

I Gusti Ngurah Rai, a Balinese hero of the Indonesian Revolution, died in a disastrous engagement with superior Dutch forces in 1946. He is shown here (on the far left) attending school in Java in 1931. In the back row, from left to right, are the future Dr A.A.M. Djelantik and his older brother, Gede Djelantik, later ruler of Karangasem. (Source: Courtesy Dr A.A.M. Djelantik)

diplomatic efforts to end it. At Linggajati, in November 1946, the Dutch and the nationalists reached agreement for the first time. Under pressure from the British, who were anxious to withdraw their occupation forces from Indonesia, the Dutch recognised *de facto* Republican authority over Java, Sumatra and Madura. The two sides also agreed to work towards a federation, to be called the United States of Indonesia, under the Dutch queen. To most nationalists, however, the proposed federation was a transparent effort to mobilise anti-Javanese sentiment in the Outer Islands against predominantly Republican Java.

While it soon became clear that the Linggajati agreement was doomed, the Dutch persevered in their efforts to establish the proposed United States of Indonesia. In December 1946, at a conference in Denpasar, they proclaimed the State of Eastern Indonesia, or Negara Indonesia Timor (NIT), including Bali and all the Dutch territory east of Bali except West New Guinea. Although the new state was suspiciously similar to a 1938 colonial realignment named the Great East, it nonetheless encouraged many hitherto undecided Balinese to support the Dutch. The discouraged Republicans argued that Bali should be included with Java in the areas under direct Republican control. They also joked that the initials for the new state really stood for 'Negara Ikut Tuan', or 'state which follows the (Dutch) master'.[1]

In fact, supporters of the concept were far from uniformly pro-Dutch or anti-nationalist. The new President of the NIT was Cokorde Gede Raka Sukawati, the man who had invited Walter Spies to Ubud. Ide Anak Agung Gede Agung left his position as ruler of Gianyar and served successively as NIT Interior Minister and Prime Minister, while his younger brother, Anak Agung Gede Oka, succeeded him as ruler of Gianyar and chaired the influential Balinese Council of Rulers. Interestingly enough, the Balinese aristocrats supporting the NIT soon fell out with the dwindling number of Dutch civil servants on Bali, who belatedly concluded that it had been a mistake to give these 'feudal' rulers so much power.

The ruler-dominated NIT regime, which had real power in Balinese affairs, may not have been popular with the Dutch, but it was certainly not sympathetic to the more fervent revolutionary youth in the Republican ranks. Geoffrey Robinson, whose book *The Dark Side of Paradise* is the definitive account of this period in Balinese history, says that Anak Agung Gde Agung 'did his best to destroy the armed resistance in Bali in efforts to ensure that "moderate" educated aristocrats like himself would dominate whatever political system emerged from the Revolution'.[2] Tension between the NIT and its opponents became one more source of conflict on Bali among armed gangs linked with rulers or political parties.

Robinson sees three underlying schismatic forces at work from 1945 to 1966. First, there was competition for leadership within many of the eight royal establishments, especially those which had been under direct rule until 1938, resulting in a proliferation of claimants for royal status. Second, the problem of caste, already controversial under the Dutch, encouraged political radicalisation as educated low-caste Balinese increasingly assumed leadership roles in the nationalist movement. Third, and perhaps most significant, were the economic inequalities related to declining rice production, increasing landlessness, and marked contrast between those regions which produced a rice surplus and those which did not. All these divisions both aggravated and were aggravated by the ingrained competition among Bali's diverse descent groups—clans, royal families and more.

The suffering that resulted is well illustrated by the story of I Ketut Ngendon, the Batuan artist who painted the 'Good bye, Good luck' painting for Margaret Mead and Gregory Bateson in 1938 (see photo page 154). The talented Ngendon was of low-caste origin. In the 1930s he graduated from peddling woodcarvings to become something of an artistic impresario for his village, arranging dance performances, elaborating new dramatic styles and hosting foreign visitors sent by Walter Spies. Following a friend who had been taught by Rudolf Bonnet, he began to paint and was one of the artists to establish what became known as the Batuan style. For Ngendon, artistic activity opened a window on the Western world, and he became dissatisfied with the inequities of colonialism and the Dutch-supported caste system.

During the Japanese occupation, Ngendon met a Javanese artist and travelled with him to Java, where he became a nationalist and is said to have met the future President Sukarno. When he returned to Bali he organised a Batuan cell of the nationalist movement, and when the Dutch military cracked down on nationalist activities he and ten or fifteen other Batuan villagers joined the armed guerilla forces. In general, the people of the area were not sympathetic to the nationalist cause; certainly the leaders of Batuan were not.

Eventually Ngendon was captured by police of the anti-revolutionary Gianyar government in 1948. They took him to the Batuan cemetery and executed him. Anthropologist Hildred Geertz, who tells his story in her book on Batuan painting, *Images of Power*, makes it clear that not all Ngendon's fellow artists shared his political views, and that his brutal death reflected a pattern of acute societal tension broadly typical of any civil war.[3]

In July 1947 the Dutch attempted to achieve a military solution by launching their first 'police action' on Java. Although they took much territory, growing pressure from the Allies, upon whom they depended for post-war reconstruction aid, soon compelled them to resume negotiations. In January 1948 the two sides agreed to a cease-fire on Java at a conference held on board the US cruiser *Renville*. As part of the *Renville* terms, the hard-pressed Republicans agreed to withdraw their troops from all Dutch-occupied territory and to recognise the NIT as an equal partner in the negotiating process.

On Bali, the *Renville* agreement seemed to undercut any further justification for opposing the NIT. At least 1000 Republican guerillas came down from the uplands of Bali and surrendered, leaving behind a small ragtag group of diehards. Henceforth the diehards did little fighting but emerged after the Republican victory in 1949 claiming 'the mantle of revolutionary purity' and were a potent force in Balinese politics thereafter.[4]

The momentum of the broader struggle soon shifted again, this time decisively against the Dutch, partly due to intense pressure for a settlement from the United States. In December 1948 the Dutch launched a second 'police action' on Java, which achieved initial success but soon led them into a diplomatic and military morass. A combination of effective guerilla resistance and growing international pressure compelled the Dutch to participate in United Nations-sponsored negotiations which over the next year led to Indonesian independence.

On Bali the 'police action' of December 1948 persuaded the ruling family of Gianyar, hitherto major supporters of the Dutch-sponsored eastern state, to change sides and back the Republic. The head of the family, Anak Agung Gede Agung, resigned from his NIT position with his entire cabinet and in due course joined the Indonesian Socialist Party (PSI) led by one of the Republic's founding fathers, Sutan Sjahrir.

In 1955 Anak Agung Gede Agung became Indonesia's Foreign Minister, in which capacity he served with distinction. The PSI was to be the favoured party of many Balinese, both aristocrats and others, in the tumultuous times that followed.

Meanwhile the Dutch presence on Bali was steadily decreasing, initially because of the apparent success of the eastern state, later because it became clear that in fact the Republicans were winning. By the end of 1949, only three Dutch officials were left on the island. The handover of sovereignty to the Republic of Indonesia took place on 27 December 1949. The war for Indonesian independence had cost Bali about 2000 casualties, of whom roughly one-third died fighting on the Dutch side.[5]

The Sukarno era

Independent Indonesia got off to a disorderly start on Bali. Unrest continued in the form of conflict between the revolutionaries and local military units which had collaborated with the Dutch, as well as among the various revolutionary factions. There was disagreement between veterans of the struggle and the authorities over who would be integrated into the new national army. In the early 1950s bands of ex-guerilla fighters again took to the hills, often in support of Balinese political factions. Violence led to more violence, and some indulged in outright banditry. All this resulted in an estimated 500 Balinese killed in 1950 alone.

One of the best known and most lethal of these private armies was LOGIS, or Continuation of the All-Indonesia Guerilla Organisation. As the 1955 national elections approached, LOGIS supported the PSI, known at the national level for its upper-crust, intellectual image. But LOGIS specialised in political intimidation, including assassinations. Those targeted were for the most part opponents of the PSI in the Nationalist Party (PNI), and by harassing them, or worse, LOGIS may have contributed to the PSI's resounding electoral success on Bali.

With the advent of Republican rule, Bali's rajas lost the official status they had enjoyed under the Dutch, but only after heated debate. Those who wanted to preserve their standing argued that the old kingdoms should be declared 'special districts' (*daerah istimewa*), as had been done in the case of the Sultanate of Jogjakarta in Central Java. While similar arrangements were informally initiated in some of the Balinese kingdoms, they were never officially confirmed. Despite their loss of state sponsorship, however, the rajas retained influence as landowners, as educated individuals, and as traditional leaders of high status. In addition to effectively denying the rajas official standing, the Sukarno regime established elected legislative councils at both province and district (*kabupaten*) levels. The provincial assembly was to elect the governor, subject to confirmation by the national president.

President Sukarno took a personal interest in Bali, at least in part because his mother was Balinese. Soon after independence he told a local audience, 'Bali has always been this country's pride and joy'.[6] From the earliest days of his presidency he intervened frequently in Balinese affairs, usually on the side of the more radical Republican elements, but also in efforts to calm things down. After one period of worsening political violence, he summoned a collection of feuding youth leaders to Jakarta and urged them to settle their differences.

In 1950 Sukarno named a left-leaning scion of the royal house of Jembrana, Anak Agung Bagus Suteja, to be regional head of Bali, and elevated him to the governorship when Bali became a province in 1958. Governor Suteja was to be an influential player throughout the Sukarno era, until he perished during the 1966 killings. In general the Balinese aristocracy remained politically conservative but, as the case of Governor Suteja illustrates, not always.

Sukarno helped obtain recognition for the Hindu-Bali religion in 1958–59, including representation in the Ministry of Religion and the creation of an official Hindu association, the Parisada Hindu Dharma Indonesia. This was a great relief to the Balinese, who had been much concerned by earlier debate over whether Indonesia should become an Islamic state, a prospect which for obvious reasons they found threatening.

The president delighted in taking world leaders, including Nehru, Tito, Ho Chi Minh, Zhou Enlai and Khrushchev to Bali. During Nehru's visit he famously referred to the island as 'the morning of the world'. One of Sukarno's pet projects was the Bali Beach Hotel at Sanur, making him the father of Bali's postwar tourism revival. Completed in 1964 with Japanese war reparations funding, it was Bali's first and for many years its only major modern hotel; its high-rise style was later deemed a mistake, and has never been repeated. Sukarno also constructed a lavish presidential guest house overlooking the ancient bathing place at Tampaksiring, allegedly so he could ogle Balinese maidens at their ablutions, and held licentious parties there, or so his detractors said.

True or not, reports of such behaviour offended conservative Balinese. Nonetheless, Indonesia's first president was generally well regarded on the island, at least in the early years of his rule. His popularity descended decades later to his daughter Megawati Sukarnoputri ('daughter of Sukarno'), who became President of Indonesia in 2001. Local affection for Sukarno contributed to the fact that Bali never developed serious regional grievances against Jakarta and displayed no sympathy for the Outer Islands rebellion of 1958. This insurrection, supported ineptly by the USA, was rooted in the economic grievances of resource-rich provinces in Sumatra and Sulawesi which wanted a greater share of their own export revenues. But Bali was still poor, if anything a financial drain on the national government.

While the downside of Republican rule on Bali was primarily economic, it was more similar to the situation on Java. Clumsy economic nationalism, manifested through interventionist policies, was easily exploited by corrupt local officials and led to inflation, growing shortages of food and declining wages. As Indonesia's currency became worthless, civil servants were guaranteed low-priced rice, while others could obtain it only with difficulty, if at all. Due in part to the exemption of some peasants from the land tax after 1951, Bali was increasingly dependent on Jakarta for revenue, but the centre was also in deepening economic trouble.

The government favoured indigenous entrepreneurs over ethnic Chinese, a policy which Governor Suteja implemented vigorously at the local level. The result may have contributed to the prevailing economic disorder, but it also encouraged Balinese to embark on business careers. The new entrepreneurs included both aristocrats and well-connected former revolutionary youth leaders.

In the late 1950s, against the background of regional rebellions in Sumatra and Sulawesi, Sukarno ended Indonesia's brief period of parliamentary democracy and proclaimed 'Guided Democracy'. This was a fluid system emphasising mass mobilisation versus reliance on political parties, which Sukarno saw as antagonistic and divisive. There were to be no more democratic national elections in Indonesia until 1999.

Guided Democracy also featured radical economic policies and a search for external enemies. First, Sukarno mobilised popular emotion to assert Indonesia's claim to West New Guinea, now the Indonesian province of Papua, which had been retained by the Dutch. After this dispute was settled diplomatically in September 1962, he embarked on a campaign to 'swallow' the nascent Federation of Malaysia. A small-scale war with Britain broke out along the border dividing Indonesian Borneo from the formerly British territories of Sarawak and North Borneo, which were being incorporated in Malaysia.

By this time Sukarno had abolished the more conservative major political parties, the socialist PSI and Muslim Masjumi, which had supported the Outer Islands rebellion of 1958. He appeared to have embarked on an increasingly reckless effort to balance the huge communist party against the politically conservative army. The political philosophy of his later years was NASAKOM, an acronym referring to a fusion of nationalism, religion and communism. All this took place in an atmosphere of escalating international tension resulting from the Cold War, heightened by the beginning of war in Vietnam. To the nervous Western powers, NASAKOM appeared to be shorthand for a rapid drift toward communist dominance.

The storm and drama of this period had great impact on Bali. At the beginning of the Republic the major national political parties had established themselves rapidly on the island. Because Muslims were a small minority, the Muslim parties Masjumi and Nahdlatul Ulama (NU) were only minor players. That left the Nationalist Party (PNI), the Socialist Party (PSI) and the Communist Party (PKI) to play major roles. All three were initially strong, but there was little ideological consistency to their popularity, another way of saying that party politics on Bali reflected the complexity of the underlying social system. A simplified scorecard would have read as follows, moving from right to left on the ideological scale:

- The PSI (Indonesian Socialist Party) was at the national level primarily appealing to Westernised intellectuals, with a genteel character and weak mass following. It was influential in the early years of the Republic, until it was banned in 1960. But on Bali the PSI developed a mass base, was aided by unruly paramilitary forces like LOGIS, and enjoyed diversified support from members of the older educated elite, from elements in the military, from factions among the young nationalists (*pemuda*), and most importantly from some of the wealthier rulers, especially the influential royal family of Gianyar.
- The PNI (Indonesian Nationalist Party) was regarded as the party of Sukarno and drew national strength from its following among high-status Javanese officials. On Bali it also had links to the security forces (especially the police), to youth elements, and to certain members of the aristocracy. After the demise of the PSI in 1960 it became the bastion of

anti-communism, again at variance with the pattern elsewhere in Indonesia.

- The PKI (Indonesian Communist Party) had relatively little following in the early years and finished in third place on Bali in the elections of 1955. It gathered strength as it appeared to be gaining favour with Sukarno, and as the overall course of Indonesian politics veered to the left. With some exceptions, it lacked the aristocratic connections of the other two parties and was more dependent on ideological and class appeal.

Aristocratic links were extremely important. Imagine what the French Revolution might have been like if the nobility had been able to rely on the support of peasant followers. That is what often happened on Bali, quite contrary to the apparent dictates of class interest. For example, Robinson notes that 'the rajas of Klungkung and Karangasem, two of the most notorious collaborators [with the Dutch] during the Revolution, became PNI supporters; they were most welcome because the substantial personal followings they commanded could be easily transformed into mass support for the party'.[7]

The same dynamic operated in the struggle over land reform. In a situation of growing absolute land shortage, some tenants who on ideological grounds might have been attracted to land reform realised that if they lost the protection of their lords they would probably be displaced by other tenants.

In August 1961 the most prominent former member of the now-banned PSI on Bali, Anak Agung Gede Agung, the former raja of Gianyar, held a grand cremation ceremony for his late father, of Fiat Phaeton fame. He invited President Sukarno only belatedly, and the President concluded that the ceremony masked a plot to assassinate him, perhaps with US complicity. Sukarno had no reason to like this talented Balinese lord, who had been a leader of the controversial State of Eastern Indonesia, and then, as Indonesian Foreign Minister, had upstaged the President by persuading the Dutch to negotiate the heated dispute over West Irian. As a result, Anak Agung Gede Agung was jailed from 1962 to 1966 along with PSI founder Sutan Sjahrir and others.

With the PSI decapitated and done for, its Balinese followers switched to either the PKI or the PNI, mostly the latter. From this period until 1966, the political contest on Bali would be between these two parties.

Prelude to cataclysm

Again reflecting national trends, the island became a political hothouse with the temperature continually ratcheted upwards. The two antagonists, PNI and PKI, and above all their mass organisations, were locked in competition for control of the local government and access to resources. The PKI's cultural front, Lekra (Institute for People's Culture), launched an assault on elements of traditional art and culture which it deemed insufficiently progressive. While this campaign was widely disliked and remembered, the main issue was land reform.

Both landlessness and tenancy had grown steadily on Bali since the Dutch conquest. About one-third of all farms were worked by tenants. Much of the problem was due to population growth; there was simply not enough land to go around. As of 1950, almost 90 per cent of all holdings were less than two hectares.[8] Thanks in part to the Dutch, there were no large plantations and no truly large private owners.

There were now roughly 1.5 million Balinese, double the number at the beginning of full Dutch control. Prime irrigated rice land, especially in the south, was under tremendous pressure, and much of the rest of the island was too dry or too mountainous for intensive cultivation. With the postwar tourist industry as yet unborn and the national economy in tatters, conflict over land reform was virtually inevitable.

Most Balinese, no matter how poor or uneducated, sensed that given the absolute shortage of land and the highly politicised context such conflict would be zero-sum in nature, meaning there would be no winners without losers, and that the losers would include many people of modest means.

Land had been an issue on Bali at least since the early 1950s, when revolutionary youth returning from the hills sometimes found that they had lost their land due to their 'illegal' activities. In March 1951 the Balinese legislature mandated a minimum share of 50 per cent of the crop for tenants as well as a land tax exemption for all holdings of less than three hectares, freeing about 80 per cent of landowners from taxation. But the tenancy provision was not enforced, thanks to a combination of landlord resistance and traditional tenant-landlord loyalties.

A decade later the national legislature passed new laws allowing a maximum of five hectares of wet rice land and six hectares of dry land per household in the most densely settled areas of the country. Excess holdings were to be redistributed by the state, preferably to the tenant cultivators. Absentee landlordism was abolished. For tenants, harvest sharing was set at fifty-fifty on wet rice land, a more favourable ratio than existing practice in many areas of Bali.

Given the nature of the problem, successful implementation of these measures on Bali would have required broad faith that the process was impartial. Instead it was relentlessly politicised. In 1963 the communists decided at the national level to pursue land reform aggressively. In effect, this was a green light to the PKI's increasingly powerful Indonesian Farmers' Front, or BTI, to seize and redistribute land according to the law, but without any semblance of due process. Also practised on Java, such seizures were known as 'unilateral action' (*aksi sepihak*). At the local level the BTI engaged in competition and conflict with the PNI farmers' organisation, Petani.

Governor Suteja did not direct the police to stop the unilateral seizures and was clearly supporting the communists, although he was never formally a member of the PKI. It was widely assumed that

President Sukarno was supporting Suteja; he had after all reappointed him in 1959 in spite of the fact that another, more moderate candidate had won election by the regional legislature.

The actual pace of land reform varied from district to district. It was rapid in the north and east, where holdings were relatively large. It was slower in south Bali, especially where strong ruling families could delay implementation. Unilateral action was widespread, supposedly targeting relatively big landholders, which included temples. Often, however, the immediate victims were tenant farmers. The result was 'deep bitterness . . . not only between landlords and tenants but also among Bali's poorest tenant farmers'.[9]

The sense of malaise engendered by the growing political turmoil was reinforced by two natural disasters, the first a plague of rats in 1962, the second an eruption of Gunung Agung in early 1963 which killed at least 1500 people and took 62 000 hectares of scarce land out of production. The eruption occurred as Bali was preparing to hold an island-wide Eka Dasa Rudra temple festival at the Besakih mother temple on the slopes of the volcano.

This ritual purification ceremony was supposed to take place only once every 100 years, according to the Balinese calendar of 200-day years, but there was no record of when the last one had been held. Its revival was not a local initiative, but had been inspired and supported by two Javanese officials, the head of police and the military commander, who apparently felt that the ritual might help to calm down what was obviously becoming an overheated political situation. President Sukarno was scheduled to attend but did not, and the ritual could not be brought to its proper conclusion.

At the time, the local press reported that the eruption was a positive sign that the gods were attending the ceremony. With hindsight, others reached different conclusions. Bali's last major volcanic event had been the great earthquake of 1917, accompanied by an eruption of the Batur volcano. This disaster had been seen by many as evidence of divine displeasure over neglected religious ceremonies, following Dutch displacement of many Balinese rulers whose job it was to conduct such ceremonies.

Similar theories on this occasion saw the 1963 eruption as godly retribution for sacrilegious behaviour, such as the redistribution of temple lands. Still later, it was seen by some as foreshadowing and perhaps legitimising the 'final cleansing' of local communists during the massacres of 1965–66.[10] The destruction wrought by the eruption was until recently clearly visible along the road from Denpasar to Karangasem.

The killings of 1965–66

On 30 September 1965, disaffected military officers in Jakarta assassinated five senior generals, leading to swift military retaliation, the eventual extermination of the Communist Party, and the establishment of the 'New Order' under General, later President, Soeharto. The army claimed the communists were responsible and the communists appeared to accept responsibility.[11] Others claimed that the army, backed by the USA, had staged the killing of the generals as a pretext for destroying the PKI. Heated controversy has swirled around this episode and its aftermath ever since.

Violence between communists and Muslims spread through Java in the months following the attempted coup. To this day there is no certainty about the total number of victims throughout Indonesia, with estimates ranging from 82 000 to more than 1 million. As military units deployed through the Javanese countryside it became crystal clear that the Communist Party was finished, and that the army was condoning and often encouraging the killing of communists by political rivals. It was this pattern which spread to Bali in early December 1965.

The Balinese were almost immediately aware of the events of 30 September, and along with other Indonesians they held their breaths waiting to see who would emerge victorious from what everyone recognised as a death struggle between the PKI and its opponents. But Bali was at the end of the process, with major killing beginning there only after the arrival of Java-based troops.

The incident that ostensibly triggered the violence on Bali was the killing of an army officer and two Ansor youths by PKI members in the village of Tegalbadeng, Jembrana, on 30 November 1965. Ansor was a Muslim youth group heavily involved in the killings on nearby Java, which had peaked in October and November. On 7–8 December, troops of the Brawijaya Division and the army's paracommando regiment, which had been spearheading the anti-communist campaign on Java, arrived on Bali. A number of other high-ranking military officers, including the future president, General Soeharto, visited Bali shortly thereafter.

The anxiety of the new army leadership is easy to understand. Troops garrisoned on Bali up to this point were suspect, notably the regional commander, Brigadier General Sjafiuddin, a loyal adherent of Sukarno whose wife was alleged to be a PKI women's front activist. By this time, Governor Suteja had departed for Jakarta, where he was caught, imprisoned and then killed under circumstances which remain unclear.

What followed was horrific. To quote from *Christian Science Monitor* correspondent John Hughes' book *Indonesian Upheaval*:

> Whole villages, including children, took part in an island-wide witch-hunt for Communists who were slashed and clubbed and chopped to death, by communal consent.
>
> Whole villages that had made the fatal mistake of embracing Communism were wiped out. Almost within view of the big new [Bali Beach] luxury hotel the government has built to woo tourists to Bali stand the charred and blackened ruins of one such village . . .
>
> Night after night flared red over Bali as villages went up in flames and thousands of Communists, or people said to be Communists, were hunted down and killed. Knowledgeable sources say 40,000 Balinese were killed in two

weeks of butchery. Estimates have gone as high as 80,000. Nobody will ever know the exact toll. As one Balinese told me, 'When people were killed in batches of less than ten, nobody even bothered to keep count'.[12]

Later research has not refined Hughes' estimate of the total killed on Bali, although Robinson seems inclined toward the higher figure, while noting there is just as much debate about the number on Bali as on Java. Eighty thousand would have approached about 5 per cent of Bali's population, in which case Bali may have been proportionately even harder hit than Java. There is to this day a distressing lack of firm evidence to support the various estimates.

Some Balinese were killed in communal massacres, as in Jembrana. In other cases the army transported the victims to selected places, including police jails, where execution was carried out by villagers, often local PNI activists. Corpses were dumped into the sea or mass graves and none were afforded the cremation which according to Balinese religion is required preparation for the afterlife.

According to some accounts, Ansor activists were imported from Java to help. PNI leaders fostered the idea that the campaign was a Balinese Hindu holy war against atheism, paralleling the declaration of a leading Muslim organisation, Muhammadiyah, that the killing on Java was an Islamic holy war, or *jihad*. Anti-communist Balinese later said that many communists had been allowed to volunteer for execution (*nyupat*). To do so was said to signify repentance, a state of mind more compatible with Balinese religious belief than unwilling execution, although by no means sufficiently so to make up for lack of cremation. Even Governor Suteja was allegedly allowed to *nyupat* when he was killed in Jakarta. But on Bali this distinction apparently meant only that those who wished to do so were allowed to come forward and move to a different part of the execution area, where they were shot just like the others.[13]

Why did it happen? Anti-communist Western commentators

favoured a cultural explanation. They agreed with Balinese conserva-
tives that this explosion of violence was, at least in part, a reaction to
communist defilement of Balinese custom. Marshall Green, US Ambas-
sador to Indonesia at the time, wrote in his memoirs:

> In the last analysis, however, the bloodbath visited on
> Indonesia can be largely attributed to the fact that com-
> munism, with its atheism and talk of class warfare, was
> abhorrent to the way of life of rural Indonesia, especially
> on Java and Bali, whose cultures place great stress on toler-
> ance, social harmony, mutual assistance . . . and resolving
> controversy through talking issues out in order to achieve
> an acceptable consensus solution.[14]

The violence, according to this explanation, also manifested the violent,
dramatic side of Balinese religion, reflected in its mixture of mysticism
and tantric-derived magic, including the phenomenon of trance which
releases the individual to commit socially unacceptable acts.

Others have little patience with such arguments, regarding them
as myth-influenced misreading of Balinese tradition, compounded in
the case of American commentators like Green by fervent US sympathy for the anti-communist cause, linked with broader Cold War
objectives. Instead, according to this viewpoint, the killings are
adequately explained by well-documented economic and political
tensions, unleashed by less than subtle military support.

Regardless of the controversy, two things are clear. First, the killings
were most severe in those regions, notably Jembrana and Buleleng,
where land reform, with its attendant political tension, had been most
rapidly and aggressively implemented. Second, the army and the police
did encourage and at minimum provide logistical support, especially
transportation, for the mass executions. In December 1965 the top
Indonesian military officer on the scene, paracommando regiment
commander Sarwo Edhie, noted:

The situation in Bali is different from the situation in Central Java. Whereas in Central Java I was concerned to encourage the people to crush the Gestapu, [acronym for *Gerakan Tigapuluh September*—30 September Movement, hence shorthand for the communists], [in Bali] on the other hand, the people were already eager to crush the Gestapu to its roots. The important thing was not to let that enthusiasm be misused by certain people, leading to anarchy. That is what we had to prevent.[15]

Here Colonel Edhie was saying in effect that tensions had been running even higher on Bali than on Java, and that the army had been concerned not to lose control, which he clearly implies it did not. Neither he nor any other senior military leader ever suggested that the massacre should have been stopped.

In addition to the killings, an estimated 100 000 Indonesians were detained following the failed coup, and many of them remained in jail for decades.[16] While there were some detentions on Bali, the number seems to have been much lower than on Java.

Was the Balinese bloodletting inevitable? Possibly not. Bali may have been unfortunate to have had in the person of Brigadier General Sjafiuddin a local military commander who was suspected of being a communist sympathiser, unusual in Indonesia at the time. An officer with the full confidence of the new army leadership just might have been able to keep matters under control on his own and avoid the fatal intervention of troops from Java, or at least reduce the extent of the violence.

In conclusion it seems apparent that the killings of 1965–66 were rooted in the darker aspects of Balinese history, that they were exacerbated by tensions and divisions originating over past decades, and that they were condoned and encouraged by the Indonesian military in what it saw as the endgame in a mortal struggle.

The killings were over by mid-January of 1966, whether from sheer exhaustion or because it was obvious, especially to the army, that the Balinese PKI was finished. Soeharto's New Order regime quickly established itself and began to make slow progress against some of the economic problems that had plagued the island. There was no more talk of land reform, which in any case would recede in importance as a new tourism-driven economy developed. Sukarno's Bali Beach Hotel was open for business, still state-owned but managed by an American company. Growing numbers of visitors were still charmed by the island, and as impressed as ever by the seemingly harmonious nature of Balinese society. Those who heard about the killings generally found it hard to comprehend that such an orgy of violence could have occurred here, of all places.

Many Balinese, in common with other Indonesians, remain deeply disturbed by the events of 1966. They worry that something in Balinese culture must have allowed this tragedy to happen, and if so they would like to identify what it was. Others have a more straightforward interest in knowing exactly what happened to friends and relatives. Even at this late date, systematic research could clarify whether or not the estimate of 80 000 deaths was substantially accurate.

Counterbalancing this desire for the truth is a multifaceted fear of reopening old wounds, plus some concern that today's democracy might not be permanent. If authoritarian right-wing rule were to return to Indonesia, any evidence of pro-communist sympathy in the past could once again be a risky proposition. The picture is further complicated by calls for investigations into more recent human rights violations in East Timor, Aceh, Papua and elsewhere. Where to begin? Just how much probing in the name of truth and reconciliation, always a painful process, can any country be expected to endure? On balance, it is far from certain that we will ever achieve substantially better understanding of the 1966 Balinese killings.

9
DICTATORSHIP, DEMOCRACY AND THE EVOLUTION OF TOURISM (1966–2002)

After 1966, politics on Bali reverted to something approaching humdrum normalcy. The New Order of General Soeharto was to last 31 years, about the same length of time as Dutch colonial rule on the island. There were other resemblances as well. Like the Dutch, the New Order put primary emphasis on 'peace and order'. With the army clearly in charge, the violent factionalism that had marked the Sukarno years came to a halt. For over a decade Bali remained under the watchful eye of Governor Sukarmen, an army colonel of Javanese origin. But there was no sign of serious unrest, and in 1978 he was replaced by a Balinese, Professor Ida Bagus Mantra, a recognised authority on Balinese culture. Since then there have been no more non-Balinese governors.

The Soeharto regime was explicitly quasi-military in nature. The army, after all, had won the struggle of 1965–66, and it espoused a doctrine, the so-called 'dual function', which was at least as important as the sketchy Indonesian constitution of 1945. Dual function doctrine asserted military responsibility for oversight of political, social and economic affairs, as well as defence. Members of the armed forces were allocated a fixed share of seats in the People's Consultative Assembly (MPR) which formally elected the President. They were favoured for all kinds of government positions, from ambassadorships to sub-district chiefs.

A system of 'territorial' military administration, parallel to the civil structure, extended down to the village level. Dual function doctrine encouraged regional commands to engage in business to support themselves, a practice which had started during the Revolution when the army took over many former Dutch enterprises. One result was a pattern of inefficient and often predatory military capitalism which has continued to plague Indonesia down to the present.

However, the new system was implemented with a relatively light hand on Bali, if only because there was no need for jackboot tactics. Surviving left-wing Balinese politicians who might most have resented army rule disappeared from public life. Everyone was still in shock from the killings, and many Balinese were understandably grateful for the end of tumult. Military participation in local government was obvious but muted—for example, military retirees were often favoured for positions as village chiefs (lurah). On a more positive note, the army became directly involved in some local development projects. These supplemented a non-military, low-interest loan programme which stimulated cottage industries with export potential.

In fact, most of the New Order's trademark policy initiatives had nothing to do with the military, but were the result of growing technocratic emphasis on economic development. Supported by substantial foreign aid from the West and Japan, they included family planning and the introduction of high-yielding rice varieties. These two programmes, discussed at greater length below, were on the whole popular on Bali despite some elements of official encouragement verging on coercion.

Like the Dutch, the Soeharto regime yearned for a more orderly structure of local administration. In 1979 the national government passed a new Village Government Law. Had this law been applied rigorously on Bali, it would have replaced community selection of hamlet (*banjar*) leaders with administrative appointment by senior authorities, and thereby radically changed the nature of local government. Nothing of the sort happened, and the *banjar* remained a vital force in Balinese political life, often to the immense benefit of New Order programmes such as family planning. Other aspects of the 1979 law were only slowly and sporadically implemented. The confusion between differently defined 'administrative' and 'customary law' villages continued.

The next great watershed in Indonesian political history was the end of the New Order and the transition to democracy in the late 1990s. As was the case elsewhere, Balinese students turned out in the streets of Denpasar and demonstrated to support their colleagues in Jakarta and to call for reform. Their protests contributed to the national unrest, further fuelled by economic crisis, which led to the resignation of President Soeharto in May 1998. He was replaced by B.J. Habibie, who ruled until genuinely democratic parliamentary elections took place on 7 June 1999. Following those elections, the People's Consultative Assembly chose Abdurrahman Wahid, better known as Gus Dur, to be Indonesia's next president, and Megawati Sukarnoputri to be his vice president. Wahid was impeached for erratic behaviour in 2001 and Megawati succeeded him as president.

President Megawati was already popular on Bali because she is Sukarno's daughter and one-quarter Balinese. Her party, the Indonesian Democracy Party (PDI), is the lineal descendant of the old Nationalist Party (PNI) which had always been strong on Bali and had been the principal local opponent of the doomed Communist Party before and during the killings of 1966. The PDI was the front-runner locally in the 1999 elections, as it was nationwide. In general, the Balinese have appreciated and taken full advantage of Indonesia's democratic reforms, which began under President Habibie and have continued to evolve. The Balinese press is lively, and local elections are sometimes hotly contested.

On the whole, however, the political history of Bali since 1966 has been relatively insignificant compared to economic and social developments. Tourism has been the key issue, but important new environmental and land-use concerns have emerged as the result of tourism and accompanying economic growth. As the tourism boom accelerated, Bali changed from a relatively poor to a relatively rich province in the Indonesian context. As the old agrarian base receded in importance and upscale resorts replaced rice paddies, the debate among Balinese over the future of their civilisation intensified.

The dialogue on this subject has become pervasive to the point where it sometimes seems that to qualify as a Balinese intellectual one has to question relentlessly the premises of modernity and the meaning of being Balinese in a globalised setting. The shock of the 12 October 2002 terrorist bombing has added a new dimension to existing concerns about the risks and costs of economic success.

In order to understand the debate, we must first track the growth of tourism and efforts at both provincial and national levels to promote, manage and profit from it.

Tourism hits high gear

I first saw Bali in the early 1970s as a junior American diplomat. Frequently, then as now, high-ranking foreign visitors to Indonesia managed to break away form their official duties to visit the fabled island, and some of them never set foot in the national capital at all.

For Americans of cabinet level or above, our embassy in Jakarta would send a substantial party by road and ferry across Java to set up the necessary clerical, communication and security arrangements at the Bali Beach Hotel. It was still the only major hotel, although there were one or two bungalow-style facilities at Sanur, as well as the old Bali Hotel in downtown Denpasar and some rustic home-stay facilities at Kuta, still little more than a village and a beach. Upcountry in Ubud there was one small hotel, the former Walter Spies residence at Campuhan, while visitors with connections were sometimes lucky enough to be guests of the hospitable ruler of Ubud, Cokorde Gede Agung Sukawati, at his residence.

Among our more memorable official guests was John Connally, Secretary of the Treasury and former Governor of Texas, who dropped in on Bali for a rest stop late in 1971. Folksy and imperious in the Texas tradition, Connally was best known for having been with John F. Kennedy at the time of his assassination. He then switched parties, and by 1971 was being touted as a potential Republican candidate for president, making him very important indeed to us. He arrived on a US Air Force plane with a large party including many aides, Secret Service agents, his wife and children.

In those days diplomatic spouses were expected to be unpaid members of the embassy team, and my wife had been tapped to help organise a cultural programme. Knowledgeable Australian friends had just set up one of the first foreign-operated tourist agencies on Bali, and through them she was able to arrange a special dinner and dance-drama performance in the palace of a Balinese prince who had never done such a thing before.

Bursting with pride, we presented what we regarded as a once-in-a-lifetime opportunity to Connally's staff. But the secretary and his family decided at the last minute that they would rather relax at the hotel and enjoy the poolside buffet, leaving only a few embassy officials plus the plane crew to attend the performance in their place. The raja put on a memorable feast, the village children turned out in force, the *topeng* (masked dance) was exquisite, and as far as we could tell our VIP was not missed.

The next morning was set aside for sightseeing. A motorcade was duly assembled in front of the Bali Beach Hotel. It was made up of ageing Chevrolet sedans with big tailfins, which somehow seemed appropriate. But the Secret Service inspected them and told our tour agent friends the cars wouldn't do—all the tyres were bald. When informed that there were no better cars or treads on Bali, the head agent shuffled the cars around to save face, and off went the Secretary, his family and entourage for a highly successful tour of temples and art shops.

We did not realise it, but John Connally was on the leading edge of a tourism boom. Bali's reputation as an exotic destination had survived and flourished in the immediate postwar years, despite political unrest and the scarcity of hotels and other infrastructure. Hollywood and Broadway both had a hand in this, and Bali-hype grew sillier than ever.

The musical *South Pacific*, set in World War II New Hebrides (now Vanuatu), immortalised 'Bali Ha'i', a mystic island across the sea evoked by Bloody Mary in her song to the star-crossed young lovers. (Author James Michener, whose *Tales of the South Pacific* inspired the musical, rather unconvincingly claimed that Bali Ha'i was wholly fictional and had nothing to do with the real Bali.)[1] A Bob Hope–Bing Crosby film, *The Road to Bali*, showed the two stars and Dorothy Lamour cavorting in front of a fake Balinese temple. And Bali's bosomy image was further uplifted by the well-advertised, American-manufactured line of Bali bras.

After 1966 the new Indonesian regime continued Sukarno's proud promotion of Bali as a showcase of Indonesian culture. But now the door was open to private enterprise, both foreign and domestic. Even more important, Bali was again at peace. It was also an overpopulated agrarian island with a serious and growing problem of landlessness.

For Bali, tourism appeared to be a heaven-sent solution to the nationwide problem of inadequate employment and income. Its development was henceforth to receive strong support from the Indonesian government and international aid donors. Critics often point out that the Balinese people were not involved in the decision to promote tourism, at least not in a formal sense. But there is no evidence of local opposition to this policy, given the alternative of reliance on an increasingly overstretched agricultural base. From the beginning, most Balinese seem to have assumed that tourism could be managed so as to minimise cultural damage. No one fully foresaw the transforming impact of the economic change that was to follow.

By the early 1970s, Balinese communities were showing some signs of irritation over the rapidly growing influx of sometimes scantily-clad foreign tourists, even while they welcomed the increased income that resulted from tourism. This sign appeared near Klungkung in 1971. (Source: Robert Pringle)

On the eve of World War II, over 2000 foreign tourists a year were visiting the island. It seemed like a large number at the time. Figures are lacking for the Sukarno era (1945–66), but by 1969 the number had grown to 86 000, presumably in large part due to the opening of the government-built Bali Beach Hotel just before the change of regime. By 1974 the number had increased to 313 000, and it had doubled again by 1982 to 642 000. Foreign exchange earnings from tourism on Bali rose from US$10.8 million in 1969 to US$359 million in 1982.[2]

By 2002 approximately 1.5 million foreign tourists were visiting Bali yearly. So were approximately the same number of Indonesian tourists, according to the provincial government. They included large numbers of Javanese students who arrived in big buses which were much in evidence, especially at school vacation time, on the island's narrow and increasingly congested roads.

If Bali did not exactly become rich, it certainly prospered, relatively speaking. In 1980, the island's per capita income was two-thirds the national figure (US$308 compared to US$456). By 1990 the figure had risen to US$592 compared to US$560 for Indonesia as a whole. Between 1980 and 1990, Balinese real per capita income rose by 4 per cent annually.[3]

Tourism-based prosperity had many side-effects, one important example being the further evolution of education. Bali was traditionally a literate society, and the first Dutch official in north Bali estimated in 1859 that half the men and as many as one-fifth of the women there could read and write.[4] Subsequently, as we have seen, progress in education was slow until after independence. But by 1985, about 85 to 90 per cent of Bali's seven- to fifteen-year-olds attended school.

Higher education has undergone a similar expansion. Udayana University opened in 1958, initially (and aptly) as a branch of Airlangga University in Surabaya. Bali's best-known public university now draws many students from beyond the island, especially to its well-known medical faculty, its foreign-language departments and its non-degree programmes serving the tourist industry. Equally well known is Bali's leading performing arts college, the College of Indonesian Arts (STSI), which integrates traditional village-level performing arts with an academic curriculum. By 1997, Bali had about 30 institutions of higher learning, the majority of them private. Literacy is close to universal.

'Tourists for Bali—not Bali for Tourists'

This slogan, written in Indonesian on a banner across a remote rural road, was encountered by a foreign visitor in the mid-1970s. The visitor was heartened by the sentiment, but also somewhat mystified. At whom was the message aimed? If at foreign tourists, why was it in Indonesian, not English? If the target was Balinese, why wasn't it in Balinese? And why was it displayed in a remote area?

In fact, the slogan had resulted from a series of seminars sponsored by the provincial government in 1971 to deal with the already well-worn question of how to profit from and simultaneously preserve Balinese culture. Its message was aimed primarily at the national government in Jakarta. The seminars were stimulated by a 1971 proposal, written by French consultants but financed by the World Bank, which led to a 1974 master plan for tourism.

The plan decreed that major Western tourist development would henceforth be concentrated in two places: at Sanur, site of the Bali Beach Hotel, and in a new 425 hectare resort enclave to be developed at Nusa Dua, south of the airport. There were to be no more high-rise hotels like the Bali Beach—nothing was to exceed 15 metres, or the height of a coconut palm. It was hoped that this strategy would minimise the impact of development on the still relatively pristine south Balinese heartland.

Written as the tourist boom was just beginning, the master plan was based on what turned out to be false premises. It assumed that first-class international tourists would be the main threat to Bali's cultural heritage and did not anticipate the flood of budget travellers who were about to transform Kuta from village to neonised strip. It did not foresee the later development of domestic tourism, much less the secondary and tertiary economic spin-offs from tourism which could hardly be fenced into a limited area.

Nevertheless, the plan had a tremendous and largely successful impact. Over the next two decades a dozen new hotels were developed in a lavishly landscaped setting at Nusa Dua, along a spine of land looking down on attractive beaches hitherto home only to scattered fishing communities.

The new hotels all followed the low-rise style originally pioneered at Sanur, albeit executed on a much larger scale, incorporating many Balinese cultural features and surrounded by superb gardens. By the time they were built, thousands of Balinese were employed in the hotel and tourism sector. The skill, charm and enthusiasm which they brought to this new vocation were an important factor in the success story.

But before the carefully planned, capital-intensive hotels of Nusa Dua could be completed, they were upstaged by spontaneous development at Kuta, just to the north on the other side of the peninsula. The small hotels established there by Robert Koke and Ktut Tantri did not survive World War II, but the coconut palms and the beautiful rural setting did, for a time. So did the surf.

Kuta was ready and waiting when the tourist boom began, made to order for young backpackers arriving on the short air-hop from Australia and looking for budget rooms. There was initially no multinational investment here. Instead, Balinese villagers began opening shops and home-stays catering to the surfing crowd. If this trend did not quite fit the master plan, it was certainly a laudable example of local participation in economic development.

Slowly but inexorably Kuta's commercialisation accelerated. By the mid-1980s it was already creating sanitation and traffic problems. By the mid-1990s there were 4600 hotel rooms, all five-star, in Nusa Dua; 5000 rooms in Sanur, mainly five-star, and 17 600 rooms, most of them starless, in Kuta.[5]

As early as the 1970s Kuta had developed a reputation for relaxed, anything-goes-that's-fun ambience. Foreigners who equated Bali with toplessness or even nudity assumed that Kuta was the place to go 'native'. Initially the Balinese authorities found this troubling, and for a time signs appeared informing visitors that topless bathing was not allowed. A few people were even arrested. This did not last long. Soon Kuta offered everything, including drugs and drink and a wide variety of nightlife. It became a small, densely packed city of restaurants, karaoke bars, fast-food outlets, hotels and shops of all descriptions, even a bungee-jumping tower. As of 2002, before the bombing, there was still no high-rise development, but at least one powerful Balinese entrepreneur was said to favour it.

One trademark attraction was and still is male prostitution. Handsome young men, often from other areas of Indonesia, are available for lonely, middle-aged Western and Japanese women, or for younger groups of Japanese women known as SOLs (for 'single office ladies'). The so-called Kuta Cowboys live by their charm. They know that to demand money upfront would shatter the image of romance which, rather than raw sex, is their stock-in-trade. They have learned to depend on their clients to proffer what is right without being asked, be it cash or maybe a trip to Australia. Bali has thus far avoided the curse of a massive sex industry, of the kind that plagues some other Asian tourist destinations. HIV/AIDS cases are still relatively few in number, but there is justifiable concern that the disease could take off on Bali and elsewhere in Indonesia.[6]

Kuta was not the only tourist destination to experience radical change. Something similar, if more muted, happened in Ubud. As late as the 1970s, this epicentre of Balinese cultural evolution was still rural. The Cokorde's palace at Ubud's crossroads and its various temples followed a classic south Balinese pattern. In most places rice fields bordered the roads, except where (as at Campuhan) the ground breaks away into a steeply carved river valley. Art shops were already proliferating both in Ubud itself and in the densely settled adjacent regions. A few Balinese families were opening small restaurants and home-stays.

In time there was more substantial investment, initiated by the Ubud ruling family and other relatively wealthy Balinese, but increasingly by outsiders as well, whether foreign or Jakarta-based. There are now several luxury hotels, and it is possible for anyone to stay in the Cokorde's palace as a paying guest. As in many other parts of Indonesia, people have preferred to build small hotels and shops flush with the roads, creating unbroken façades which block the view of the rice fields on either side. By 2000, Ubud did not look or feel at all the way it had 30 years previously. It had become a small city.

The master planners' intention to concentrate tourism infrastructure in the south came under immediate pressure from other regions which felt left out. In response, in 1988 the governor proclaimed a 'Spatial Arrangement Plan' which authorised fifteen (eventually sixteen) new locations for tourist infrastructure and development. Among the first areas to be developed were Candidasa, on the coast near Karangasem, and another coastal resort area around Lovina in north Bali. In both cases prominent Balinese were instrumental in promoting the developments.

Large-scale tourism also spread to the ethnically Balinese west coast of Lombok, where magnificent temples and unspoiled beaches remained unvisited for years after major development on Bali itself. On Lombok, interests controlled by President Suharto's youngest son, Hutomo 'Tommy' Mandala Putra, were behind most of the new hotels.

By the early 1990s, two new trends in Balinese tourism were well underway. The first, little documented, was the development of a robust domestic tourist industry. It has been a boon to small business, because most Indonesian tourists patronise small hotels and eat at roadside stalls. But the habits of some can be as expensive as those of any foreigner. For the wealthiest of the Soeharto-era Indonesian elite, a trip to Bali to celebrate New Year's Eve became a must.

The second trend was toward high-end, capital-intensive investment sponsored by alliances between wealthy, politically prominent Balinese, other Indonesian capitalists, military and ex-military entrepreneurs, and the Udayana regional military command based in Denpasar. In 1995, journalist and scholar George Junus Aditjondro published a monograph entitled 'Bali, Jakarta's Colony', which highlighted the prominence of President Soeharto's family in numerous Bali tourist investments, from hotels to white-water rafting. Aditjondro, an Indonesian scholar resident in Australia, emphasised that Bali's tourist boom resulted from decisions in which the people of Bali had no say. He also cited social and environmental costs, from water shortages to the profanation of sacred sites.

In a national context of growing demands for political and economic reform, Balinese for the first time protested against a tourist project. The Meridien Nirwana Golf and Spa Resort, backed by a wealthy Jakarta-based conglomerate, overlooks the Tanah Lot temple, one of Bali's most holy. It is located on a formerly pristine stretch of

Tanah Lot temple, as seen from the Nirwana Resort and Golf Club. Construction of this resort, which opened in 1999, was delayed but not stopped by protests resulting from its proximity to one of Bali's holiest places and the displacement of farmers. The trestle-like structure in the background is being used to place giant concrete tetrapods to halt ocean erosion at the base of the temple. (Source: Robert Pringle)

the Tabanan coast, where rice terraces cascade down to the sea. The temple is clearly visible from both the golf course and the hotel lobby.

The resort was planned in 1991, but engendered years of objections from farmers who resented losing their land, from Hindus who believed it would violate a religious stricture against development close to a holy site, and from a group of sympathetic foreign scholars. Compromises eliminated some of the more egregious features, such as a spotlight which would have illuminated the temple at night for the benefit of hotel guests. The 1997 financial crash caused further delay, but the hotel opened under French management in 1999.

Tanah Lot is now besieged by tourists, both foreign and domestic, who come by bus and car to view it at sunset, requiring a large parking lot and stimulating a small city of food and souvenir stalls. The islet on which the temple sits is being undermined by Indian Ocean swells which crash picturesquely against its base, necessitating construction of an ugly if temporary trestle so that huge concrete pylons can be placed to block the surf. The surrounding rice fields are giving way to development, with the Nirwana resort complex being the closest and most obvious (but not the only) offender. The hotel has been cleverly designed to minimise its visibility from the temple, although not vice versa, and is arguably less obtrusive than the growing clutter of shops and stalls. Only the sea will remain as it was after the unavoidable anti-erosion construction work is completed. Tanah Lot has become a sad spectacle, and future generations, both Balinese and foreign, will probably regret that more effective measures were not taken to preserve both the temple and its natural setting.

Protests also erupted over plans to build a huge statue of the Hindu god Vishnu mounted on the mythical bird Garuda, just south of Bali's international airport. Announced in 1990, the monument was conceived by a Balinese artist resident in Bandung and is intended to appeal primarily to Indonesian, not foreign, tourists. The gold-plated Garuda will be 146 metres high, supposedly the world's tallest statue. Originally estimated to cost $83 million, it will include a complex of restaurants, a 700-seat amphitheatre, and yet another shopping mall. Stylistically it is the culmination of a trend toward large, often garish statues depicting Hindu-Balinese themes which have been in vogue for some time at town crossroads across the island.

For many Balinese intellectuals and foreigners, the great golden Garuda epitomises everything wrong with Bali today, especially uncontrolled development. For its promoters it demonstrates Indonesia's emergence from financial crisis, the diversity of Indonesian culture, and the blending of traditional values with the latest construction technology. Although stalled for a time by the 1997–98 economic slump, the project is now under construction, with strong support at both the national and provincial level.

The economic offspring of tourism

Sometime in the mid-1990s tourism overtook agriculture as Bali's leading economic activity. According to a Balinese economist, the total contribution of the tourism sector to provincial finances, including both income and investment, was 51.6 per cent in 1998. At the same time tourism was generating 38 per cent of Bali's formal employment.[7] These figures probably fall far short of capturing tourism's full importance because they do not include its impact on other sectors, or its spin-off effects.

By imprinting Bali on both national and international consciousness, tourism led to major new economic activity. Thanks to its world-class hotel infrastructure, the 'resort island', as it was now being called, became a regional gathering ground for conferences and meetings of all kinds. It also became a place where both foreigners and Indonesians like to do business, resulting in a remarkable surge in what amounts to entrepot trade activity.

For example, furniture is now manufactured in nearby Java, sent to Bali for final finishing and sale, and then sent back to the port of Surabaya in East Java for export to foreign destinations. Handicrafts from other parts of Indonesia as far away as Papua are shipped to Bali both for sale to tourists and for export, along with Balinese handicrafts. There has been similar impact on the important garment-manufacturing industry. Little of this economic activity is ascribed to tourism, yet without tourism it would not have developed.

Bali also became a political and financial safe-haven, especially for Indonesia's ethnic Chinese, who were traumatised by unprecedented anti-Chinese riots in Jakarta in 1998. (Contrary to what many non-Indonesians believe, the 1965–66 killings on Bali, Java, and to lesser extent elsewhere, were only marginally directed against ethnic Chinese.) Indonesian Chinese have invested or bought homes in Bali as a prudent alternative, 'a place where they can send the children at election time', as one observer told me. Whether the terrorist bombing of October 2002 will permanently affect this pattern remains to be seen. Some of these investments, often made in partnership with Hong Kong or Singapore Chinese, have been substantial. Others consist of little more than a structure which combines downstairs business space with upstairs family quarters. Known as '*rukos*' (for *rumah-toko*, or 'house-shop'), they are another cause of rapid urbanisation throughout south Bali. Other immigrants, less affluent, arrived in larger numbers to escape unrest elsewhere in the country or to seek employment generated by tourism and its side-effects. In late 1998, according to one source, at least 760 non-Balinese were moving to Denpasar monthly.[8]

Demographic trends: Family planning

The early phase of the tourism boom was accompanied by remarkable and positive changes in Bali's demographic makeup. By the early postwar years, the island appeared to be facing a Malthusian crisis. Population was spiralling upwards, outstripping locally grown rice supplies and forcing poorer Balinese to rely on less nutritious substitutes, mainly the starchy root known as cassava. Today, however, there are substantially fewer Balinese than was anticipated.

When the Dutch established full control over the island in 1908, it had a population of perhaps 750 000. In 1930 the population stood at 1 101 000. According to census figures, it had grown to 1 519 000 by 1957; to 2 100 000 by 1971; to 2 470 000 by 1980 and to 2 716 000 by 1991. Population density increased from 381 per square kilometre in 1971 to 500 per square kilometre in 1990 (dense indeed, but not quite as dense as East or Central Java)[9]. In the mid-1970s experts were predicting that the number would almost double by 2000, to 4.4 million.[10] Instead, the 2000 census recorded 3 147 000 inhabitants.

From 1950 to 1971, Bali's population grew at slightly less than 2 per cent per year. From 1980 to 1990 the growth rate was only 1.2 per cent, the third lowest for any Indonesian province. One reason for the declining rate of increase was an extraordinarily successful family planning programme.

Like the Javanese, many Balinese were aware by the 1950s that uncontrolled family size was no longer rational, but they did not know what to do about it. President Sukarno believed that there could never be too many Indonesians. He accepted the communist position that population control was a capitalist plot—the West was simply trying to keep the developing countries small and weak. His successor, Soeharto, was willing to listen to those who argued that Java and Bali were sinking beneath a burden of population growth which was making it impossible to provide a decent standard of living.

Bali's population growth rate had started to drop compared with the colonial period even before the fall of Sukarno. In 1961 a Dutch-trained chief medical officer and scion of the Karangasem royal family, Dr A.A. Made Djelantik, began an informal family planning programme with the help of a non-governmental organisation, Planned Parenthood International. The villagers proved extraordinarily receptive, and after 1966 the programme, now a national priority, continued to grow with assistance from international aid agencies. In the 1970s Balinese fertility dropped at the fastest rate of any province in Indonesia, while the number of Balinese accepting contraception was the highest. The method of choice was, and still is, the IUD.

Family planning experts credit the decision-making ability of the *banjar*, the lowest unit of local government, with Bali's success. 'The *banjar* were able to make a collective decision and then execute it', according to one Balinese familiar with the history of the programme.[11] While this is no doubt true, something similar happened in Javanese villages, which do not have *banjar*.

Did strong government support for family planning verge on coercion? Perhaps, but it seems clear that the majority of Balinese, exercising their preferences through their neighbourhood-based *banjar*, were strongly supportive of the programme. On both Java and Bali, widespread desire to reduce the burden of large families, at a time when fewer children were dying in infancy, appears to have been the critical factor. Today some estimate that population growth on Bali would be nearing replacement rate—meaning only sufficient growth to maintain the current population—were it not for the influx of non-Balinese attracted by job opportunities.

O Pioneers! Transmigration

'Transmigration' was another government programme designed in part to relieve overcrowding. Initiated by the Dutch shortly after 1900, and continued by both Sukarno and Soeharto, it aimed to relocate peasant families from overpopulated Java and Bali to the Outer Islands. The Dutch hoped it would also help develop remote provinces through the introduction of wet rice technology. Sukarno in particular believed it would further his nationalist aims by integrating the Outer Islands with Java.

During the Soeharto era, the World Bank supported transmigration for years, despite strenuous attack from critics who claimed, with some reason, that it was environmentally unsound, did not significantly slow population growth, and simply replicated Javanese (and Balinese) poverty elsewhere. Be that as it may, the Balinese programme achieved surprising success at both ends of the transfer process.

The earliest Balinese transmigrants had been exiled for political misbehaviour to Banda, a dry coral island in Maluku Province, renowned as the original home of nutmeg. They were unhappy and asked to be transferred to another location where they could farm. In 1906 the Dutch allowed them to move to Parigi in Central Sulawesi, a fertile, well-watered but under-populated area, in the hope that they would introduce their sophisticated methods of rice cultivation. Later they were joined by men guilty of marrying higher caste women. Under traditional Balinese law such individuals might have faced the death penalty. Instead the new Dutch rulers sent them to the wilds of Sulawesi.

The Parigi programme had a chequered history. The early migrants faced every conceivable hardship, including isolation, land disputes with the local population, disease, and almost constant political unrest during the Sukarno era. At one point many of them went home to Bali. Beginning in 1957, those who stayed were joined by an influx of several hundred Christian Balinese originally resettled by the Dutch in western Bali because of friction with their Hindu neighbours. In the early 1970s, the government's transmigration programme gathered momentum and more than 15 000 Hindu Balinese migrated to Parigi.

Some of the transmigrants were government-sponsored, meaning they received transportation, land and initial support from the Department of Transmigration. Others were volunteers, so-called 'spontaneous' transmigrants, who paid their own way and were supported by those who had preceded them. Some were farmers whose lands had been destroyed by the eruption of Gunung Agung in 1963, while others were fleeing violence and uncertainty after the 1966 killings.

As the earlier settlers on Parigi flourished, increasing numbers of Balinese followed them voluntarily. While the transmigrant communities around Parigi were initially dominated by Christians, they became strongly Hindu following the massive arrival of Hindus in the 1970s.

The Parigi case seems to have been broadly typical of Balinese transmigration. As with family planning, the organising ability of the *banjar* helped the Balinese to succeed, in this case as pioneers in a strange land. From 1953 to 1999 a total of 219 000 people left Bali as transmigrants, the largest numbers from Buleleng and Jembrana, for destinations in Kalimantan (Borneo), Maluku, Sulawesi, Sumatra, Sumbawa and Papua. Some undoubtedly returned home, but a large proportion remained, as witness the thriving communities they founded. The government-sponsored programme is now over, but a trickle of voluntary transmigration has continued.[12]

As hoped, the pioneers were able to replicate the complex irrigation technology of their home island. In general they have been eager to maintain ties with Bali, and to recreate and uphold Balinese culture.

Often, as soon as a transmigrant community is able to save enough money, it orders a gamelan orchestra to be made and sent from Bali so that a proper ceremonial life can begin. Today some migrants are even critical of what they see as a 'false prosperity' in their old home, dependent on outsiders and, in their view, increasingly divergent from Balinese tradition.[13]

Balinese agriculture transformed

If Bali now has fewer mouths to feed than was anticipated, it is also producing more rice to feed them. During the early 1970s, the International Rice Research Institute developed new high-yielding varieties of 'miracle rice'. The government introduced them throughout Indonesia with strong support from foreign aid donors. Combined with improvements in irrigation methods, the new varieties led to a 50 per cent increase in rice production between 1969 and 1982. Both Bali and Indonesia as a whole regained self-sufficiency in rice, regarded by most Indonesians as very desirable, regardless of whether or not some importation might make sense in purely economic terms. Bali began exporting rice to the rest of Indonesia.

The Green Revolution, as it was labelled, has nonetheless been a mixed blessing on Bali, as elsewhere. Despite higher yields overall, the new varieties turned out to be much less dependable, in part due to pest and disease problems, with heightened risk of wide variation in yield from one harvest to the next. The new rice has a pasty, insipid taste compared to traditional strains. Most important, the increase in yields is dependent on regular applications of chemical fertilisers and pesticides, which are an added expense for farmers.[14]

In the early 1970s, the government required farmers to switch to the 'miracle' varieties and pressured them to plant as often as possible, eliminating traditional fallow periods and the rotation of dry crops in the paddy fields. Government agents, backed by foreign advisors, dictated to farmers when they should plant and how fertilisers and pesticides should be applied, usurping both the function of the *subak* irrigation societies and the broader coordinating role of the water temples located at the volcanic lakes, Bratan and Batur.

One result was an upsurge of pest problems, which had traditionally been controlled by carefully timed crop rotation. After complaints from farmers supported by social scientists, the agricultural technicians began to allow the *subak* once again to help decide how the planting cycle should be managed. In the mid-1980s the government dropped its emphasis on continuous rice cultivation and began to encourage both fallow periods and rotation of dry crops such as soybeans and corn between the rice cycles. But overall the Green Revolution is still in place.

Critics wonder whether 'miracle' rice technology is sustainable over the long run. Traditional methods required no artificial imported fertiliser, although manure and other organic matter was applied. This plus natural nutrients generated by the rich stew of the paddy fields created a stable system in which soil fertility did not decline over time. Under the new system, the use of pesticides has a sterilising effect, killing many organisms other than those targeted. Some research has indicated that soil quality on Bali is now declining. And the application of large amounts of hydrocarbon-based fertiliser is overloading the rivers with phosphorus, potassium and nitrogen, contributing to the pollution of the streams themselves and degrading the coral reefs and shallow marine ecosystems offshore.

The result is one of several emerging environmental problems discussed in the next chapter. It is true that the new system of agriculture, dependent on heavy injections of energy in the form of fertiliser, is part of a worldwide phenomenon, as typical of American corn as it is of Balinese rice. If change is needed, it is needed everywhere, not just on Bali.

Today Balinese farmers are free to plant as they wish, normally by collective decision at the *subak* level, and approximately 5 to 10 per cent of the total crop once again consists of traditional varieties.

A complete reversion to pre-'miracle' methods would entail a substantial reduction of current rice production, and no one is suggesting that this is likely or even desirable. Most experts feel that the harmful side-effects of the Green Revolution can be mitigated by a middle-ground approach, including renewed respect for the value of traditional cultivation and water management technologies.

Bali's experiences with expanding tourism, family planning and the Green Revolution all demonstrated a new range of opportunities and attendant problems at the end of the twentieth century. As the new millennium dawned the island faced additional challenges, and would soon experience a shock unlike anything in its often turbulent past.

10
BALI IN THE TWENTY-FIRST CENTURY: NEW CHALLENGES, INCLUDING TERRORISM

On the evening of 12 October 2002, violent explosions tore through the most crowded area of the Kuta strip, incinerating two nightclubs frequented by young Westerners, mostly Australians. A third, much less powerful bomb exploded harmlessly several miles away near the modest US Consulate. The Kuta blasts killed at least 202 people, about three-quarters of them foreigners, of whom 88 were Australians. Suddenly, and for the first time in its history, Bali was front-page news around the world.

The Indonesian police, working as a team with Australians and a few Americans, made surprisingly rapid progress in the subsequent investigation. Good forensic work on the principal bomb-carrying vehicle led to an East Javanese suspect whose testimony rapidly led to others. It soon became clear that the radical Islamic organisation Jemaah

Islamiah was the main source of funding and operational support. Links to the al-Qaeda network seem almost certain. In a mid-November 2002 radio broadcast someone claiming to be Osama bin Laden took credit for the attack. He said it was aimed at Australia, but other sources have suggested that Americans were the main target. It is equally likely that the attacks were aimed against the West in general, as well as at the insufficiently Islamic Republic of Indonesia. Trials of 33 suspects began in June 2003, and two months later the first trial ended with the conviction of Amrozi, who was sentenced to death.

A Balinese police officer, Major General I Made Mangku Pastika, returned to Bali to head the investigation and rapidly achieved international star status for his frankness and professional demeanour. Pastika, the son of a primary school teacher, had once served with the United Nations in Namibia. More recently, in Papua, he had demonstrated a refreshing capacity for honesty and effectiveness in dealing with possible military involvement in high-profile killings. *Time* Magazine named him 'Asian Newsmaker of the Year' for 2002. Jakarta then appointed him to be police commander for all Bali, a clear recognition of his excellent leadership of the investigation and of the national importance of Bali in both symbolic and economic terms.

Bali's tourist industry, just recovering from the impact of the World Trade Center attack a year previously, was devastated. Hotel occupancy rates plunged to near single digits. Major hotels tried not to lay off workers, but thousands of small businesses were pushed to the brink of collapse.

Many observers feared that the damage would be compounded by a violent Balinese reaction against the local Muslim minority, which was almost certainly blameless. But the provincial authorities, from Governor Dewa Made Beratha on down, worked hard to prevent this, in part by mobilising the *banjar* network to warn against such violence, in part by sponsoring a series of cleansing and reconciliation rituals. Balinese Hindus believe that without proper observances the spirits of people killed remain abroad in the land, dangerous and malevolent.

Following the 12 October 2002 bombing in Kuta, the Balinese placed offerings and held ritual observances at the disaster site to cleanse it, to prevent dangerous behaviour by the spirits of the dead, and to promote reconciliation. The climax of this ritual process was a major ceremony on 15 November. (Source: AP/World Wide Photos)

The ceremonies required to ward off this danger were held in a way that underscored Bali's hard-won image as a sanctuary of harmony. The island's long experience with lethal natural disasters may have helped its people to cope on a spiritual level with this man-made cataclysm.

Before the Kuta explosion, the Balinese had assumed that their island was safe from terrorism, already looming as a problem elsewhere in Indonesia. They had apparently forgotten that in March 1985 a group of Islamic radicals based on Java, who had previously detonated a bomb at the Borobodur in Central Java, tried to send another bomb to Bali, possibly to Kuta. Before the bus the terrorists were on could reach the ferry across the Bali Strait, the bomb exploded, killing three of them. One crucial difference this time was that the accused perpetrators of the 2002 Kuta terrorism had been trained by veterans of the anti-Soviet *jihad* in Afghanistan and were far more technically proficient.[1]

The Balinese had been greatly annoyed when, in the aftermath of the World Trade Center attack, Western governments warned their citizens to stay away from Indonesia, without exempting Hindu Bali. In the months after September 11, Balinese taxi drivers routinely gave foreign clients polite but pointed lectures explaining the difference between safe, peaceful Bali and riot-prone Jakarta, coupled with expressions of hope that tourists would soon get over their overwrought reaction to 'Waytaysay' (WTC) and return to Bali in droves.

The traumatic impact of the totally unexpected bombing in Kuta was accordingly profound, and it is too soon to judge its long-term consequences. Some Balinese immediately pointed fingers at over-reliance on tourism and argued for a re-emphasis on agriculture. Indeed, the tragedy may well stimulate some healthy re-examination of the island's recent economic management. But for the moment the national and provincial governments, together with the private sector, focused on repairing the immediate damage.

Hotels and airlines offered deep discounts. A big cultural mission flew to Tokyo with the objective of reassuring the notoriously crisis-sensitive Japanese. Aid donors and private sources pitched in with emergency assistance. The national Minister of Tourism, himself a Balinese, took a diplomatic delegation around his home province, Buleleng. Plans to hold a series of international conferences on Bali were reconfirmed. New security measures were introduced at hotels, at the airport, and on the ferry from Java. Central government concern was understandable: Bali accounts for at least half of all national tourism revenue, and the tragedy dealt a big blow to Indonesia's already bruised political image.

Ten weeks after the bombing, President Megawati and other high officials came to Bali to celebrate New Year's Eve in style, and some of the big hotels at Nusa Dua were once again filled to capacity. The celebratory mood was abruptly jarred a few days later when President Megawati announced extremely unpopular national price hikes for hitherto subsidised fuel and utilities, with no exceptions for Bali. Moreover, no sooner had the impact of the bombing started to recede when Bali's tourism industry was hammered by the cumulative impact of the Iraq War and the SARS (Severe Acute Respiratory Syndrome) epidemic, leaving many hotels still struggling and small businesses in even worse shape. A United Nations survey conducted in mid-2003 found that average incomes across Bali had dropped by 40 per cent since the crisis began.

A whiff of paranoia

Assuming that the Indonesian government can respond effectively to the threat of terrorism nationwide, its impact on Bali will diminish with time. A happy outcome will depend on more than tough, effective sleuthing, however. Indonesia will need greatly enhanced capacity to deal wisely with separatism and ethnic unrest. Reform of the military, police and legal institutions is urgent. The Balinese can contribute in only a minor way to this national effort. But they also face a complex array of social, religious and environmental problems on their own island. Temporarily overshadowed by the Kuta tragedy, these challenges will remain alive and in need of attention. Some of them are urgent. And unlike terrorism, they can only be addressed at home.

Thus far the island has escaped the kind of ethnic turmoil that has plagued some other regions of Indonesia, but there have been a few disturbing indications that Bali might not be immune from the disease. For one thing, the Balinese seems to be increasingly anti-foreign. This does not mean they harbour sentiments against visitors from other countries who come to Bali for pleasure. Such people are seen as 'tourists', not foreigners, and by and large are regarded with mercenary affection.

'Foreigners' in the negative sense are other Indonesians who come to Bali to work and maybe to live. They include, for example, the Javanese farm labourers who work the rice harvests in south Bali, the local labour force being largely occupied in the hotel, handicraft and restaurant businesses. Matters are arranged so that these workers return to Java soon as the harvest is over. But many other people who come to Bali for employment remain there.

Anti-'foreign' sentiment has been reported among the increasingly prominent, *banjar*-based religious security police, or *pacalang*. These units were traditionally responsible for maintaining order at religious processions and ceremonies, but they can be quick to mete out vigilante justice to suspected criminals, and are sometimes prone to stirring up trouble with neighbouring *banjars*. They are a reminder of the paramilitary violence which plagued Bali during the Revolution and in the Sukarno era. That said, the *pacalang* turned out to be an asset following the Kuta bombing, as Bali struggled to strengthen local security.

Then there is the hardy perennial of angst about Balinese identity in a rapidly changing world. It centres around the reconciliation of tradition with modernity. How, for example, can a busy professional be expected to meet personal obligations as a member of a *banjar* which may be hours away from his or her place of employment? Yet *banjar* obligations, such as helping to prepare for funerals, lie at the heart of Balinese culture.

What about the role of the Balinese calendar, with its intricate guidance on when things should be done? How can this convoluted system dictate the activities of a businessman or tour operator? Yet if the way Balinese tell time—not *what* time it is, but what *kind* of time it is—is consigned to the ash heap of progress, some of the island's charm will go with it.

What about the substitution of money and modern technology for the painstaking labour that traditionally went into temple offerings? Already these offerings are often purchased at a neighbourhood offering stall, rather than being made by the devotee. The use of blowtorches has become commonplace as an aid to cremation, with the requisite equipment and fuel tank transported by pickup truck, the workers of course arrayed in proper customary dress.

Similar dilemmas have been faced by many other societies seeking to reconcile religious practices with the demands of modernity. And certainly the Balinese debate over modernity does not imply any diminution of religious vitality; quite the contrary. Any visitor will soon observe the active use of wayside shrines and household temples, even in the most urban of settings. The Kuta tragedy evoked new proof that Balinese Hinduism remains a potent force. But it is also true that the Balinese are experiencing a surge of anxiety, aggravated by the rapidity of social change, which is stirring up some old religious divisions, especially on the matter of caste.

The Hindu schism

The Parisada Hindu Dharma Indonesia (Indonesian Hindu Council), created at the time that Sukarno gave official status to Balinese religion, is more involved than ever before in trying to define what is acceptable Hinduism. For example, it has attempted to set guidelines for the creation of ogoh-ogoh, the huge papier-mâché monsters which are now paraded through the streets of Bali in Mardi Gras-like celebrations on the night before Nyepi. This occasion, often referred to as the Balinese New Year, must be preceded by an annual cleansing of evil spirits. On Nyepi Bali shuts down; by law no one is to work, tourists are not allowed outside their hotels and even the airport closes.

Nyepi was not legally recognised until 1983, and the huge papier-mâché ogoh-ogoh are a relatively new phenomenon. The Hindu Council would like all of them to reflect proper Hindu themes. But the Balinese youth who make them sometimes prefer ogoh-ogoh modelled on pop culture, equipped with cell phones, celebrating drugs and drink, or replicating Spiderman. The role of the monsters is after all to represent about-to-be-cleansed evil spirits in preparation for the New Year, and the kids argue that their creations are just as realistic as the orthodox models, whatever those might be. At the first Nyepi following the

Kuta bombing there was an *ogoh-ogoh* depicting Amrozi, one of the accused terrorists. Perched on his shoulder was the demon-sorceress Rangda, goading him to do unspeakable things.

For several years the Hindu Council has been at the centre of a much more serious dispute over what kind of priests should be allowed to officiate at ceremonies. Until recently, customary practice gave an important role in some ceremonies to priests from the important non-caste clans which have roots going back to the Old Bali kingdoms. But in recent years the high-caste priests, tracing their descent and authority to the Majapahit invaders from Java, have attempted to improve on custom by asserting that only they are legitimate.

The dispute sharpened when, in September 2000, the non-caste group succeeded in taking over the central, all-Indonesia Parisada Hindu Dharma, issued decrees legitimising a role for all priests, regardless of caste, and even recommended abolition of the entire caste system. The high-caste group retaliated by seizing control of the provincial council on Bali and disavowing the decisions of the national council. Things began to get heated, and a December 2001 press report in the *Jakarta Post* was headlined 'Balinese Hinduism on the Brink of Violent Conflict'.

The headline may have been overblown. However, anyone familiar with Bali's history can understand why this contretemps is potentially more serious than disputes in European or American Christian churches over such matters as the ordination of homosexuals and women. Arguments about social status on Bali have often really been about political power and all too frequently settled by bloodshed. Moreover, the current disagreement has sharpened old resentments on the part of non-caste Balinese intellectuals, which were being debated in the provincial press as long ago as the 1930s.

Interestingly enough, the non-caste leaders have been able to bolster their case by reference to ancient Indian texts, pointing out that the oldest Hindu scriptures say nothing about caste. For this and other reasons, Balinese Hindus are increasingly travelling to India as religious tourists. The controversy has generated volumes of coverage in the provincial press and is not settled at this writing.

Religious tolerance on Bali

Interfaith relations, traditionally excellent, have eroded somewhat, particularly between Hindus and the small (about 2 per cent) Christian minority, divided fairly evenly between Catholics and Protestants. By its nature Christianity is a proselytising religion, and some of the Balinese churches have offended Hindu sentiment by (among other things) using Hindu terminology in their liturgy, apparently in an effort to attract converts.

Because Christian communities tend to be ethnically Balinese, there is likely to be tension when Christians neglect customary obligations centred around temples and other predominantly Hindu institutions. This was apparently the cause of anti-Christian rioting in the upland town of Kintamani in 2001, when Hindus attacked and burned the residences of several of their Christian neighbours.

The majority of Muslims, by contrast, are 'foreigners', that is, non-Balinese Indonesians, although some have been on Bali for a very long time. They have rarely attempted to proselytise and the majority of conversions to Islam have come about through marriage. Although their proportion of the population has more than doubled since colonial times, to just under 10 per cent, Bali's Muslims have usually remained in discrete communities and do not seem to be regarded as a threat by the majority of Hindus.

Mutual tolerance is partly a matter of familiarity; as noted in an earlier chapter, some Islamic communities on Bali are hundreds of years old. Moreover, the older Muslim communities have a history of syncretic accommodation with their Hindu neighbours, extending even to the use of Balinese motifs in the pulpit carvings found in some old mosques. However, the Kuta bombing undoubtedly placed a new strain on

Hindu-Muslim relations. Until Bali recovers from terrorist-induced recession, the danger of anti-Muslim violence will persist.

The arts: Still lively...

Well before World War II, Western observers were predicting that commercialism would swamp creativity and ruin Bali, at the same time that they were overlooking the poverty, landlessless and lack of social services that were the flip-side of their idyll. We have seen, however, that Balinese art, music and drama, essential to the island's appeal, have all demonstrated a remarkable aptitude for change, whether or not Western observers approved. The same pattern has continued under new circumstances.

The fundamental fascination of the Balinese for their own culture is alive and well. The melodic crash of urban gamelan music, from a *banjar* ensemble gathering for regular evening practice, is still intriguing, for all that the musicians must now compete with the noise of traffic on nearby streets. As the agrarian sector waned, tourism and the growth of service industries injected large sums of money into the Balinese economy. This strengthened the economic foundation necessary for a rich cultural life and helped to maintain traditional pride in Balinese culture, now linked with economic well-being. As in the 1930s, not everyone is enthralled by the results in their entirety. But, on balance, money and pride intermingled have been a stimulus to artistic activity.

Both old and new forms continue to abound and proliferate. At last count, there were about 35 types of gamelan extant on Bali. *Jegog*, an ancient type of bamboo orchestra from West Bali, had fallen into decay by the 1930s, but now has been revived as a tourist attraction. The *ogogogoh* phenomenon described above is an example of recent innovation. Balinese culture continues to find new and spontaneous expression, from cartoon magazines to dump trucks adorned with *barong* paintings.

Robust state sponsorship has played a part. In 1961, a high school for the performing arts elaborated a new dance-drama form called *sendratari*, in which a narrator seated with the gamelan orchestra relates the story while dancers act it out in pantomime. A new one is created each year for the annual Bali Arts Festival.

Community troupes still produce dramatic performances of high quality for tourists. It continues to be true, as Margaret Mead noted decades ago, that a Balinese ceremony financed by outsiders is not necessarily deprived of genuine religious content, even when it happens on schedule three times a week. Much traditional culture is televised, although there is concern about the consequences of endlessly repeating dramatic performances removed from their traditional village settings.

No doubt some homogenisation and poor quality is inevitably resulting from commercialisation. The key question for Balinese artists is still, as it was in the 1930s, whether this negative impact outweighs the positive stimulus of economic support. Controversy continues. A few years ago, the students of the leading Balinese art institute in Denpasar embarrassed their school president by turning a major painting exhibit into a noisy protest against the rampant commercialisation of Balinese art. Yet Bali's annual Arts Festival, initiated by the province in 1979 primarily to stimulate tourism, was immediately popular among the Balinese themselves and has remained so.

… but is it sustainable?

If Bali's cultural soul moved into the second millennium in remarkably good health, the same cannot be said for Bali's physical body. The island is plagued with environmental problems of many kinds, virtually all of them the result of too many people combined with increasing affluence, the downside of the economic success story. As noted, Green Revolution agriculture is degrading soils and overloading Bali's streams and coastal waters with chemical pollutants, raising the question of whether the new farming methods are sustainable over the long run.

There has been enormous, human-induced physical change, the majority of it in the last 50 years. Bali's Indian-derived civilisation was born on an island which was still largely uninhabited and mostly under forest. Except for remnants in areas which are either too high, too dry or too rugged for agriculture, the last significant old-growth forest was cleared long ago. The most extensive wild area, the West Bali National Park, on land which falls in the 'too dry' category, is experiencing management problems similar to those which plague other national parks in Indonesia.

Arid as it is, the west is no longer empty, and the tigers which once prowled the highway from Denpasar to the ferry landing at Gilimanuk had disappeared by World War II. Meanwhile Bali's woodcarving industry has become a major consumer of exotic wood from elsewhere in the archipelago, much of it illegally harvested.

Bali was originally surrounded by coral reefs, the same reefs that provided heaven-sent shipwrecks to be plundered by the local rulers. Today this colourful underwater habitat has suffered heavy damage from villagers who mine the coral to make lime for cement and, together with fishermen from other islands, use explosives and poisons for fishing. This is especially unfortunate at a time when tourist interests are trying to promote diving and snorkelling as one more reason for a Balinese vacation.

The odds are stacked against any effective conservation effort. There are still too many poor Balinese living near the reefs, and it is hard for them to abandon any activity that will provide some income. In the early 1990s an expatriate began a project to persuade north Balinese villagers to try ecotourism instead of dynamite fishing by hosting divers and snorkellers. He finally gave up under threats from the local population and decided to develop horse-riding instead.

In addition, most of Bali's coral reefs are exposed to the full impact of rising ocean temperatures caused by global warming, which have been damaging and in some cases killing reefs across the Pacific. Those near Nusa Penida, off the south coast, are about the only ones bathed by

SAVE OUR LAST TURTLE
SELAMATKAN PENYU YANG SEMAKIN LANGKA

The World Wide Fund for Nature has successfully campaigned to end Bali's role
as a regional market for sea turtle meat, and enlisted the support of the tourist industry
to safeguard the few remaining turtle nesting sites on Bali. (Source: World Wide
Fund for Nature Wallacea Program, Denpasar)

upwellings of cold water, without which experts feel that preservation efforts, always an uphill battle, are likely to be futile. Elsewhere, along the heavily travelled coastal route between the airport and Sanur, the elimination of mangrove habitat is causing salt water to invade the water supply in this most populated area of the island.

As anywhere else in the world, environmental issues stir passionate debate, especially when conservation clashes with customary behaviour. Such has been the case with sea turtles. Readers of Colin McPhee's pre-war classic A House in Bali may recall references to the consumption of turtle kebabs (saté) on ceremonial occasions. The turtle figures prominently in Hindu mythology as the foundation on which earth itself rests. Turtle shell was used to make valuable handicrafts and, as tourism developed, turtle meat even appeared on hotel menus.

As a result of this dietary preference, Bali became a regional hub for the sea turtle trade. Turtles were being imported from all over eastern Indonesia, kept live in pens at the Balinese port of Benoa, then sold for local consumption or re-exported. On Bali itself, coastal development has eliminated many of the beaches suitable for use as nesting areas by the light-sensitive creatures.

Enter the World Wide Fund for Nature (WWF), with a programme based on Bali to help save the globally endangered sea turtles in Indonesian waters. In 1999 the Fund persuaded Governor Beratha to issue a decree shutting down the turtle trade. Pro-turtle forces appealed to the Balinese to make their ceremonial kebabs from something else. Duck meat was suggested, the duck being another creature esteemed in Balinese culture. The result was strenuous protest from the turtle traders, the great majority of whom were not from Bali, but just doing business there. In November 2000, the angry traders organised a march on the WWF offices in Denpasar. They chanted, 'If we can't eat turtle meat, we'll eat you instead.'

Understandably alarmed, the Balinese director of the WWF turtle programme appealed to Governor Beratha, who defused the situation by personally receiving the demonstrators. However, he stood behind his turtle decree, several of the traders were jailed, a prominent Hindu cleric supported the ban on trade, and the turtle pens at Benoa went out of business. Now the project has set aside a strip of Balinese coast where WWF is paying local fishermen, formerly turtle hunters, to protect nesting turtles, while distributing publicity at hotels encouraging tourists to support its efforts.

The turtle episode was a skirmish won in a war which is generally being lost. It was manageable because there were no powerful interests arrayed against a favourable outcome. The really big battles revolve mainly around land use and are far more problematic.

'Bali makin jelek'

My taxi was crawling through traffic in Denpasar, surrounded by the usual swarm of motorcycles. As one foreign scholar observed, the provincial capital has changed in recent years 'from a noisy but comfortable small town to a wildly getting out of hand metropolis whose long fingers grab out along the highway in all directions all over the island'.[2]

The taxi driver wondered out loud what could be done about the traffic. Maybe, he suggested, the government should build elevated freeways, as in Jakarta (which in spite of them has some of the most ghastly traffic in the world). At one point he observed, *'Bali makin jelek.'* It means, 'Bali is getting ugly.'

The idea that Bali, of all places, should be getting ugly, not just in a few areas, but generally ugly, still comes as shock. But although much remains beautiful, there is no doubt that uglification is beginning.

Despite the slowing of population growth, Bali is ever more crowded. The population density of the province is five times the national average, exceeded only by Central and East Java. Moreover, today's increasingly affluent Balinese take up a lot more space than their parents did. Urban sprawl extends from the provincial capital into the south Bali heartland and beyond. From Sanur to Karangasem one is rarely out of densely congested areas. Glorious views of rice terraces carved from the long volcanic slopes are increasingly obscured by houses and shops.

To escape one must go to the eastern end of the island, or high on the flanks of Gunung Agung, where the kind of scenery commonplace on Bali 30 years ago remains accessible. Toward the sea, around the most famous cultural centres—places like Mas, Batuan, Pejeng, Bedulu and dozens more—much of the development is directly tourist related—art galleries, handicraft manufacturers and outlets for their products. But elsewhere, as much or more commercial activity serves Balinese or other Indonesian markets. There is a long strip which sells

A Balinese view of the hazards of urban sprawl, by cartoonist Surya Dharma.
(Source: *Surya Dharma*)

nothing but bamboo furniture, another specialising in stone carving (very few tourists go home with large stone carvings), yet another devoted to pottery, and so on. Everywhere there is incessant new construction.

One result is that Bali is losing irrigated rice land at an accelerating rate. In the mid-1980s an Australian ecologist calculated that the rate of loss was about one per cent a year, and it has certainly gone up since then. The erosion of Bali's agriculture is a symptom of either economic success or overdependence on tourism, depending on how you look at it. But it could, by contributing to uglification, damage the very foundation on which tourism rests.

A related problem is water. Famous for its verdant, sculptured landscape, with rivulets trickling from every crevice, all artfully channelled and managed, south Bali was saturated literally and spiritually with water. But now the heavily urbanised south faces an imminent water crisis. Badung, the district around Denpasar, will soon need to import water from other districts. The *subak* societies, charged with managing irrigation, are willy-nilly being drawn into disputes with city-dwellers and businesses. In one recent case a group of *subak* in Badung cut off water to a municipality because their farmer members did not have enough to grow rice.

Bali's uncontrolled development puts at risk a vital relationship between culture, aesthetic appeal and natural surroundings. Aesthetic appeal was and to a large extent remains the bedrock foundation of Balinese tourism. As discussed earlier, the artists, social scientists and globetrotters of the 1930s were attracted by a high culture, richly endowed with artistic creativity, set in a magnificent rural setting. Although Balinese culture derived from one of the great traditions of Asia, there was nothing like it elsewhere. Early observers worried that the culture would be destroyed by exposure to outside influence, but foresaw no threat to the physical setting—what today we call the environment. It can now be safely concluded that they had it pretty much backwards.

We cannot be absolutely sure that environmental degradation will ruin Bali's resort industry. Tourist motivations no doubt vary by nationality and age. The Western aesthetes who dominated pre-war tourism are now a minority. In 2001, Japanese were the most numerous foreign tourists, followed in descending order by Australians, Taiwanese, British, Germans and Americans. The Kuta surf-and-nightlife crowd is presumably less interested in Balinese culture than is the educated, middle-aged constituency staying at five-star hotels. Asians may be more partial than Dutch to karaoke bars, and so on.

But in general, and despite all the uncertainties, it is safe to conclude that Bali's attraction will diminish if the island develops a reputation for incipient physical ugliness. There are, after all, good hotels, beaches, nightclubs and golf courses in many other places in Asia and beyond. What Bali has that the others do not is the same cultural and aesthetic heritage that first made it famous.

As this suggests, the island requires a determined, coherent land-use regime. It would be based on the premise that the preservation of

219

Bali's landscape, including its water resources, is a fundamental provincial and national interest for long-term economic reasons. There are plenty of precedents elsewhere in the world for land-use regimes of this nature in areas of great historic or cultural interest. But on Bali the only land-use rule which has been respected up to now is the old one restricting the height of buildings to 15 metres, the approximate height of a coconut palm.

Meanwhile, some of the rules that do exist are generally ignored. Although it is still technically illegal for foreigners to own land on Bali, the prohibition is widely circumvented by building houses and leasing the land they stand on. According to one estimate there are now about 5000 expatriate landholders on Bali, and trendy expatriate bungalows are all the rage in the prime scenic areas of the south.[3]

The cynical conclusion, which appears almost universal among the Balinese, is that money can buy anything. That viewpoint is no doubt exaggerated. There is evidence, for example, that Balinese communities, acting at either the *banjar* or the customary village level, can sometimes bring effective pressure to bear on local development initiatives when they feel that customary law is being violated. In one case in 1997, the governor of Bali, Ida Bagus Oka, withdrew his support from a controversial coastal resort development in which his family had interests after his own village threatened him with expulsion for transgressing local custom.[4]

But the speed with which the overdevelopment problem has arisen, plus the factionalism of Balinese society, has made concerted action on a wider scale difficult. And, as anywhere else, Balinese elites are divided between an intelligentsia which is becoming quite sensitive to the dangers of uncontrolled physical development and a business community more interested in making money.

Some Balinese—how many is not clear—will welcome the proposed expansion of the Benoa port, or perhaps the construction of a new port in north Bali which would require road links across the already environmentally stressed interior of the island. Some may even support the construction of a bridge to Java, announced in 2002 as an objective by President Megawati, although the Kuta bombing (staged from Java) will make many others think twice about it, and the current governor of Bali is flatly against it. All these projects will be strongly opposed by other Balinese on environmental grounds and as fundamental threats, not only to tourism, but to the island's embattled identity as a place of beauty.

An optimistic Balinese proponent of developmental moderation told me it was like the classic battle between 'good' Pendawa and 'evil' Kurawa families in the Indian-origin *Mahabharata* epic, a mainstay of the shadow puppet theatre repertory on both Java and Bali. The Kurawas are more active, more numerous and have more physical assets. The Pendawas are slower to mobilise, wiser and more subtle, and in the end they win. Perhaps this is true, but time is running out.

The challenge of decentralisation

Until quite recently, critics often blamed Bali's more controversial tourism-related projects on the absence of democracy. As noted above, under the Soeharto regime alliances between the first family, the military and business interests, both foreign and domestic, were behind many big hotel developments. They were not sensitive to popular opinion. In the case of the Tanah Lot (Nirwana) project, for example, it proved easy to stifle or ignore grassroots opposition.

Today the political process is very different. The provincial governor is indirectly elected by the provincial legislature (DPRD), although he (or potentially she) is still subject to presidential confirmation. The heads of the districts (*kabupaten*) are also indirectly elected by their local assemblies. The provincial and district assemblies are elected by popular vote, as is the national parliament. In 2004 Indonesia's president, until now chosen by the People's Consultative Assembly (MPR), will also for the first time be directly elected.

The system has many flaws, on Bali as elsewhere, but no one denies that it is increasingly democratic. Thus far, however, the new provincial democracy has had little visible impact on development issues. Meanwhile Bali, along with the rest of the country, is faced with the new and troubling challenge of decentralisation.

In 1999, Indonesia's parliament passed decentralisation legislation which gave great but ill-defined powers, as well as new financial resources, to the country's 357 district and city governments. In theory, the powers devolved include all major categories except police, judicial, monetary, religious, defence and foreign affairs. The law responded to widespread agreement that a healthy democracy in Indonesia would require the abandonment of the old, highly centralised system and a greater degree of local participation.

Under the old system, provincial governors and regional military commanders, both in fact responsible only to Jakarta, were the key figures in local power structures. District heads were appointed, often from the ranks of the military. But under the 1999 law, not yet fully implemented, sweeping new powers would go directly to the districts, and the 27 provinces would be largely bypassed.

Many observers immediately concluded that Jakarta was practising divide-and-rule tactics; it did not want to devolve power to the provincial level because it feared this kind of decentralisation might stimulate additional secessionist movements similar to those in Aceh and Papua. Proponents of the reform countered that most of the provinces are artificial creations without ethnic or historic rationale, and that the districts and cities are therefore a sounder basis for local autonomy.

Because the powers being transferred have not yet been well defined, decentralisation has led to considerable confusion. Some districts aggressively seized the initiative, going so far as to impose new taxes on inter-district commerce or to claim control over maritime traffic. Confusion or not, two-thirds of the national civil servants formerly paid by Jakarta have already become the responsibility of the districts and cities.[5] Since 2001 the districts have received cash subsidies from Jakarta to cope with this new responsibility, but they predictably complain that the money is not sufficient.

Everyone agrees that it will be a long time before the districts have the necessary expertise to cope with their new authority, however it may eventually be defined. The government of Megawati Sukarnoputri, which took office in 2001, has added to the confusion by signalling that it will be less enthusiastic than its predecessor about giving away central authority and by launching a very slow review of the entire decentralisation process.

Decentralisation is particularly interesting in Bali because its nine districts are for the most part identical to the nine traditional kingdoms. (Denpasar, once the capital of Badung, now has separate status as a municipality.) This might raise the spectre of resurgent dynastic rivalry were it not for the fact that historically the most lethal Balinese factionalism rarely coincided with the chronically unstable kingdoms, but was manifested at lower levels of the political process.

Some of the poorer districts—those with minimal returns from the tourist bonanza—quickly saw decentralisation as an opportunity to make up for lost time. The district head of Buleleng, for example, announced plans for an exclusive resort and a cable car in the middle of the island, near Buleleng's border with Tabanan.

Cynics may wonder whether chaotic competition among districts could be any more damaging to the island's environment than what is already happening in south Bali. But most Balinese seem convinced that regardless of the track record to date, the small island needs an integrated planning capability, not nine rival jurisdictions each out to maximise its own benefit. The governor has pointed out that many issues are not amenable to district-level control, one example being the administration of the mother temple, Besakih, which serves all Balinese. He has created a unit to refine a provincial policy on decentralisation. Jakarta has asked all the provinces to submit recommendations and the provincial government of Bali hopes that it will be able to persuade Jakarta to give it the coordinating authority it needs.

Up to this writing, many Balinese have remained dubious about the whole thing. 'Let's not have a policy that will hurt the Balinese people,' remarked one.[6] Another commented, 'Suddenly, local officials feel they have new power and authority to do whatever they want. Small-scale tyrants are everywhere.'[7] Bali is hardly anticipating either economic ruin or civil war as a result of decentralisation, if and when it is fully implemented. But the outcome of the undertaking may determine whether the island can manage its challenging environmental and social agenda in the years ahead.

Conclusion

As this is written, the island province of Bali stands as an economic and political success story. It has found a significant place in the disorderly, democratic Indonesia of 2003. Tourism and its spin-offs have made the province relatively prosperous compared to many others. Bali's economy expanded robustly in the 1970s and '80s and for much of this period its growth was almost 10 per cent a year, 2 percentage points higher than the national economy.[8] The growth rate slowed in the downturn of 1997–98, and Bali remains far from wealthy in absolute terms. There are still many very poor people, tourism revenue is concentrated in the south, and the growth process has increased the gap between relatively rich and relatively poor.

Nevertheless, and not withstanding the need for better environmental policy, it is unlikely that many Balinese would want to turn the clock back to the overcrowded, underfed agrarian blind alley of the past. They are in general fiercely proud of what they have accomplished, viewing their progress as primarily the result of their own hard work, whatever the role of outside capital and national policy may have been.

Individual Balinese are playing a vigorous role in the Indonesian state. They have a higher percentage of positions in the military than their share, less than two per cent, of the national population. They continue to succeed as officials, businessmen and artists in the broader national context. From an Indonesian perspective, Bali remains a source of pride both as a lucrative source of foreign exchange and as a show-case of Indonesian culture.

The Balinese are not too worried about being a Hindu island in a sea of resurgent Islam. They realise, as foreign observers often do not, that their Hindu-animist culture may be closer to the syncretic brand of Islam espoused by most Javanese, hence by most Indonesians, than is the fundamentalist, *jihad*-prone variety professed by an extremist minority. In other words, the Balinese are more in tune with the polit-ical and cultural mainstream of Indonesia than religious nomenclature suggests. They sense that Megawati Sukarnoputri is their kind of Muslim, just as her late father was. Of course they were traumatised by the Kuta terrorism, but they also realise, cold comfort though it may be, that the problem is indeed worldwide.

For more than 70 years, outsiders have been warning that Bali is on the verge of ruin, one way or another. It still isn't true. The envi-ronmental problems are serious, but by no means beyond the capacity of the island's talented population to solve. Hopefully the Balinese will use their new, as-yet evolving democratic institutions to do so. The threat of terrorism, which emerged so tragically on 12 October 2002, will have to be addressed primarily at the national level, but the Bali-nese have already demonstrated that there is much they themselves can do at the local level.

Terrorism aside, today's challenges are after all the side-effects of an economic success which would have amazed and perhaps even pleased the pessimists of yesteryear. None of the environmental and land-use issues are unique to Bali. They are for the most part variations on a global challenge: how to achieve sustainable development, defined as using natural resources without destroying them and thereby denying future generations the opportunity to do the same.

Bali's economic resource base happens to be dominated to an unusual degree by cultural and aesthetic content. But the beauty and creativity which have made the island famous depend as never before on a carefully nurtured environmental foundation. Creating public policy and private investment based on that premise is easy to propose, but extremely difficult to implement. It is without doubt the greatest challenge facing Bali today.

11
SOME CLOSING
THOUGHTS

What conclusions can be drawn from the history of Bali? What is unusual, what worth remembering about this one province of a far-flung island republic? What are the most important themes in Bali's history? What are the issues which, if better understood by a new generation, might help them to deal with the future?

Bali's history has its share of intriguing questions and 'what ifs', and a number relate to the pre-colonial period, where evidence is often very thin. One of them is the reason for the survival of Balinese Hinduism. As discussed in Chapter 3, the conventional explanation is not, in my view, persuasive.

Another durable riddle is the radical divergence between the characters of Javanese and Balinese culture, especially in matters of aesthetics and organisational behaviour. Again in my view, history does not shed any more light on this subject than it does on the stylistic differences between the French, the Italians and the English, but the subject needs more research.

More recently, Bali has been fortunate at a number of key points. Freedom from direct European control in the seventeenth and eighteenth centuries spared Bali the worst excesses of colonialism and shaped its subsequent development. Bali is lucky to have possessed no spices, no precious minerals, no wide expanses of land suitable for plantation agriculture, or other enticements which might have drawn the Dutch in sooner, and with heavier hands.

The delayed arrival of colonialism meant that it came to Bali with a guilty conscience, in the form of a local variation of the Indonesia-wide Ethical Policy. On balance, its positive aspects outweighed its considerable failings. The Dutch have not often received high marks for their governance in the Indies, but their policy of protecting Bali from disruptive intrusion, including large-scale European investment and missionary activity, was preferable in hindsight to any conceivable alternatives. Like other colonial powers, the Dutch were parsimonious with social services, including health and education, yet what they did provide became the basis for independence. The central paradox of Dutch rule was that in their eagerness to preserve, they were sometimes driven to invent what they concluded *ought* to have existed. In so doing, they ended up making significant and sometimes unfortunate changes. From the vantage point of 2002, their 'reform' and strengthening of the caste system is probably the most important example.

Partly because of fortuitous timing and colonial restraint, Balinese civilisation came to be recognised as something special, a kind of hot spot in the world's cultural landscape. The Western artists and social scientists who visited between the two world wars publicised this heritage, and it rapidly emerged as Bali's most important economic asset as well. Nothing similar happened in other parts of Indonesia and there are few parallels elsewhere in the world. As a result, physical modernisation has paradoxically imperilled the basis of the modern Balinese economy, while the rapid pace of change is making rational responses to developmental and environmental policy issues particularly difficult, yet essential.

Bali has been a success story in the Republic of Indonesia at many levels. All Indonesian governments have regarded Bali with pride as a showcase of national culture. Relations between Denpasar and Jakarta have been correct if not always cordial both before the development of tourism, when the island was a financial liability, and more recently, when it has been an asset to the centre. It is true that since independence Bali, until recently, has had little control of its own destiny, yet at no time have there been symptoms of severe unrest, much less of secessionist sentiment.

From a political perspective, Balinese culture seems almost a mixed blessing. It combines cohesiveness with divisiveness, a passion for status with a yen for democracy, sparkling humour with morbid fear—the list of apparently contradictory traits could be extended. But one thing is certain—the Balinese sense of pride in being Balinese is very strong, and all the overblown rhetoric about Balinese creativity should not obscure its reality. This creativity will continue to be a tremendous asset in dealing with future challenges of all kinds.

The Balinese are passionately interested in their own history insofar as it affects personal or community status and power. It is not clear whether beyond academia they are especially interested in history as a source of social truth or as a guide to future policy, in Santayana's sense that ignorance of history dooms us to repetition of past mistakes. Like everyone else, the Balinese people would profit from more attention of this kind to history. As a case in point, it seems high time to deflate the mythology of Majapahit origins, which does no justice at all to the first half millennium of Balinese history, functions as a defence of the caste system, and is therefore a source of considerable antagonism.

Caste itself remains a big problem, as the Balinese are well aware. Perhaps the time will come when they find another way of measuring personal status, as all people do in one way or another, and modify or abandon the misleading terminology of caste. Although Bali's past is full of unanswered questions, it seems clear from the historical record that the modern caste system is largely a product of colonial rule. If so, there is little reason to preserve it in the name of tradition.

Another area that needs more attention is the study of the earliest periods, prehistory and Old Bali (the term I have used to cover events from the adoption of Indian religion to the Majapahit conquest). There is plenty of talent available on Bali and elsewhere to pursue more research in these fields, but few people recognise their importance and there is accordingly little money available. A better understanding of their ancient past would help the Balinese sort through the problems that beset them today. Aside from that, the history of the Old Bali kingdoms is fascinating in its own right, and has been unduly neglected since the departure of the Dutch.

The bloody events of 1965–66 remain unsettling to many Balinese, with reason. Although there is growing interest in analysis of the killings and some relevant research is underway, it is still difficult to penetrate the phobias that surround this subject. It is to be hoped that the necessary work can be done before those who were present are all deceased. Better understanding could help dispel the perverse notion that such violence is somehow inherent in Balinese character and that it is likely to resurface in the absence of strong authoritarian government.

The Balinese have recently been handed a hot potato in the form of an ill-defined decentralisation policy. On Bali as elsewhere in Indonesia, empowering local jurisdictions seems essential to achieve sustainable democracy, but devolving authority to the level of the old kingdoms may not be prudent given the urgent need for harmonisation of land-use issues on this small island. Some degree of provincial authority will be essential, whether it is proffered by Jakarta or, more likely, must be elaborated by the Balinese themselves. Perhaps the issue will have been solved by the time this book is published, but that seems unlikely.

Few Balinese seem to have much patience with the foreign penchant for discussing Bali in sweeping terms—has it been spoiled, or worse, and so on. What does interest them, and what they debate endlessly among themselves, is the kind of modulated change which will be necessary to allow cultural requirements and the demands of modern life to coexist. At times it almost seems as if the Balinese are unaware that they are not the only ones faced with conflict between tradition and modernisation, made more acute when tradition has ongoing economic value. The same dilemma is, for example, faced in many areas of Europe, where tourism is equally dependent on careful management of aesthetic and environmental capital. While few solutions are perfect, and none are easy, there is ample evidence elsewhere that such challenges can be met and mastered, with adequate attention to the well-being of future generations.

Terrorism has now cast another shadow over Bali's future. Yet there is every reason to believe that the Balinese will be able to surmount this challenge, much as New Yorkers and others are doing. For outsiders, Bali will remain a literally wonder-full place to experience. But it can only be appreciated, not as a false paradise, but as one particularly fascinating example of humans struggling to maintain a unique heritage while deriving advantage from what the world has to offer.

Glossary

Adat Customary law, from Arabic.

Anak Agung Royal title often bestowed by the Dutch.

Babad Balinese history or chronicle.

Banjar The lowest level of civic organisation, often translated 'ward' or 'hamlet'.

Barong Benevolent, lion-like figure prominent in Balinese ritual, representing the forces of 'good'.

Brahmana The highest caste category, from which priests and senior advisers to kings, and occasionally royalty, were drawn.

Candi Funerary monument where deceased monarchs of the Old Bali period were memorialised and worshipped.

Cili Stylised image of the rice goddess Dewi Sri.

Cokorde Royal title.

Controleur The equivalent of a district officer in the Dutch colonial service.

Desa Village. Bali has two types; the customary village (*desa adat*) and the formerly government-mandated 'service' or official village (*desa dinas*); they do not necessarily coincide.

Gamelan Percussion orchestra consisting primarily of gongs and xylophone-type instruments; also refers to the type of music played by such an orchestra.

Gandrung Flirtatious, sometimes bisexual male dancers.

Gde or Gede Big or large, used as a status-elevating modifier.

Gusti Title indicating *wesia* status, the lowest order of caste or nobility.

Ikat Tie-dyed fabric.

Janger Dance done in rectangular format, which in the 1930s became a vehicle for satirical depiction of foreigners.

Jegog   Bamboo orchestra and accompanying dance, disappearing in the 1930s but recently revived.

Kabupaten   Administrative district on modern Bali.

Kawi   Old Javanese language, considered sacred on Bali, the vehicle for much traditional literature.

Kebiar   Variety of music which evolved in north Bali in the 1920s; also the dance which accompanies it, done from the waist up in a sitting posture.

Kecak   'Monkey dance', a chattering male chorus originally used in ritual *sanghyang* trance dance. In the 1930s an expanded *kecak* chorus was integrated with the *Ramayana* story to create a new dance-drama form, now a standard tourist attraction.

Kepeng   Strings of Chinese copper coins used as currency.

Kris   Wavy-bladed dagger, sometimes with magical properties.

Lamak   Decorative palm-leaf panel used in temple festivals.

Legong   Famous dance for young girls.

Lontar   Palm-leaf material used to write on.

Lurah   Government-appointed village headman.

Mekel   Official who mobilised manpower to serve the palace.

Nyepi   A festival at the beginning of the Balinese year, before which evil spirits must be cleansed away.

Nyupat   To volunteer for execution.

Ogoh-ogoh   Papier-mâché monsters paraded through the streets on the eve of Nyepi.

Pacalang   Unofficial community-based security units.

Padmi   Highest ranking wife of a monarch.

Pandé   High-status descent group of iron and gold smiths which is not part of the caste system.

Pasek   Term sometimes used for all high-status clans or descent groups which predated and are not part of the modern caste system.

Pemaksan   Temple membership or congregation.

Pemuda   Youth, especially radical young supporters of the Indonesian Revolution.

Perbekel   Royal official charged with mobilising manpower; later, Dutch-appointed Balinese village official.

Punggawa   District chief.

Puputan   Literally 'finishing'; a desperate last stand against overwhelming odds, sometimes suicidal.

Pura   Temple.

Puri   Palace.

Raja   Ruler or king.

Rangda   Witch or sorceress (literally 'widow') who represents malevolent forces in Balinese legend and drama, often in opposition to the benevolent Barong.

Regent   An Indonesian ruler holding authority under the Dutch.

Sakti   Supernatural power.

Sanghyang   Kind of trance dance.

Saté   Meat kebabs.

Satria   Second ranking (after *brahmana*) caste category, in India the warrior caste; on Bali associated with kings.

Sedehan   Royal official who collected taxes and managed irrigation.

Sendratari   Type of dance-drama which evolved in the early 1960s; from the Indonesian words *seni* (art), *drama* (drama) and *tari* (dance).

Stamboel   Dance style of the 1930s with comical European features.

Stedehouder   Another term for an Indonesian ruler holding authority under the Dutch, implying somewhat more autonomy than 'regent'.

Subak   Irrigation society.

Sudra   Those without high-caste status; often translated 'commoner'.

Topeng   Masked dance.

Triwangsa   The three high castes: *brahmana*, *satria* and *wesia*.

Wayang   Puppet theatre often based on the Indian-origin *Mahabharata* epic, popular on both Bali and Java.

Wesia   Third of the three high-caste categories; the merchant caste in India, on Bali more typically associated with officials.

Notes

Chapter 1　A snug little amphitheatre

1. Clifford Geertz, *Negara: The Theatre State in Ninteenth-Century Bali*, Princeton University Press, Princeton, 1980, p. 20.
2. The term 'favored trading coast' is from O.W. Wolters, *Early Indonesian Commerce: The Origins of Srivijaya*, Cornell University Press, Ithaca, 1967, p. 196.
3. Margaret Mead, 'The arts in Bali' in *Traditional Balinese Culture*, ed. Jane Belo, Columbia University Press, New York, 1970, p. 333.
4. Clifford Geertz, *Person, Time and Conduct in Bali: An Essay in Cultural Analysis*, Cultural Report Series No. 14, Yale University Southeast Asian Studies, New Haven, 1966, p. 47.
5. Clifford and Hildred Geertz, *Kinship in Bali*, University of Chicago Press, Chicago, 1975, p. 30.
6. Geertz, *Negara*, p. 48.
7. Henk Schulte Nordholt, *The Spell of Power: A History of Balinese Politics*, KITLV Press, Leiden, 1996, p. 152.

Chapter 2　Moonset at Pejeng

1. This point is based on conversation with Balinese prehistorian I Wayan Ardika.
2. Marx-Engels letter, 14 June 1853, Marx-Engels Internet Archive, www.marxists.org

Chapter 3　From Indianisation to the Majapahit Empire

1. J.C. van Leur, *Indonesian Trade and Society*, W. van Hoeve, The Hague, 1955, p. 98.

2. John Miksic, *Borobudur, Golden Tales of the Buddha*, Periplus, Singapore, 1990, pp. 34–35.
3. W.F. Stutterheim, *Indian Influences in Old-Balinese Art*, The Indian Society, London, 1935, p. 12.
4. Georges Coedès, *Les états hindouisés d'Indochine et d'Indonésie*, Editions E. de Boccard, Paris, 1964, p. 239 (author's translation).
5. Stutterheim, *Indian Influences*, pp. 28–29.
6. O.W. Wolters, *History, Culture and Region in Southeast Asian Perspectives*, Institute of Southeast Asian Studies, Singapore, 1982, p. 16.
7. Sembiran C inscription, cited in I Wayan Ardika, 'Archaeological Research in Northeastern Bali Indonesia,' PhD Thesis, Australian National University, 1991, pp. 258 ff.
8. Headhunting on Java and Bali is discussed in Theodore G.Th. Pigeaud, *Java in the Fourteenth Century*, Martinus Nijhoff, The Hague, 1962, Vol. III, p. 127; Vol. IV, pp. 358–59.
9. Coedès, *États hindouisés*, pp. 220, 248fn; Lawrence Palmer Briggs, *The Ancient Khmer Empire*, Transactions of the American Philosophical Society, Philadelphia, 1951, p. 148.
10. Stutterheim, *Indian Influences*, p. 36.
11. Barbara Lovric, 'Bali: Myth, magic and morbidity' in *Death and Disease in Southeast Asia*, ed. Norman G. Owen, Oxford University Press, Singapore, 1987, pp. 123–25.
12. Stuart O. Robson, *Desawarnana (Nagarakertagama) by Mpu Prapanca*, KITLV Press, Leiden, 1995, p. 59.
13. ibid., p. 82.
14. Pigeaut, *Java in the Fourteenth Century*, Vol. IV, p. 255.
15. Claire Holt, *Art in Indonesia: Continuities and Change*, Cornell University Press, Ithaca, 1967, p. 85.
16. Henk Schulte Nordholt, *The Spell of Power: A History of Balinese Politics*, KITLV Press, Leiden, 1996, p. 23.
17. Clifford Geertz, *Negara: The Theatre State in Nineteenth-Century Bali*, Princeton University Press, Princeton, 1980, p. 16.
18. ibid., p. 14.

Chapter 4 The Balinese state to the eve of Dutch control

1. Henk Schulte Nordholt, *The Spell of Power: A History of Balinese Politics*, KITLV Press, Leiden, 1996, p. 68.
2. ibid., p. 125.
3. Quoted in ibid., p. 87.
4. Quoted in ibid., pp. 86–87.
5. ibid., p. 154.

Chapter 5 The Dutch arrive

1. James A. Boon, *The Anthropological Romance of Bali, 1597–1972: Dynamic Perspectives in Marriage, Caste, Politics and Religion*, Cambridge University Press, Cambridge, 1977, p. 10.
2. Geoffrey Robinson, *The Dark Side of Paradise: Political Violence in Bali*, Cornell University Press, Ithaca, 1995, p. 22.
3. From Dutch records in the Indonesian archives cited by Henk Schulte Nordholt, *The Spell of Power: A History of Balinese Politics*, KITLV Press, Leiden, 1996, p. 41.
4. ibid., p. 43.
5. Henk Schulte Nordholt, 'The Mads Lange connection: a Danish trader on Bali in the middle of the nineteenth century: broker and buffer' *Indonesia*, 32, Oct. 1981, p. 19.
6. M.C. Ricklefs, *A History of Modern Indonesia Since c.1200*, 3rd edn., Stanford University Press, Stanford, 2001, p. 107. (I have substituted 'Company' for 'VOC'.)
7. Cited in Alfons Van der Kraan, 'Bali: Slavery and slave trade' in *Slavery, Bondage and Dependency in Southeast Asia*, ed. A. Reid, University of Queensland Press, St Lucia, 1983, p. 335.
8. Willard Hanna, *Bali Profile: People, Events, Circumstances, 1001–1976*, American Universities Field Staff, New York, 1976, p. 14.

9. Thomas Stamford Raffles, *The History of Java*, Black, Parbury & Allen, London, 1817, Vol. II, p. ccxxxvi.

10. ibid., p. ccxxxi.

11. Ludvig Verner Helms, *Pioneering in the Far East, and Journeys to California in 1849, and to the White Sea in 1878*, W.H. Allen, London, 1882, pp. 70–71.

12. Adrian Vickers, 'Ritual written: The Song of the Ligya, or the Killing of the Rhinoceros,' in *State and Society in Bali: Historical, Textual and Anthropological Approaches*, ed. Hildred Geertz, KITLV Press, Leiden, 1991, p. 92–93.

13. Hanna, *Bali Profile*, p. 33; for a somewhat different version see Nordholt, *The Spell of Power*, p. 163.

14. Cited in Nordholt, *The Spell of Power*, p. 163.

15. ibid., p. 160fn.

16. Hanna, *Bali Profile*, p. 73.

17. Clifford Geertz, *Negara*, pp. 11, 13.

18. Personal communication with Henk Schulte Nordholt; in *The Spell of Power: A History of Balinese Politics*, KITLV Press, Leiden, 1996 he estimates total *puputan* deaths at 'more than a thousand' (*Spell*, p. 214).

19. Personal communication with Henk Schulte Nordholt.

20. Margaret Wiener, *Visible and Invisible Realms: Power, Magic and Colonial Conquest in Bali*, University of Chicago Press, Chicago, 1995, p. 327.

Chapter 6 Pax and poverty Neerlandica

1. The term is from James A. Boon, *The Anthropological Romance of Bali, 1597–1972: Dynamic Perspectives in Marriage, Caste, Politics and Religion*, Cambridge University Press, Cambridge, 1977, p. 149.

2. H. van Kol, *Uit Onze Kolonien*, A.W. Sijthoff, Leiden, 1903, p. 465 as cited in Willand Hanna, *Bali Profile: People, Events, Circumstances, 1001–1976*, American Universities Field Staff, New York, 1976, p. 89.

3. V.E. Korn cited in Geertz, *Negara: The Theatre State in Ninteenth-Century Bali*, Princeton University Press, Princeton, 1980, p. 68.

4. Henk Schulte Nordholt, *Bali: Colonial Conceptions and Political Change, 1700–1940*, Erasmus University, Rotterdam, 1986, p. 40.

5. V.E. Korn quoted in Nordholt, *ibid.*, p. 42.

6. Cited in Geoffrey Robinson, *The Dark Side of Paradise: Political Violence in Bali*, Cornell University Press, Ithaca, 1995, p. 53, n. 7.

7. Willard Hanna, *Bali Profile: People, Events, Circumstances, 1001–1976*, American Universities Field Staff, New York, 1976, p. 95.

8. Willard Hanna, *Bali Profile*, p. 99; see also Robinson, *Dark Side*, p. 54 for further information on opium revenue.

9. Henk Schulte Nordholt, *Bali: Colonial Conceptions and Political Change, 1700–1940*, Erasmus University, Rotterdam, 1986, p. 47.

10. The entire discussion of coinage is drawn from ibid, pp. 97–98.

11. Nordholt, *Bali: Colonial Conceptions*, p. 41.

12. ibid., p. 46.

13. Robinson, *Dark Side*, p. 33.

14. Nordholt, *Bali: Colonial Conceptions*, p. 36.

15. ibid., p. 47.

16. ibid., p. 47.

17. Cited in Robinson, *Dark Side*, p. 41.

Chapter 7   The world discovers Bali

1. Cited in Tilman Seebass, 'Change in Balinese musical life' in *Being Modern in Bali: Image and Change*, ed. Adrian Vickers, Yale Southeast Asia Studies, New Haven, 1996, p. 79.

2. Miguel Covarrubias, *Island of Bali*, Alfred A. Knopf, New York, 1936, p. xvi.

3. The notion of van Kol as 'first tourist' along with the discussion of his stay is drawn from Willard Hanna, *Bali Profile: People, Events, Circumstances, 1001–1976*, American Universities Field Staff, New York, 1976, pp. 83ff.

4. ibid., p. 87. Hanna, p. 86, also refers to von Kol's observation about Karangasem's overpopulation.
5. ibid., p. 105.
6. A.A.M. Djelantik, *The Birthmark: Memoirs of a Balinese Prince*, Periplus, Hong Kong, 1996, pp. 129–30.
7. Gregor Krause, *Bali 1912*, Pepper Publications, Singapore, 1998, p. 55.
8. Seebass, 'Changes in Balinese musical life,' p. 79.
9. ibid., pp. 87–88.
10. Covarrubias, *Island of Bali*, p. 251.
11. Quoted in Ruud Spruit, *Artists on Bali*, Peplin Press, Amsterdam, 1995, p. 61.
12. Hanna, *Bali Profile*, pp. 122–23.
13. Margaret Mead, *Letters from the Field 1925–1975*, Harper & Row, New York, 1977, p. 171; Gregory Bateson and Margaret Mead, *Balinese Character: A Photographic Analysis*, New York Academy of Sciences, New York, 1942, p. 263.
14. First quoted in Frank Clune, *Islands of Spice*, E.P. Dutton, New York, 1942, p. 319.
15. Jane Howard, *Margaret Mead*, Simon & Schuster, New York, 1984, p. 196.
16. Margaret Mead, *Blackberry Winter: My Earlier Years*, Simon & Schuster, New York, 1972, p. 229. The quotation has also been rendered as 'excessive' ritual, possibly drawn from a different version in archival sources (see Adrian Vickers, *Bali: A Paradise Created*, p. 121) but 'expressive' makes better sense in the context of Mead's other comments on the subject.
17. Mead, *Blackberry Winter*, p. 230.
18. Mead, *Letters from the Field*, p. 161.
19. Bateson and Mead, *Balinese Character*, p. xiii.
20. Mead, *Letters from the Field*, p. 191.
21. ibid., p. 160.
22. Bateson and Mead, *Balinese Character*, p. 47.

23. ibid, p. 36.
24. Mead, *Blackberry Winter*, p. 231.
25. Beryl de Zoete and Walter Spies, *Dance and Drama in Bali*, Faber & Faber, London, 1938, p. 2. The reference to 'mixed race' is puzzling.
26. ibid., p. 45.
27. ibid., pp. 211ff.
28. Hans Rhodius and John Darling, *Walter Spies and Balinese Art*, Tropical Museum, Amsterdam, 1980, p. 77.
29. Paul Morand, 'Bali, or paradise regained,' *Vanity Fair* (New York), May 1932, p. 40.
30. Clune, *Islands of Spice*, p. 315.

Chapter 8   Occupation, revolution and bloodbath

1. M.C. Ricklefs, *A History of Modern Indonesia Since c.1200*, 3rd edn, Stanford University Press, Stanford, 2001, p. 276.
2. Geoffrey Robinson, *The Dark Side of Paradise: Political Violence in Bali*, Cornell University Press, Ithaca, 1995, pp. 171–72; for a different account of Anak Agung Gde Agung's career, focusing mainly on his undoubted diplomatic achievements, see Willard Hanna, *Bali Profile: People, Events, Circumstances, 1001–1976*, American University Field Staff, New York, 1976, pp. 118–28.
3. Hildred Geertz, *Images of Power: Balinese Paintings made for Gregory Bateson and Margaret Mead*, University of Hawaii Press, Honolulu, 1995, pp. 18–19.
4. Robinson, *The Dark Side*, p. 158.
5. ibid., p. 15.
6. Cited in ibid., p. 186.
7. ibid., p. 207.
8. ibid., p. 254. My account of land reform is based on Robinson's *The Dark Side*, Chapter 10.
9. ibid., p. 27.

10. Henk Schulte Nordholt, *State, Village and Ritual in Bali*, VU University Press, Amsterdam, 1991, p. 20.
11. Ricklefs, *A History of Modern Indonesia*, p. 340. On 2 October, two days after the generals were killed, the PKI newspaper in Jakarta published an editorial praising the rebel movement. Like virtually everything else about the affair, this aspect remains controversial.
12. John Hughes, *Indonesian Upheaval*, student edn, Fawcett, New York, 1967, pp. 151–2.
13. Robinson, *The Dark Side*, p. 301.
14. Marshall Green, *Indonesia: Crisis and Transformation, 1965–68*, Compass Press, Washington DC, 1990, pp. 59–60.
15. Cited in Robinson, *The Dark Side*, p. 296.
16. Ricklefs, *A History of Modern Indonesia*, p. 348; information on relatively fewer detentions on Bali is from personal communication with Geoffrey Robinson.

Chapter 9 Dictatorship, democracy and the evolution of tourism

1. Hugh Mabbett, *The Balinese*, Pepper Publications, Singapore, 2001, p. 113.
2. Tourism statistics are drawn from I Nyoman Erawan, *Parawisata dan Pembangunan Ekonomi (Bali Sebagai Kasus)*, Upada Sastra, Denpasar, 1994; *Bali 97, Bali Tourism Statistics*, Bali Government Tourism Office, Denpasar, 1997; and interviews with the provincial tourism office.
3. Carol Warren, *Centre and Periphery in Indonesia: Environment and Human Rights in the Regional Press*, Working Paper No. 42, Asia Research Centre, Murdoch University, July 1994, p. 14n.2.
4. Lynette Parker, 'The introduction of Western-style education to Bali: Domination by consent?' in *To Change Bali: Essays in Honor of I Gusti Ngurah Bagus*, eds Adrian Vickers and I Nyoman Darma Putra, *Bali Post*, Denpasar, 2000, p. 49.

5. Putu Suasta, 'Between holy waters and highways' in *Bali Living in Two Worlds*, eds Urs Ramseyer and I Gusti Raka Panji Tisna, Museum der Kulturen, Basel, 2001, p. 39.
6. See 'Seven housewives infected with HIV/AIDS in Bali,' *Jakarta Post*, 2 Dec. 2002.
7. Figures are from I Nyoman Erawan, 'Keparawisataan dan Otonomi Daerah,' unpublished ms, Denpasar, 2001.
8. Suasta, 'Between holy waters and highways' in Ramseyer, *Bali Living in Two Worlds*, p. 44.
9. Census figures are rounded from Indonesian Government census reports.
10. Willard Hanna, *Bali Profile: People, Events, Circumstances, 1001–1976*, American Universities Field Staff, New York, 1976, p. xii.
11. Interview with Dr Dewa N. Wirawan, Denpasar, 6 March 2002.
12. History of transmigration is from Gloria Davis, 'Parigi: A Social History of the Balinese Movement to Central Sulwesi, 1907–1974', unpublished PhD dissertation, Department of Anthropology, Stanford University, 1976. More recent statistics are courtesy of the provincial government transmigration office in Denpasar.
13. I Gusti Made Sutjaja, 'Where's the real Bali? Transmigration and the transmission of culture,' *Latitudes*, Vol. 7, August 2001, p. 76.
14. For a critical analysis of the Green Revolution on Bali see Sean Foley, 'Rice Cultivation in Bali: An Energy Analysis,' honours thesis, School of Environmental and Life Science, Murdoch University, 1979.

Chapter 10   Bali in the twenty-first century

1. Background on the group which perpetrated the 1985 bombings and its relationship to Jemaah Islamiah are explored in the International Crisis Group report, 'Al-Qaeda in Southeast Asia: the Case of the "Ngruki Network"', 10 Jan. 2003, at www.intl-crisis-group.org.

The abortive 1985 attack on Bali is also described in court records of the verdict from the trial of the Borobodur bombers, consulted courtesy Sidney Jones of the International Crisis Group.

2. *Bali Living in Two Worlds*, eds Urs Ramseyer and I Gusti Raka Panji Tisna, Museum der Kulturen, Basel, 2001, p. 11.

3. Eric Ellis, 'Why I bought a home in Bali,' *Financial Times*, 10 August 2002.

4. Carol Warren, 'Adat and the discourses of modernity in Bali' in *To Change Bali: Essays in Honour of I Gusti Ngurah Bagus*, eds Adrian Vickers and I Nyoman Darma Putra, *Bali Post*, Denpasar, 2000, pp. 7–8.

5. Bert Hofman and Kai Kaiser, World Bank, 'The Making of the Big Bang and its Aftermath,' paper presented at a conference, 'Can Decentralization Help Rebuild Indonesia,' Atlanta, Georgia, May 1–3, 2002.

6. Agus Astapa, 'Jangan ada Kebijaksanaan yang Rugikan Masyarakat Bali,' *Bali Post*, 21 December 2001.

7. Rita A. Widiadana, 'Bali demands a greater share in autonomy era,' *Jakarta Post*, 27 December 2001.

8. Sisira Jayasuriya and I Ketut Nehen, 'Bali: Economic growth and tourism' in Hal Hill ed., *Unity and Diversity: Regional Economic Development in Indonesia since 1970*, Oxford University Press, Oxford, 1989, p. 332; Angela Hobart, Urs Ramseyer and Albert Leemann, *The People of Bali*, Blackwell, Oxford, p. 219.

Selected further reading

Bali's international allure has generated a flood of writing. It began with chronicles and poems by the Balinese themselves. Then came travellers' tales and studies by colonial administrators. Today there is prolific discussion of contemporary topics by both foreign and Balinese authors, including those who publish in the very lively local press. David Stuart-Fox's *Bibliography of Bali: Publications from 1920 to 1990* (KITLV Press, Leiden, 1992) has over 9000 entries. By now the number would no doubt be over 10 000. No other province of Indonesia has been bathed in so much ink, and no short guide to further reading can do more than scratch the surface. What follows is restricted to publications in English. Those interested in Dutch and Indonesian language writings should refer initially to the excellent bibliographies in *Negara* by Clifford Geertz, *The Spell of Power* by Henk Schulte Nordholt and *The Dark Side of Paradise* by Geoffrey Robinson, all cited at greater length below, as well as to the Stuart-Fox bibliography.

General works

A number of books illuminate the island's entire past and present, sometimes brilliantly. These are my choices of the very best among them: those I would want if marooned at the South Pole with only six books about Bali. Henk Schulte Nordholt, *The Spell of Power: A History of Balinese Politics* (KITLV Press, Leiden, 1996) is the best book written thus far on Balinese history. Clifford Geertz, *Negara: The Theater State in Nineteenth-Century Bali* (Princeton University Press, Princeton, 1980) provides a different perspective on the same subject matter, along with a juicy dose of the author's verbal and theoretical pyrotechnics. Beryl de Zoete and Walter Spies, *Dance and Drama in Bali* (Faber & Faber, London, 1938), with its elegant prose and luminous photographs, sometimes badly reproduced in reprint editions, is the most memorable literary product of the 1930s. Miguel Covarrubias, *Island of Bali* (Alfred Knopf, New York, 1937), another 1930s classic, combines sympathetic ethnography with great illustrations by the author and his wife. Geoffrey Robinson, *The Dark Side of Paradise: Political Violence in Bali* (Cornell University Press, Ithaca, 1995) fills an enormous gap in our knowledge of the troubled years culminating in the killings of 1966. A.A.M. Djelantik, *The Birthmark: Memoirs of a Balinese Prince* (Periplus, Hong Kong, 1997) is a charming and informative memoir by a prominent Balinese prince and public servant.

Merle Ricklefs, *A History of Modern Indonesia since c.1200* (3rd edn, Stanford University Press, Stanford, 2001) is a thorough, reliable source on the Indonesian historical context. Willard Hanna, *Bali Profile: People, Events, Circumstances 1001–1976* (American Universities Field Staff, New York, 1976) is a very readable history of Bali to the early 1970s. Of the many photographic books on Bali one stands out: Leonard Lueras (ed.), *Fire: A Journey of the Balinese Soul* (Yayasan Sekar Manggis, Gianyar, 1994). Sponsored by the Gianyar royal family to record a lavish cremation ceremony held in 1992, this spectacular volume is out of print and hard to find, but well worth a trip to your nearest rare book library.

Chapter 1   A snug little amphitheatre

For background basics, W.F. Wertheim et al., eds, *Bali: Studies in Life, Thought and Ritual* (W. van Hoeve, The Hague, 1960) remains indispensable; begin with the introduction by J.L. Swellengrebel and don't miss the contributions by Roelof Goris and C.J. Grader. Hildred and Clifford Geertz, *Kinship in Bali* (University of Chicago Press, Chicago, 1975), is the best account of social organisation. J. Stephen Lansing, *The Balinese* (Harcourt Brace College Publishers, Fort Worth, 1995), is another excellent overview of Balinese culture. Fred B. Eiseman, Jr, *Bali: Sekala and Niskala: Essays on Religion, Ritual and Art* (Periplus Editions, Berkeley, 1989), and the same author's companion volume,

Bali: Sekala and Niskala: Essays on Society, Tradition and Craft (Periplus Editions, Berkeley, 1990), comprise a potpourri of essays, including one of the few discussions of Bali's Chinese community. Thomas Anton Reuter's *Customs of the Sacred Mountains: Culture and Society in the Highlands of Bali* (University of Hawaii Press, Honolulu, 2002) is the definitive work on the Bali Aga, including analysis of their role in Old Balinese history. David Stuart-Fox, *Pura Besakih: Temple, Religion and Society in Bali* (KITLV Press, Leiden, 2002) and the same author's *Once a Century: Pura Besakih and the Eka Dasa Rudra Festival* (Penerbit Sinar Harapan and Citra Indonesia, Jakarta, 1982) are beautifully illustrated scholarly works on the mother temple and its role. Major recent additions to the anthropological literature include Unni Wikan, *Managing Turbulent Hearts: A Balinese Formula for Living* (University of Chicago Press, Chicago, 1990) and Frederik Barth, *Balinese Worlds* (University of Chicago Press, Chicago, 1993).

Chapter 2   Moonset at Pejeng

Peter Bellwood, *Prehistory of the Indo-Malaysian Archipelago* (University of Hawaii Press, Honolulu, revised edn, 1997) is an authoritative source on regional prehistory, especially valuable in this context because of the author's research on Bali. H.R. van Heekeren, *The Bronze–Iron Age of Indonesia* (Martinus Nijhoff, [The Hague] 1958) is still an excellent introduction. I Wayan Ardika and Peter Bellwood, 'Sembiran: The beginnings of Indian contact with Bali', *Antiquities* Vol. 65, 1991, pp. 221–32, describes the important archaeological work in the north. Vernon L. Scarborough, John W. Schoenfelder and J. Stephen Lansing, 'Early statecraft on Bali: The water temple complex and the decentralisation of the political economy', *Research in Economic Anthropology*, Vol. 20, 1999, pp. 299–330, offers an intriguing new interpretation of irrigated rice origins.

Chapter 3   From Indianisation to Majapahit Empire

A.J. Bernet Kempers, *Monumental Bali: Introduction to Balinese Archaeology and Guide to the Monuments* (Periplus Editions, Berkeley, 1991) doubles as scholarly field guide and account of the prehistoric and Old Bali periods. It should be read along with W.F. Stutterheim's *Indian Influences in Old Balinese Art* (The India Society, London, 1935). For a good general discussion of the Old Bali period, see Chapter 16 of Angela Hobart, Urs Ramseyer and Albert Leeman, *The Peoples of Bali* (Blackwell, Oxford, 2001). Helen Creese, 'In search of Majapahit: The transformation of Balinese identities' in *To Change Bali: Essays in Honor of I Gusti Ngurah Bagus*, eds Adrian Vickers and I Nyoman Darma Putra (*Bali Post*, Denpasar, 2000), pp. 15–46, is a fine analysis of the Majapahit interregnum, balancing myth against historical likelihood. Stuart Robson, *Desawarnana (Nagarakrtagama) by Mpu Prapanca* (KITLV Press, Leiden, 1995) is the best translation of our main source for the Majapahit conquest of Bali. On the Balinese expansion to Lombok, see A.Van der Kraan, *Lombok: Conquest, Colonization and Underdevelopment* (Heinemann, Singapore, 1980) and Hans Hägerdal, *Hindu Rulers, Muslim Subjects: Lombok and Bali in the Seventeenth and Eighteenth Centuries* (White Lotus Press, Bangkok, 2001). On the use of Balinese chronicles, see H.I.R. Hinzler, 'The Balinese Babad' in *Profiles of Malay Culture: Historiography, Religion and Politics*, ed. Sartono Kartodirdjo (Ministry of Education and Culture, Jakarta, 1976), pp. 39–52.

Chapter 4   The Balinese state to the eve of Dutch control

Anyone wanting to know more about pre-colonial politics in Bali should begin with Henk Schulte Nordholt's *The Spell of Power*, on which this chapter is largely based, and continue with Clifford Geertz, *Negara: The Theatre State*.

248

Chapter 5 The Dutch arrive

For the first Dutch visitors, see Aernoudt Lintgenzoon, 'Meeting a King and his Chancellor' in *Travelling to Bali: Four Hundred Years of Journeys*, ed. Adrian Vickers, (Oxford University Press, Kuala Lumpur, 1994), pp. 36–45. For background on slavery see (in addition to Nordholt's *Spell of Power*) Alfons van der Kraan, 'Bali: Slavery and slave trade' in *Slavery, Bondage and Dependency in Southeast Asia*, ed. Anthony Reid (St Martin's Press, New York, 1983), pp. 315–40. Ann Kumar, *Surapati: Man and Legend* (E.J. Brill, Leiden, 1976) is a fine account of the Balinese hero. For descendants of Balinese slaves in modern Jakarta see Rizal, 'The Depok Dutch of Jakarta', *Latitudes* Vol. 25, February 2003, pp. 28–35. Alfons van der Kraan, *Bali at War: A History of the Dutch-Balinese Conflict of 1846–49* (Monash University, Clayton, 1995) covers the 1846–49 war from Dutch archival sources. On the Banjar War in north Bali, see Raechelle Rubinstein, 'Allegiance and alliance: The Banjar War of 1868' in *Being Modern in Bali: Image and Change*, ed. Adrian Vickers (Yale Southeast Asia Program, New Haven, 1996), pp. 38–70. Henk Schulte Nordholt, 'The Mads Lange connection: A Danish trader on Bali in the middle of the nineteenth century: Broker and buffer', *Indonesia*, no. 32, 1981, pp. 16–47, puts the Danish proto-diplomat in historical context. Ide Anak Agung Gde Agung, *Bali in the 19th Century* (Yayasan Obor Indonesia, Jakarta, 1991) is a detailed account of Dutch conquest by a man who himself was a major figure in Balinese and Indonesian history. Margaret J. Wiener, *Visible and Invisible Realms: Power, Magic and Colonial Conquest in Bali* (University of Chicago Press, Chicago, 1995) superbly analyses the 1908 'finishing' in Klungkung.

Chapter 6 Pax and poverty Neerlandica

Robinson's *The Dark Side of Paradise* and Nordholt's *Spell of Power* contain a wealth of additional material on the impact of colonialism.

See also Henk Schulte Nordholt, *Bali: Colonial Conceptions and Political Change, 1700–1940: From Shifting Hierarchies to Fixed Order* (Erasmus University, Rotterdam, 1986) and, by the same author, *State, Village and Ritual in Bali: A Historical Perspective* (VU University Press, Amsterdam, 1991). For background on the opium monopoly see James R. Rush, *Opium to Java: Revenue Farming and Chinese Enterprise in Colonial Indonesia* (Cornell University Press, Ithaca, 1990).

Chapter 7 The world discovers Bali

Adrian Vickers, *Bali: A Paradise Created* (Penguin Books, Victoria, 1989) is a mainly cultural romp through history emphasising the creation of Bali's image as the 'last paradise', particularly useful for the 1930s. Ruud Spruit, *Artists on Bali* (The Pepin Press, Amsterdam, 1997) features biographical background and well-reproduced paintings by six leading expatriate artists in Bali, including Spies and Bonnet. On Walter Spies' life and influence see Hans Rhodius and John Darling, *Walter Spies and Balinese Art* (Tropical Museum, Amsterdam, 1980). Michael Hitchcock and Lucy Norris, *Bali: The Imaginary Museum: The Photographs of Walter Spies and Beryl de Zoete* (Oxford University Press, Kuala Lumpur, 1995) describes among other things how *Dance and Drama in Bali* was produced. Jane Belo, ed., *Traditional Balinese Culture* (Columbia University Press, New York, 1970) is a collection of articles by the scholars of the 1930s. The literature on Margaret Mead is voluminous, including her own *Letters from the Field, 1925–1975* (Harper & Row, New York, 1977) and her autobiography, *Blackberry Winter: My Earlier Years* (Simon & Schuster, New York, 1972). For analysis of her work in Bayunggede see Walter Sullivan, *Margaret Mead, Gregory Bateson and Highland Bali: Fieldwork Photographs of Bayung Gede, 1936–39* (University of Chicago Press, Chicago, 1999). Additional books by 1930s' expatriates, including Vicki Baum, Colin McPhee, Robert Koke and Ktut Tantri, most of them still in print and good reading, are mentioned in the text. The best short overview of Western influence on Balinese art is the chapter by Jean Cocteau in *Museum Puri Lukisan* (Yayasan Ratna Warta, Ubud, 1999). See also the more extended treatment in Urs Ramseyer, *The Art and Culture of Bali* (Oxford University Press, Oxford, 1977) and A.A.M. Djelantik, *Balinese Painting* (2nd edn, Oxford University Press, Kuala Lumpur, 1990). Hildred Geertz, *Images of Power: Balinese Paintings made for Margaret Mead and Gregory Bateson* (University of Hawaii Press, Honolulu, 1994) covers the history and characteristics of Batuan style. Claire Holt's *Art in Indonesia: Continuities and Change* (Cornell University Press, Ithaca, 1967) remains the best discussion of Balinese art in the Indonesian context. On gamelan history, begin with Michael Tenzer, *Balinese Music* (Periplus Editions, Hong Kong, 1998). Cokorde Gede Agung Sukawati, *Reminiscences of a Balinese Prince*, as told to Rosemary Hilbery (Southeast Asian Studies, University of Hawaii, Honolulu, 1979), is the autobiography of the Raja of Ubud, covering the period 1910–78, including the creation of Pita Maha and much more.

Chapter 8 Occupation, revolution and bloodbath

Robinson's *The Dark Side* is the only adequate account in English of the Japanese occupation and of Bali's role in the Indonesian Revolution. On youth in the revolution, see I Gusti Ngurah Bagus, 'Bali in the 1950s: the role of the Pemuda Pejuang in Balinese political processes' in *State and Society in Bali: Historical, Textual and Anthropological Approachs*, ed. Hildred Geertz (KITLV Press, Leiden, 1991), pp. 199–212. John Hughes, *Indonesian Upheaval* (Fawcett Publications, student edn, New York, 1967) remains the only contemporary report on the killings on Bali. The best overview is Robert Cribb, ed., *The Indonesian Killings of 1965–66: Studies from Java and Bali* (Monash University, Clayton, 1990).

Chapter 9 Dictatorship, democracy and the evolution of tourism

Carol Warren, *Adat and Dinas: Balinese Communities in the Indonesian State* (Oxford University Press, Kuala Lumpur, 1993) discusses the New Order on Bali. On the history of tourism, see the writings of Michel Picard, especially *Bali: Cultural Tourism and Touristic Culture* (Archipelago Press, Singapore, 1996), and, from an economic perspective, Sisira Jayasuriya and I Ketut Nehen, 'Bali: Economic growth and tourism' in *Unity and Diversity: Regional Economic Development in Indonesia since 1970*, ed. Hal Hill (Oxford University Press, Singapore, 1989), pp. 330–48. Hugh Mabbett, *In Praise of Kuta: From Slave Port to Fishing Village to the Most Popular Resort in Bali* (January Books, Wellington, 1987) makes poignant reading since 12 October 2002. On the 'Kuta Cowboys' see Degung Santikarma and Leslie Dwyer, 'Intimate exchanges: Selling lust and love in Bali', *Latitudes*, Vol. 7, Aug 2001, pp. 10–17. For the recent history of Ubud, see Graeme MacCrae, 'Acting global, thinking local in a Balinese tourism town' in *Staying Local in the Global Village: Bali in the Twentieth Century*, eds Raechelle Rubinstein and Linda H. Connor (University of Hawaii Press, Honolulu, 1999), pp. 123–54. New Order involvement in tourism is skewered in George Aditjondro, *Bali: Jakarta's Colony: Social and Ecological Impacts of Jakarta-Based Conglomerates in Bali's Tourism Industry*, (Asia Research Centre on Social, Political and Economic Change, Murdoch University, Perth, 1995). For Tanah Lot development and the Great Golden Garuda, see Putu Suasta and Linda H. Connor, 'Democratic mobilization and political authoritarianism: Tourist developments in Bali' in Rubinstein and Connor, *Staying Local*, pp. 91–122. Putu Suasta treats urbanisation in 'Between holy waters and highways' in *Bali: Living in Two Worlds: A Critical Self-Portrait*, eds Urs Ramseyer and I Gusti Raka Panji Tisna (Museum der Kulturen, Basel, 2001), pp. 38–44. For a history of family planning see Kim Streatfield, *Fertility Decline in a Traditional Society: The*

Case of Bali (Department of Demography, Australian National University, Canberra, 1986). For a Balinese scholar's view of transmigration see I Gusti Made Sutjaja, 'Balinese transmigrants in Lampung: Language change and transition' in *Being Modern in Bali*, ed. Vickers, pp. 212–22. J. Stephen Lansing gives a critical assessment of the Green Revolution in *Priests and Programmers: Technologies of Power in the Engineered Landscape of Bali* (Princeton University Press, Princeton, 1991).

Chapter 10   Bali in the twenty-first century

An initial account of the Kuta bombing is Alan Atkinson's *Three Weeks in Bali* (Australian Broadcasting Corporation, Sydney, 2003). For many of the other issues discussed in this chapter see Bali's outstanding English-language monthly *Latitudes*, especially the following: Degung Santikarma, 'Modern guardians of tradition', Vol. 6, July 2001, pp. 7–8; Bodrek Arsana, 'The blowtorch business in Bali', Vol. 7, Aug 2001, pp. 35–7; Bodrek Arsana and Degung Santikarma, 'Bali's modern day demons', Vol. 16, May 2002, pp. 73–7 and Andre Syahreza, 'Culture, conservation or cuisine? The embattled turtles of Bali', Vol. 6, July 2001, pp. 68–73. On the Hindu schism see the writings of I Gede Pitana, including 'Sociology of the temple: Issues related to rivalry in status and power' in *Living in Two Worlds*, ed. Ramseyer, pp. 118–27. On the influence of traditional communities on decision making, see Carol Warren, 'Adat and the discourses of modernity in Bali' in *To Change Bali*, eds Vickers and Darma Putra, pp. 1–14.

Index